Handbook of Screen Format Design
THIRD EDITION

Books and Training Products From QED

DATABASE

Data Analysis: The Key to Data Base Design
The Data Dictionary: Concepts and Uses
DB2: The Complete Guide to Implementation and Use
Logical Data Base Design
DB2 Design Review Guidelines
DB2: Maximizing Performance of Online Production Systems
Entity-Relationship Approach to Logical Data Base Design
How to Use ORACLE SQL*PLUS
ORACLE: Building High Performance Online Systems
Embedded SQL for DB2: Application Design and Programming
SQL for dBASE IV
Introduction to Data and Activity Analysis
ORACLE Design Review Guidelines
Using DB2 to Build Decision Support Systems
How to Use SQL for DB2

SYSTEMS ENGINEERING

Handbook of Screen Format Design
Managing Projects: Selecting and Using PC-Based Project Management Systems
The Complete Guide to Software Testing
A User's Guide for Defining Software Requirements
A Structured Approach to Systems Testing
Practical Applications of Expert Systems
Expert Systems Development: Building PC-Based Applications
Storyboard Prototyping: A New Approach to User Requirements Analysis
The Software Factory: Managing Software Development and Maintenance
Data Architecture: The Information Paradigm
Advanced Topics in Information Engineering

MANAGEMENT

CASE: The Potential and the Pitfalls
Strategic and Operational Planning for Information Services
The State of the Art in Decision Support Systems
The Management Handbook for Information Center and End-User Computing
Disaster Recovery: Contingency Planning and Program Analysis

MANAGEMENT (cont'd)

Winning the Change Game
Information Systems Planning for Competitive Advantage
Critical Issues in Information Processing Management and Technology
Developing the World Class Information Systems Organization
The Technical Instructor's Handbook: From Techie to Teacher
Collision: Theory vs. Reality in Expert System
How to Automate Your Computer Center: Achieving Unattended Operations
Ethical Conflicts in Information and Computer Science, Technology, and Business

DATA COMMUNICATIONS

Data Communications: Concepts and Solutions
Designing and Implementing Ethernet Networks
Network Concepts and Architectures
Open Systems: The Guide to OSI and its Implementation
VAX/VMS: Mastering DCL Commands and Utilities

PROGRAMMING

VSAM Techniques: Systems Concepts and Programming Procedures
How to Use CICS to Create On-Line Applications: Methods and Solutions
DOS/VSE/SP Guide for Systems Programming: Concepts, Programs, Macros, Subroutines
Systems Programmer's Problem Solver
VSAM: Guide to Optimization and Design
MVS/TSO: Mastering CLISTS
MVS/TSO: Mastering Native Mode and ISPF
VAX/VMS: Mastering DCL Commands and Utilities

SELF-PACED TRAINING

SQL as a Second Language
Building Online Production Systems with DB2 (Video)
Introduction to UNIX (CBT)
Building Production Applications with ORACLE (Video)

For Additional Information or a Free Catalog contact

QED INFORMATION SCIENCES, INC. • P. O. Box 82-181 • Wellesley, MA 02181
Telephone: 800-343-4848 or 617-237-5656

THIRD EDITION

Handbook of Screen Format Design

Wilbert O. Galitz

QED Information Sciences, Inc.
Wellesley, Massachusetts

© 1981, 1985, 1989 by QED Information Sciences, Inc.
P.O. Box 181
Wellesley, MA 02181

Library of Congress Catalog Number: 88-15849
International Standard Book Number: 0-89435-258-X

Printed in the United States of America
    90 10 9 8 7 6 5 4 3

Library of Congress Cataloging-in-Publication Data

Galitz, Wilbert O.
    Handbook of screen format design / Wilbert O. Galitz.—3rd ed.
        p.   cm.
    Bibliography: p.
    ISBN 0-89435-258-X
    1. Information display systems—Formatting.   I. Title.
TK7882.I6G34   1988
    005.7—dc19   88-15849
                                                               CIP

To Sharon, who so ably handles all the many other things that must be done with a business so that this book could be written.

Contents

Introduction

Today the most common communication bridge between a person and a computer system is a visual display terminal. The medium of this communication is a cathode ray tube upon which data and information are electronically inscribed. What information or data is placed on a display tube, how it is structured, and where it is located is called screen format design.

A well designed screen format can increase human processing speed, reduce human errors, and speed computer processing time. A poorly designed screen has the opposite effect: it will decrease human processing speed, provoke mistakes, and complicate machine operations. A well designed screen, then, will increase human productivity; a poorly designed screen will reduce it.

Screen format design, or screen design, as it is commonly called, is the topic of this handbook. In some quarters screen design is perceived as encompassing the programming steps necessary to provide a finished product to a user. It should be recognized that a discussion of this design activity is beyond the scope of this book. This document will only be concerned with how a screen looks and behaves for a user. It is directed toward developing a screen product that is easily used and visually clear. Simple programming concepts introduced are only those necessary to accomplish this objective.

AN HISTORICAL REVIEW

During its first twenty years, the data processing industry paid little attention to the human/computer interface in system design. The focus instead was on efficient use of central processing units and storage media. The high cost of technology and the fact that computers were used by a relatively few specialists sublimated the interface between humans and computers. Systems were, in effect, designed from the "inside out."

As computing power increased and computing costs decreased, computers touched more work lives. Computer usage by several users became usage by several hundred users, and, thus, personnel costs became a dominant factor in total systems costs. In the early 1980s the ratio of office workers to display terminals was on the order of 10 to 1. That is, for every ten white collar workers, there was one display terminal to be found in offices across the country. With the increasing popularity of the personal computer, this ratio has dropped dramatically.

Economics have thus forced a refocusing of system design emphasis onto the user. It has become more widely recognized that the ease and effectiveness of human interaction with computers depends on how well the interface reflects people's needs. Thus, the system design emphasis has shifted to the "outside in." Effective screen design from a user's perspective has assumed increasing importance.

Historically, screen design responsibility has fallen on programmers and systems analysts—those charged with designing and building computer systems. The design process, unfortunately, has developed with few guidelines. Technical considerations have received the most attention, and the human factors involved have not been well understood or have been neglected entirely. As a result, screen design has tended to be unsystematic and inconsistent, and has failed to adequately reflect human perceptual and processing capabilities. As a result, many screens in today's office systems are difficult to use and lack visual clarity.

At best, a poorly designed screen can exact a toll in human productivity, as illustrated in figure 1.1.

Based on an actual system requiring processing of 4.8 million screens per year, an analysis established that if poor clarity forced screen users to spend one extra second per screen, almost 1 additional person-year would be required to process all screens. A 20-second degradation in screen processing time would cost an additional 14 person-years.

At its worst, a poorly designed screen can create an impression that understanding it will require more time than one can afford to commit, or that it is too complex to understand at all. Those who have the luxury of doing so (managers and professionals) may refuse to use it, and the objectives of the system for which it was designed will never be achieved.

The benefits of a well designed screen are coming under much closer experimental scrutiny. Dunsmore (1982) attempted to improve screen clarity and readability by making screens less crowded. Separate items, which had been combined on the same display line to conserve space, were placed on separate lines instead. The result: screen users were about 20 percent more productive with the less-crowded version. Keister and Gallaway (1983) reformatted a series of screens following many of the same concepts to be described in this handbook. The result: screen users of the modified screens completed transactions in 25 percent less time and with 25 percent fewer errors than those who used the original screens.

Figure 1.1   Impact of inefficient screen design on processing time.

Additional Seconds Required per Screen in Seconds	Additional Person-Years Required to Process 4.8 Million Screens per Year
1	.7
5	3.6
10	7.1
20	14.2

Tullis (1981) has reported how reformatting inquiry screens following good design principles reduced decision-making time by about 40 percent, resulting in a savings of 79 person-years in the affected system.

Screen design may also be contributing to the visual fatigue reported by some system users. Studies of people's eye movements in using screens have uncovered instances where visual movements between screen and source documents exceed several thousand for one work day. At this number of movements, a significant difference in the brightness level between display screen and source document can fatigue the muscle of the eye. This has led to attempts to brighten the display screen or lower the illumination to try to achieve the proper balance. But what about the design of the screen? Several thousand eye movements a day may reflect poor screen design rather than an unsatisfactory environment or terminal. The symptoms of a problem rather than the cause are perhaps being addressed in some cases.

What can be done, then, to improve the screen design process? Plenty. While screen design is not yet a precise science, the body of knowledge derived from experimental studies is growing. And a wealth of information derived from printed material research (e.g., books and newspapers) and the graphics arts discipline is available to provide guidance until more research questions are answered. This material simply awaits conscientious application to the screen design process.

HANDBOOK OBJECTIVES

The purpose of this handbook is to assist a designer in developing an effective screen interface between a program and its users. It is intended as a ready reference source for all screen design. Its specific objectives are to enable the reader to:

- describe the considerations that must be applied to the screen design process,
- describe a series of design rules that can be applied to the several categories of screens,
- perform the design steps necessary to develop and lay out effective screens.

HANDBOOK SCOPE

The materials in this handbook, although far from exhaustive, represent an attempt to identify, collect and/or deduce, and ultimately document a useful set of guidelines for screen design. This handbook is the most complete and thorough reference source available to the screen designer today. The guidelines have been culled from a variety of sources:

- known human factors and psychological principles,
- analysis of the results of experimental studies in the behavioral disciplines,
- available guideline documents for people/machine interfaces,
- informal studies conducted by the author,
- the author's experience.

Although the validity of some guidelines cannot be absolutely guaranteed, as a whole they will provide a solid foundation for most screen design activities, at least until experimental evidence is available to prove, disprove, or modify them.

These guidelines will not answer every design problem that may be encountered. Application-specific requirements and guideline incompatibilities will never free the designer from performing design tradeoffs. It is hoped, however, that these guidelines will promote "wiser" decisions than have been possible in the past.

Types of Screens

Screens can be developed for a wide variety of purposes and in a wide variety of styles. Unfortunately, no consistent naming conventions exist in current documentation, various names being affixed to screens whose purpose seems similar. For this handbook, screen types will be catalogued as described below. This categorization is based on differences in screen functions that cause fundamental differences in screen structure and layout.

Data entry screens. Data entry screens are designed to collect information quickly and accurately. Commonly called data collection screens, they usually contain a number of captioned fields into which data is keyed. Data entry screens are sometimes referred to as fixed form or form fill-in screens.

All data entry screens are not alike. Whether or not data keying is being performed from a specially designed (or dedicated) source document to be used with the screen will cause fundamental differences in screen design.

- *With a Dedicated Source Document*—When keying is performed from a dedicated source document, the document will be the visual focus of the user's attention. Keying aids will be built into the document itself, and the design of the screen will be interwoven with the design of the document.

* *Without a Dedicated Source Document*—When there is no dedicated document from which keying is performed, the primary visual focus of the user will be the screen itself. Screen clarity as an end in itself will assume a much more important role in the design process.

Both kinds of data entry screens are discussed in this handbook.

Inquiry screens. Inquiry screens are used for displaying the contents of computer files. Data on these screens does not change, and they are designed for ease of information location and visual clarity.

Multipurpose screens. Multipurpose screens are combination screens achieving more than one objective. They may be used to enter data into the system, review what is there, and possibly change what is displayed. As such, they combine the characteristics of the data entry and inquiry screens.

Question and answer screens. A question and answer screen consists of alternating communications between the computer and the user. Each communication is short and contains one idea at a time. Communications may contain captions or be free-form (without captions).

Menu screens. The primary purpose of a menu screen is to permit a user to select one or more alternatives from a variety of alternatives. As such, it combines the characteristics of both data collection and inquiry screens.

These screens may be designed for use on a monochromatic (one-color) alphanumeric terminal, a color alphanumeric terminal, or a graphics terminal. Separate chapters will be devoted to color and graphics and the unique considerations they present.

OVERVIEW

Chapter 2 sets the stage for the screen design guidelines by looking at the user, discussing why people have trouble with computer systems and their typical responses to poor design. It explains the differences between discretionary and nondiscretionary system use and then sets forth four commandments for designing for users. The chapter concludes with a review of critical human considerations in screen design. Chapter 3 addresses the dialogue between people and computers. It defines the concept of ease of use and the kinds of dialogues available, and presents directions and guidelines for achieving an effective people/computer interface. Chapter 4 focuses on actual screen design. It discusses a test for good design, visually pleasing composition, objective measures of a well-designed screen, the structure of words and messages, and how to use the various monochromatic display features.

Following chapter 4 emphasis shifts to specific types of screens. Chapter 5 treats data collection or data entry screens; chapter 6, inquiry screens; and chapter 7, multipurpose screens. Chapters 8 and 9 deal with question and answer screens and menu screens respectively.

As color displays are becoming more prominent, the use of color in screen design is discussed in chapter 10. Chapter 11 surveys new directions in the use of graphics.

Also, since effective data entry screen design frequently involves development of source documents, chapter 12 presents guidelines for good source document design.

The concluding chapter 13 provides an illustrated review of the design steps necessary to define, design, and lay out a typical data entry screen.

HOW TO USE THIS HANDBOOK

This handbook provides some general design considerations and guidelines (chapters 2, 3, 4), guidelines applicable to specific kinds of screens (chapters 5 through 9), unique situation design guidelines (chapters 10, 11, 12), and a design steps review (chapter 13). After an initial reading, the handbook user need only be concerned with the chapters relevant to the kind of screen being designed. Table 1.1 serves as an aid in determining chapter relevancy.

Table 1.1 Chapter relevancy for various types of screens.

If you are going to design ...	See chapter ...
A data entry screen and related source document	2, 3, 4, 5-1, 5-2, 12
A data entry screen to be used without a related source document	2, 3, 4, 5-1, 5-3
An inquiry screen	2, 3, 4, 6
A question and answer screen	2, 3, 4, 8
A menu screen	2, 3, 4, 9
A multipurpose screen	7, plus chapters relevant to the particular kind of screen
A screen using color	10, plus chapters relevant to the particular kind of screen
A screen using graphics	11, plus chapters relevant to the particular kind of screen

Topic Organization and Illustrations

Each handbook chapter contains important points, concepts, or guidelines organized by topic and presented in a highlighted checklist format. Following each checklist is a narrative that provides further detail on much of the high-lighted material. The reader who finds the checklists of satisfactory clarity and scope need not be concerned with the narrative. The reader desiring more information on any topic will find the narrative valuable.

The guidelines also contains many illustrations and examples. These illustrations of screen display will be designated as follows:

```
NUMBER:x_____xxxTIME:x_____


MODEL            YEAR
_____xxx____
_____      ____
_____      ____
```

For clarity of interpretation, spaces in a screen example important to a particular guideline are designated by the lowercase letter x.

A FINAL WORD

While this handbook contains much to aid the screen format designer, there may be shortcomings in its organization, content, or clarity. Readers having comments or suggestions concerning screen design, or the design process, are urged to communicate them to the author so they may be incorporated into subsequent editions. It is only by working together that we can provide an efficient and effective product.

The System User   2

The journey into the world of screen design must begin with a discussion of the system user, the most important part of any computer system, whose needs the systems are built to serve. We will start by looking at why people have had trouble with computer systems and the past results of poor design. Then we will explore the nature of the user, including such characteristics as non-discretionary vs. discretionary use and varying levels of expertise. Finally, we will look at several human considerations that are critical to the screen design guidelines.

WHY PEOPLE HAVE TROUBLE WITH COMPUTER SYSTEMS

Although system design and its behavioral implications have come under intense scrutiny in the past decade, as we have seen, this has not always been the case. Historically, the design of computer systems has been the responsibility of programmers, systems analysts, and system designers, many of whom possess extensive technical knowledge but little behavioral training. Design decisions have thus rested mostly upon the designers' intuition and wealth of specialized knowledge, and, consequently, poorly designed interfaces often go unrecognized.

The intuition of designers or of anyone else, no matter how good or bad they may be at what they do, is error-prone. It is too shallow a foundation on which to base design decisions. Specialized knowledge lulls one into a false sense of security. It enables one to interpret and deal with complex or ambiguous situations on the basis of context cues not visible to users, as well as knowledge of the computer system they do not possess. The result is a perfectly usable system to its designers but one the office worker is unable or unwilling to face up to and master.

What makes a system complex in the eyes of its user? Listed below are five contributing factors.

Use of jargon.   Systems often talk in a strange language. Words alien to the office environment or used in different contexts, such as filespec, abend, segment, and boot proliferate. Learning to use a system requires learning a new language.

Non-obvious design.   Complex or novel design elements are not obvious or intuitive, but they must nevertheless be mastered. Operations may have prerequisite conditions that must be satisfied before they can be accomplished, or outcomes may not always be immediate, obvious, or visible. The overall framework of the system may be invisible, with the effect that results cannot always be related to the actions that accomplish them.

Fine distinctions.   Different actions may accomplish the same thing, depending upon when they are performed, or different things may result from the same action. Often these distinctions are minute and difficult to keep track of. Critical distinctions are not made at the appropriate time, or distinctions having no real consequence are made instead, as illustrated by the user who insisted that problems were caused by pressing the ENTER key "in the wrong way" (Carroll, 1984).

Disparity in problem-solving strategies.   People learn best by doing. They have trouble following directions and do not always read instructions before taking an action. Human problem solving can best be characterized as "error-correcting" or "trial-and-error," whereby a tentative solution is formulated based upon the available evidence and then tried. This tentative solution often has a low chance of success, but the results are used to modify one's next attempt and so increase the chances of success. Most computers, however, enforce an "error-preventing" strategy, which assumes that a person will not take an action until a high degree of confidence exists in its success. The result is that people often head down wrong paths, or get entangled in situations difficult if not impossible to get out of (Reed, 1982).

Design inconsistency.   The same action may have different names: for example, "save" and "keep," "write" and "list." Or the same result may be described differently: for example, "not legal" and "not valid." The result is that system learning becomes an exercise in rote memorization. Meaningful or conceptual learning becomes very difficult.

RESPONSES TO POOR DESIGN

Unfortunately, people remember the one thing that went wrong, not the many that go right, so problems achieve an abnormal level of importance. Errors are a symptom of problems. The magnitude of errors in a computer-based system has been found to be as high as 46 percent for commands, tasks, or transactions (Barber, 1979; Card et al., 1980; and Ledgard et al., 1980).

Errors, and other problems that befuddle, lead to a variety of psychological to physical user responses. Some psychological responses are listed below (Foley and Wallace, 1974).

Confusion. Detail overwhelms the perceived structure. Meaningful patterns are difficult to ascertain, and the conceptual model or underlying framework cannot be established.

Panic. Panic may be introduced by unexpectedly long delays during times of severe or unusual pressure. The chief causes are unavailable systems and long response times.

Boredom. Boredom results from improper computer pacing (slow response times) and overly simplistic jobs.

Frustration. An inability to easily convey one's intentions to the computer causes frustration, which is heightened if an unexpected response cannot be undone or if what really took place cannot be determined. Inflexible and unforgiving systems are a major source of frustration.

These psychological responses diminish user effectiveness because they are severe blocks to concentration. Thoughts irrelevant to the task at hand are forced to attention and necessary concentration is impossible. The result, in addition to higher error rates, is poor performance, anxiety, and job dissatisfaction. Further, these psychological responses frequently lead to, or are accompanied by, the following physical responses (Eason, 1979; Stewart, 1976).

Abandonment of the system. The system is rejected and other information sources are relied upon. These sources must be available, and the user must have the discretion to perform the rejection. This is a common reaction of managerial and professional personnel. One study (Hiltz, 1984) found the system abandonment rate to be 40 percent.

Incomplete use of the system. Only a portion of the system's capabilities are used, usually those operations that are easiest to perform or that provide the most benefits. Historically, this has been the most common reaction to most systems.

Indirect use of the system. An intermediary is placed between the would-be user and the computer. Again, since this requires high status and discretion, it is another typical response of managers.

Modification of the task. The task is changed to match the capabilities of the system. This is a prevalent reaction when the tools are rigid and the problem is unstructured, as in scientific problem solving.

Compensatory activity. Additional actions are performed to compensate for system inadequacies. A common example is the manual reformatting of information to match the structure required by the computer. This is a reaction common to workers whose discretion is limited, such as clerical personnel.

Misuse of the system. The rules are bent to shortcut operational difficulties. This requires significant knowledge of the system and may affect system integrity.

Direct programming. The system is reprogrammed by its user to meet specific needs. This is a typical response of the sophisticated worker.

THE NATURE OF THE USER

While we would like to think the system user sits idly at his desk anxiously awaiting the arrival of the computer system and the salvation it will afford, the truth is mostly the opposite. The user in today's office is usually overworked, fatigued, and continually interrupted. Documentation tends not to be read and problems are not well understood, and little is known about what information is available to meet one's needs. Moreover, the user's skills have been greatly overestimated by the system designer, who is often isolated psychologically and physically from the user's situation. Unlike the user, the designer is capable of resolving most system problems and ambiguities through application of experience and background and technical knowledge. Yet, often, the designer cannot really believe that anyone is incapable of using the system created.

The user, while being subjected to the everyday pressures of the office, is probably technologically unsophisticated, computer illiterate, and possibly even antagonistic. He wants to spend time using a system, not learning to use it. His objective is simply to get some work done.

In reality, there is not just one kind of system user, but many. From a design perspective, what distinguishes users are discretionary capability and level of expertise.

Nondiscretionary Versus Discretionary Use

Nondiscretionary use. Users of the earliest computer systems were nondiscretionary. That is, they required the computer to perform a task that, for all practical purposes, could be performed no other way. Characteristics of nondiscretionary use can be summarized as follows:

- the computer is used as part of employment;
- time and effort in learning to use the computer are willingly invested;
- high motivation is often used to overcome low usability characteristics;
- the user may possess a technical background;
- the job may consist of a single task or function.

The nondiscretionary user must learn to live comfortably with a computer, for there is really no other choice. Examples of nondiscretionary use today include a flight reservations clerk booking seats, an insurance company employee entering data into the computer so a policy can be issued, and a programmer writing and debugging a program. The toll exacted by a poorly designed system in nondiscretionary use is measured primarily by productivity—e.g., speed and errors—and poor customer satisfaction with the product of the system.

Discretionary use. In recent years, as computers have become more common in the office, the discretionary user has become exposed to the benefits, and costs, of technology. He is much more self-directed than the nondiscretionary user—not being told how to work but being evaluated on the results of his efforts. For him, it is not means but the results that are most important. In short, this user has never been told how to work in the past and refuses to be told so now. This newer kind of user is the office executive, manager, or other professional, whose computer use is completely discretionary. Common characteristics of the discretionary user are as follows:

- his use of the system is not necessary;
- his job can be performed without the system;
- he will not invest extra effort to use the system;
- technical details are of no interest to him;
- he does not show high motivation to use the system;
- he is easily disenchanted;
- his voluntary use must be encouraged;
- he is a multi-function knowledge worker;
- he is from a heterogeneous culture;
- he did not expect to use system;
- his career path did not prepare him for system use.

Quite simply, the discretionary user often judges a system on the basis expected effort versus results to be gained. If the benefits are seen to exceed the effort, the system will be used. If the effort is expected to exceed the benefits, it will not be used. Just the perception of a great effort to achieve minimal results is often enough to completely discourage system use, leading to system rejection, a common discretionary reaction.

Novice Versus Expert Use

At one time or another, various schemes have been proposed to classify the different and sometimes changing characteristics of people as they become more experienced using a system. Words to describe the new, relatively new, or infrequent user have included *naive, casual, inexperienced,* or *novice.* At the other end of the experience continuum lie terms such as *experienced, full-time,* or *expert.* The words themselves are less important than the behavioral characteristics they imply. For experience to date is uncovering some basic differences in feelings of ease of use based upon proficiency level. What is easy for the new user is not perceived as easy for the "old hand," and vice versa.

For consistency in our discussion, the term "novice" will be used for the new user; the term "expert," for the most proficient.

Novice users have been found to:

- depend upon system features that assist recognition memory: menus, prompting information, and instructional and help screens;
- need restricted vocabularies, simple tasks, small numbers of possibilities, and very informative feedback;
- view practice as an aid to moving up to expert status.

Whereas, experts:

- rely upon free recall;
- expect rapid performance;
- need less informative feedback;
- seek efficiency by bypassing novice memory aids, reducing keystrokes, chunking and summarizing information, and introducing new vocabularies.

In actuality, the user population of most systems is spread out along the continuum anchored by these two extremes. And, equally important, the behavior of any one user at different times may be closer to one extreme or the other. A person may be very proficient, an expert, in one aspect of a system and ignorant, a novice, in other aspects at the same time (Draper, 1984).

A well designed system, therefore, must support at the same time novice and expert behavior, as well as all levels of behavior in between.

DESIGNING FOR USERS—THE FOUR COMMANDMENTS

Designing a computer system is never easy. The development path is littered with obstacles and traps, many of them human in nature. The process can be simplified, however, if four basic commandments are followed by the designer.

I. Understand the user. This is a difficult and undervalued goal but extremely important because of the gap in skills and attitudes between system users and designers. The following profiles are necessary:

- gender
- age
- education
- training

- ethnic background
- cultural heritage
- motivation
- personality
- physical abilities

The job or task, as well as the user, must be understood through direct contact prior to design. The first successful step is recognizing that users are individuals whose outlook is probably different from your own.

II. Involve the user in design.   Involving the user in design from the beginning provides a direct source to the extensive knowledge he possesses. It also allows the designer to confront the user's resistance to change. People dislike change for a variety of reasons, among them fear of the unknown and lack of identification. Involvement in design removes the unknown and gives the user a stake in the system, or an identification with it. One caution, however: user involvement in design should be based on job or task knowledge, not status or position.

III. Test the system on actual users.   Something that is still not well understood is the human mind. No mathematical formula exists to describe it. While the design guidelines that follow go a long way toward making systems and screens easier to comprehend, factors like ease of learning, the most useful system features, and all possible problems cannot be predicted. So pilot, prototype, and acceptance testing with actual users is a necessity and must be included as part of the design process itself. If it is not built into the design process, the testing must occur in the user's office, often leaving a negative first impression in the user's mind. First impressions harden quickly, causing attitudes that may be difficult to change. The testing process should record any difficulties, errors, or hesitations, and users should be interviewed to uncover what was difficult, what problems existed, what was not understood, and what could have been done differently.

IV. Refine as necessary.   Since testing is an iterative process, system refinement will be ongoing as testing proceeds. A good benchmark for success is the point at which 95 percent of the typical users are performing the tasks without difficulty and without consulting manuals, help facilities, or other users.

HUMAN CONSIDERATIONS IN DESIGN

A human being is a complex organism with a variety of attributes that have an important influence on screen design. Of particular importance are perception, memory, visual acuity, learning, skill, and individual differences.

Perception

Perception is our awareness and understanding of the elements of our environment through physical sensation of our various senses. It is influenced, in part, by achieved experience: we classify stimuli based upon models stored in our memories and in this way achieve understanding. Comparing the accumulated knowledge of the child with that of an adult in interpreting the world is a vivid example of the role of experience in perception. Perception is also influenced by expectancies. Proofreading errors are a perceptual expectancy error: we see not how a word is spelled but how we expect to see it spelled. Context, environment, and surroundings also influence individual perception. For example, two drawn lines of the same length may look the same length or a different length depending upon the angle of adjacent lines, or what other people have said about the size of the lines.

The human sensing mechanisms are bombarded by many stimuli, some of which are important and some of which are not. Important stimuli are called signals; those that are not important are called noise. Signals are more quickly comprehended if they are easily distinguishable from noise in the sensory environment. Noise interferes with the perception of signals to the extent that they are similar to one another. Noise can even mask a critical signal. For example, imagine a hidden word puzzle where meaningful words are buried in a large block matrix of alphabetic characters. The signals, alphabetic characters constituting meaningful words, are masked by the matrix of meaningless letters.

Stimuli may also assume the quality of signals in one situation and that of noise in another. Just as things may be important in one context and unimportant in another. Imagine, for example, walking on a downtown sidewalk in a large city and hearing a train whistle in the distance. Then imagine walking down a train track and hearing the same whistle in the distance. On the sidewalk the train whistle may not even be perceived, but walking down the train track, it will most certainly be heard loud and clear.

Other perceptual characteristics include the following.

Proximity. The eye and mind see objects as belonging together if they are near each other in space.

Similarity. The eye and mind see objects as belonging together if they share a common visual property, such as color, size, shape, brightness, or orientation.

Matching patterns. We respond similarly to the same shape in different sizes. The letters of the alphabet, for example, possess the same meaning, regardless of physical size.

Closure. Perception is synthetic; it establishes meaningful wholes. If something does not quite close itself, such as a circle, square, triangle, or word, we see it closed anyway.

Balance. We desire stabilization or equilibrium in our viewing environment. Vertical, horizontal, and right angles are the most visually satisfying and easiest to look at.

The human perceptual mechanism has significant implications in the screen design process.

Memory

Memory is not one of the most developed of human attributes. Short-term memory is highly susceptible to the interference of such distracting tasks as thinking, reciting, or listening, which are constantly erasing and overwriting it. Remembering a telephone number long enough to complete the dialing operation taxes the memory of many people. The short-term memory limit is generally viewed as 7 ± 2 "chunks" of information (Miller, 1956), and knowledge and experience govern the size and complexity of chunks that can be recalled. To illustrate, most native English-speaking people would find recalling seven English words much easier than recalling seven Russian words. Short-term memory is thought to last 15 to 30 seconds. Unlike short-term memory, with its distinct limitations, long-term memory is thought to be unlimited. An important memory consideration, with significant implications for screen design, is the difference in ability to recognize or recall words. The human active vocabulary (words that can be recalled) typically ranges between 2,000 and 3,000 words. Passive vocabulary (words that can be recognized) typically numbers about 100,000. Our powers of recognition are much greater than our powers of recall.

Visual Acuity

The capacity of the eye to resolve details is called visual acuity. It is the phenomenon which results in an object becoming more distinct as we turn our eyes toward it, and rapidly loses distinctness as we turn our eyes away, that is, as the visual angle from the point of fixation increases. It has been shown that relative visual acuity is approximately halved at a distance of 2.5 degrees from the point of eye fixation (e.g., Bouma, 1970). Therefore, a 5-degree diameter circle centered around an eye "fixation" character on a display has been recommended as the area "near" that character (Tullis, 1983) or the maximum length for a displayed word (Danchak, 1976).

If one assumes that the average viewing distance of a display screen is 19 inches (475 mm), the size of the area on the screen of optimum visual acuity is 1.67 inches (41.8 mm). Assuming "average" character sizes and character and line spacings, the number of characters on a screen falling within this visual acuity circle is 88, with 15 characters being contained on the widest line, and 7 rows being consumed, as illustrated below.

```
            3 2 1 3 1 2 3
          5 4 3 2 1 2 1 2 3 4 5
        6 5 4 3 2 1 1 1 2 3 4 5 6
      7 6 5 4 3 2 1 0 1 2 3 4 5 6 7
        6 5 4 3 2 1 1 1 2 3 4 5 6
          5 4 3 2 1 2 1 2 3 4 5
            3 2 1 3 1 2 3
```

The eye's sensitivity increases for those characters closest to the fixation point (the "O") and decreases for those characters at the extreme edges of the circle (A 50/50 chance exists for getting these characters correctly identified). This may be presumed to be a visual "chunk" of a screen.

Learning

The human ability to learn is important—it clearly differentiates people from machines. A design developed to minimize human learning time can accelerate human performance. Given enough time, of course, people can improve their performance in almost any task. Most people can be taught to walk a tightrope, but a designer should not incorporate a tightrope into his design if a walkway is feasible.

Evidence derived from studies of computer system learning parallels that found in studies of learning in other areas. Users prefer to be active (Carroll, 1984), to explore (Robert, 1986) and to use a trial-and-error approach (Hiltz and Kerr, 1986). There is also evidence that users are very sensitive to even minor changes in the user interface, and that such changes may lead to problems in transferring from one system to another (Karat, 1986). Moreover, just the "perception" of having to learn huge amounts of information is enough to keep some people from using a system (Nielson et al., 1986).

Learning can be enhanced if it:

- allows skills acquired in one situation to be used in another somewhat like it (design consistency accomplishes this),
- provides complete and prompt feedback,
- is phased, that is, it requires a person to know only the information needed at that stage of the learning process.

Skill

The goal of human performance is to perform skillfully. To do so requires linking inputs and outputs into a sequence of action. The essence of skill is performance of actions in the correct time sequence with adequate precision. It is characterized by consistency and economy of effort. Economy of effort is achieved by establishing a work pace that represents optimum efficiency. It is accomplished by increasing mastery of the system through such things as progressive learning of shortcuts, increased speed, and easier access to information or data.

Skills are hierarchical in nature, and many basic skills may be integrated to form increasingly complex ones. Lower order skills tend to become routine and may drop out of consciousness. Screen design must permit development of more skillful performance.

Individual Differences

A complicating but very advantageous human characteristic is that we all differ—in looks, feelings, motor abilities, intellectual abilities, learning abilities and speeds, and so on. In a keyboard data entry task, for example, the best operators will probably be twice as fast as the poorest and make ten times fewer errors.

Individual differences complicate design because the design must permit people with widely varying characteristics to satisfactorily and comfortably learn the task or job. In the past this has usually resulted in bringing designs down to the level of lowest abilities or selecting people with the minimum skills necessary to perform a job. But office technology now offers the possibility of tailoring jobs to the specific needs of people with varying and changing learning or skill levels. Screen design must permit this to occur.

System Considerations 3

A computer, the most powerful tool in the array of office equipment, must be an extension of the worker. This means the system and its software must reflect a person's capabilities and respond to his or her specific needs. It should be useful, accomplishing some business objective faster and more efficiently than did the previously used method or tool. It must also be easy to learn, for people want to do, not learn to do. Finally, the system must be easy and fun to use, evoking a sense of pleasure and accomplishment, not tedium and frustration.

The system interface itself should serve as both a connector and a separator: a connector in that it ties the user to the power of the computer, and a separator in that it minimizes the possibility of the participants damaging one another. While the damage the user inflicts upon the computer tends to be physical (a frustrated pounding of the keyboard), the damage caused by the computer is more psychological (a threat to one's self-esteem).

As part of the overall person/computer interface, system design focuses on these three considerations:

- the language by which people express their needs and desires to the computer,
- the display representations that show the state of the system to workers,
- the more abstract issues that affect a person's understanding of the system's behavior.

Ideally, a system's design should enable a person to develop a conceptual model of the system itself.

CONCEPTUAL OR MENTAL MODELS

A conceptual or mental model of a system is what a person gradually develops in order to understand, explain, and interact with the computer. A well established mental model of a system enables a person to predict the necessary actions to do things if the necessary action has been forgotten, or has not yet been encountered.

A mental model is derived from the system image presented to the user. This system image is shaped by the system's input requirements, its outputs, including screens and messages, and its help facilities. System manuals and training sessions also play a formative role.

The development of a mental model can be aided by the following:

Providing design consistency.   Design consistency greatly reduces the number of concepts to be learned. Inconsistency requires the mastery of multiple models.

Drawing physical analogies.   Replicate the environment that has become familiar and well known. Use words and symbols in their customary ways. Duplicate actions that are already learned, such as changing screens by paging rather than scrolling.

Complying with expectancies and stereotypes.   Avoid new and unfamiliar associations. With color, for example, accepted meanings for red, amber, and green are already well established. Directional movement is strongly associated with the face of the compass so directional orientation should mimic this expectancy.

Providing action-response compatibility.   All system responses should be compatible with the actions that elicit them. Command names, for example, should reflect the actions that will occur. Organization of function key names on menus or help screens should reflect the spatial organization of the keys themselves on the keyboard. Action-response compatibility promotes rapid transfer of information between the user and the system.

Providing necessary and proper feedback.   Feedback shapes human performance. Efficient learning of the mental model will not occur unless feedback is provided concerning the correctness of all actions taken.

EASE OF USE

Ease of use is frequently mentioned as an ultimate design criterion for a system. Although it is a simple expression, it has complicated implications. It may apply to a single operation, task, or procedure, or to an entire job. The following

13 criteria, some of which were first described by Miller (1971), can measure a system's ease of use.

1. *The training time required to achieve satisfactory performance* is important because in office systems, brevity equals goodness. Most managerial and professional personnel are too busy to devote much time to training in new technologies. In light of this, and considering high turnover rates, satisfactory performance levels must be achieved as soon as possible. It is critical that people be able to learn to operate a system within the time they allot to the learning process.

2. *Number of errors* refers to the maintenance of a reasonable error rate by competent people measured in units of time or number of operations.

3. *Integration of automated and nonautomated tasks* means that there must be a good fit between automated tasks and tasks the technology does not address. That fit must be achieved quickly and with few errors.

4. *Exasperation responses* are the "Oh damn!" reactions that express user annoyance or frustration. Their frequency may foretell a strong rejection of a tool or technology. The absence of exasperation, however, may not represent acceptance.

5. *Habit formation rate* refers to how quickly people learn to use a facility and how quickly that use becomes more or less automatic, so that they no longer have to think about what they are doing. This variable can be measured by observing a person's speed, lack of hesitation, and apparent ease in working with a device or system.

6. *How many people want to use the system* reflects the attitude of actual or potential users toward a device or system. There are, of course, many reasons for liking or disliking a system, and not all of them are necessarily connected with the device itself or the service it provides. In any case, these attitudes may be a more powerful factor than any other in a given system's acceptance.

7. *Irrelevant supporting actions required to perform a task* are the incidental actions required for, but not directly related to, doing a job. They include translating computer code into English, performing frequent or extensive *log-on* procedures, or going through several operations to find the right page in an instruction manual.

8. *Irrelevant display events* include information items that must be disregarded but that use up part of the capacities an individual could devote to relevant tasks.

9. *Time and frequency for user warm-up* means how long it takes to relearn the necessary skills involved in using infrequently used tools or procedures. It also refers to the number of minutes required for warm-up each time a frequently used tool is used before satisfactory speed and accuracy are achieved.

10. *Decision-making time* is the amount of time required to decide what to do after receiving all the information necessary to analyze a problem and select a suitable action.
11. *Shift or work time* is the length of time a person can work without becoming fatigued.
12. *Failure recovery time* includes the amount of time, the number of operations, and the cost of resources required for the user to recover from failures caused by either operator or system errors.
13. *Technology transition time* means the time necessary, where multiple systems are employed, to achieve a satisfactory performance level after shifting from one tool to another.

FRIENDLY SYSTEMS

Another descriptive term commonly used in today's systems literature is *friendly*—a quality that well-designed office systems are supposed to possess. However, the definition of *friendly* (relating to or befitting a friend; showing kindly interest or goodwill; not hostile; inclined to favor; comforting or cheerful) from *Webster's Seventh New Collegiate Dictionary* provides designers with little useful information for developing a friendly system. Much is left to the imagination.

To put the term in a systems context, let us say that any design decision that allows a system to achieve a high score in ease-of-use criteria will get a high score in friendliness. But friendliness may mean something more—the harmonious interaction of all the ease-of-use criteria. Achieving this will be slow, as systems implementors gain a better understanding of the role of people in systems, and as they test and then modify those systems.

THE DESIRABLE QUALITIES OF A SYSTEM

The computer, as the office worker's major tool, should, like a friend, be pleasant to be with. It should be seen as possessing a variety of desirable qualities. In recent years, a number of writers and researchers (e.g. Nemeth, 1982) have begun to describe what these desired qualities are. While too abstract to serve as design guidelines themselves, they provide useful criteria toward which design guidelines my be directed. They are discussed in the following paragraphs.

Adaptive. A system must be adaptable to the physical, emotional, intellectual, and knowledge traits of the people whom it serves. All office workers should be permitted to interact with a computer in a manner and style that best suit their needs. In essence, the system should be responsive to individual differences in interaction manner, depth, and style.

Transparent. A system must permit one's attention to be focused entirely on the task or job being performed, without concern for the mechanics of the interface. One's thoughts must be directed to the application, not the communication. Any operations which remind a worker of their presence are distracting.

Comprehensible. A system should be understandable. A person should know what to look at, what to do, when to do it, why to do it, and how to do it (Treu, 1977). The flow of information, commands, responses, and visual presentations should be in a sensible order that is easy to recollect and place in context (Kaplow and Molnar, 1976).

Natural. Operations should mimic the office worker's behavior patterns. Dialogues should mimic his thought processes and vocabulary (Foley and Wallace, 1974).

Predictable. System actions should be expected, within the context of other actions that are performed. All expectations should be fulfilled uniformly and completely (Martin, 1973; Treu, 1977).

Responsive. Every human request should be acknowledged, every system reaction clearly described. Feedback is the critical ingredient in shaping a user's performance.

Self-explanatory. Steps to complete a process should be obvious and, where not, supported and clarified by the system itself. Reading and digesting long explanations should never be necessary (Eason, 1979).

Forgiving. A system should be tolerant of the human capacity to make errors, at least up to the point where the task or the integrity of the system are affected. Inflexible, unforgiving systems are a major cause of system dissatisfaction. The fear of making a mistake and not being able to recover from it is a primary contributor to a fear of dealing with computers (Eason, 1979; Hansen, 1976).

Efficient. Eye and hand movements must not be wasted. Attention should be directed to relevant controls and displays of information. Visual and manual transitions between various system components should proceed easily and freely.

Flexible. People should be able to structure or change a system to meet their particular needs. Inexperienced people may wish to confront and use only a small portion of a system's capabilities in a specific manner. With experience, they may wish to utilize extended capabilities in some other way. This extension and modification of interaction and control procedures should be permitted at the discretion of the users (Kaplow and Molnar, 1976; Shneiderman, 1980).

Available. Like any tool, an office system must be available if it is to be effective. Any system unreliability, no matter how good normal system performance is, will create dissatisfaction (Miller and Thomas, 1977).

DIALOGUES

"Dialogue" is the word now commonly used to describe the exchange of information, or communication, between the computer and its user. The dialogue style chosen reflects the forms of communication available and computer and user capabilities.

Forms of Communication

The need for people to communicate with each other has existed since we first walked upon this planet. The lowest level, and most common, communication modes we share are movements and gestures. Movements and gestures are language-independent, that is, they permit people who do not speak the same language to deal with one another.

The next level, in terms of universality and complexity, is spoken language. Most people can speak one language, some two or more. A spoken language is a very efficient mode of communication, if both parties to the communication understand it.

At the third level of complexity is written language. While most people speak, not all can write. But for those who can, writing is still nowhere near as efficient a means of communication.

In modern times, we have the typewriter, another step upward in complexity. Significantly fewer people type than write, yet a practiced typist can find typing faster and more efficient than handwriting. (The unskilled may not find this the case). Spoken language is still more efficient than typing, regardless of typing skill level.

From the computer's perspective, these four forms of communication are inversely related to its ease of understanding. The easiest and best way for a computer to communicate is through typed input. It can accept a handwritten input, but only if the message contains carefully formed letters or symbols. Some computers can be taught to recognize spoken words, but even greater limitations exist in terms of vocabulary size and inflection variation. Computers that can respond to human gestures and movements do not exist, except in a few experimental laboratories. The computer does best, then, with what people do worst, and vice-versa. So the dialogue style chosen reflects a compromise by the user. This does not mean, however, that an effective human-computer interaction is not attainable today. It means that things will move from good today to better tomorrow.

Interaction Styles

An interaction style is the particular technique used for providing an orderly exchange of information between people and computers. Styles include question and answer, menu selection, form fill-in, command language, natural language, and direct manipulation, as described by Chapanis (1984) and Shneiderman (1987).

Question and answer. The computer asks a series of questions and the user responds to each in turn. Its advantage is minimal training, making it especially useful for the novice or casual user. This approach can become cumbersome for the more frequent system user.

Menu selection. A list, or menu, of items or alternatives is presented and the appropriate one selected, either by pointing at it, keying the applicable code, or pressing the proper key. One advantage of a menu is that it structures the decision-making process and reduces learning and keystrokes, making it useful to the novice or casual user. Disadvantages include the necessity to consume screen space to list the alternatives, the danger of too many menus, and the requirement for fast response times. While small numbers of menus and fast response times may not always hinder frequent users, overall, menu dialogues do tend to slow down experts.

Form fill-in. The computer presents the user with a series of captioned blank fields which the user fills in with the required information. This style requires that the user understand the captions, know the method of entry and the permissable values to be keyed, and be able to respond to and correct errors. Therefore, some knowledge and training is usually necessary. The process is similar to filling out a paper form and it is fairly easy for the system to provide assistance in the event of problems. It is faster than question and answer dialogue because of multiple responses for each computer communication.

Command languages. The user types a command to which the computer responds. This interaction gives the user a strong feeling of control. Also, complex instructions can be expressed rapidly. Other advantages include minimal screen space requirements and lessened impact of slow response times. To master a command language dialogue typically requires a great deal of memorization and learning, placing it in the domain of the expert user. Its big disadvantage is its training requirements, which are difficult for the novice or casual user to cope with. Error rates for this kind of dialogue tend to be high.

Natural language. Computer natural languages are sometimes considered synonymous with English prose. Many argue that systems must accept natural language sentences or phrases if they are to move smoothly into the office. The advantage of a natural language is that it is flexible, powerful, and requires no special learning. On the negative side, a natural language interaction provides little context for specifying the next command, frequently requires clarification, and may be slower and more cumbersome than some of the other alternatives.

Natural human communications are characterized by an apparent unruliness. Gould et al. (1976) found that slight variations in instructions for achieving a goal led to large variations in the expressions people used to achieve the goal. There was no particularly strong natural tendency, but the adaptiveness of human linguistic and cognitive systems was apparent. Procedure manuals written by different analysts describing the same activity, or forms they design to collect the same data, are classic examples of this adaptiveness. Chapanis el al. (1977), in a study of communication modes, found numerous errors and irregularities, and grammatical rules repeatedly violated or ignored in natural language interactions.

If computers are ever to interact with people on human terms, the irregularities and inconsistencies that characterize natural languages must be confronted. Although human communication appears to have no strict standards, it obviously follows some rules because information gets conveyed and quite complex problems get solved.

But perhaps a totally natural language is not necessary. Seeking economy of effort, people tend to be impatient with redundancy (Nickerson, 1969), something which English has in abundance. The objective of any communication is to transmit an idea quickly and accurately. The transmitter's degree of redundancy depends on the recipient's ability to understand. If the communicator limits redundancies, will the message still be effectively conveyed?

The study by Kelly and Chapanis (1977) has a bearing on this question. They required subjects communicating by teletypewriter to use either 300-word, 500-word, or unlimited vocabularies. Subjects who worked with the restricted vocabularies interacted and solved problems as successfully as those who worked with no restrictions. Thus it appears possible, at least for the types of communications studied in this experiment, to develop limited vocabularies for use in human/machine interactions.

Another pertinent study is Gould et al. (1976), which found that subjects who showed a low preference for a restricted-syntax language would readily and sometimes spontaneously use such a language when called upon to communicate.

Schoonard and Boies (1975) tested the ability of typists to type abbreviated words (of one to three characters) in a text-entry process. The typists recognized and typed 93 percent of the abbreviated words, with an error rate no greater than when they were typing unabbreviated words. And the substitution process did not affect the keystroke rate.

The results of these studies and evidence from operating data-processing systems (Galitz, 1979) indicate that well-designed, restricted vocabularies can provide effective language interfaces between users and office systems. But the language must be natural from an application and job-related standpoint.

The search for the ideal language or languages must continue if people and machines are to work in total harmony. The ultimate solution is probably beyond today's technology and will require further refinement and the use of voice and touch. But for now, designs must be developed within the limits of today's technology.

Direct manipulation (iconic). The newest interaction style is direct manipulation of visual objects representing the world of interest. By pointing at pictures of objects or actions, the user can quickly perform tasks and watch the results immediately. Direct manipulation is believed to be superior to other styles because it is simple, natural, and direct, the keyboard keys being replaced by cursor movement devices (the Mouse, for example). For novice and casual users direct manipulation is appealing. It does have disadvantages, however, in that it is harder to program and requires graphics and a pointing device.

In conclusion, the above interaction styles each have certain advantages and disadvantages for users with differing levels of experience. Are these differences always generalizable, and is interaction style the most critical consideration in ease of use? The evidence indicates no. Whiteside et al. (1985) compared seven different interactive systems possessing three different styles: command language, menu selection, and iconic (direct manipulation). They found that interaction style is not related to user performance or preference, but that careful design is. The care with which an interface is crafted is more important than the style of interface chosen; new interface technology has not solved old usability problems. This, of course, is not to say that interaction style is irrelevant, however. It simply means that poor design can mask any differences that do exist.

CURRENT DIRECTIONS AND GUIDELINES

Design of the human–computer interface still remains more an art than a science. The body of research needed to develop truly effective interfaces is small, and only now is this needed research effort showing signs of awakening. Also, the design issues also have great depth and subtlety. Even seemingly straightforward considerations, such as minimizing the number of keystrokes, may not make a system easier to use. Therefore, we cannot be optimistic that all the answers will be forthcoming in the years ahead.

The office and technology, however, will not wait. We must move forward with what is known today, making decisions as best we can. Toward that goal, what follows is a series of guidelines addressing system design. They reflect not only what we know today but what we think we know today. Many are based on research; others, on the collective thinking of behaviorists working in office automation. The guidelines address only general behavioral considerations when nothing is known about individuals and their functions. Final system design will, of course, require understanding of specific user tasks and goals.

Consistency

A system should look, act, and feel the same throughout.

Design consistency is the common thread that runs throughout these guidelines. It is the cardinal rule of all design activities. Consistency is important because it can reduce requirements for human learning by allowing skills learned in one situation to be transferred to another like it. While any new automated system must impose some learning requirements on its users, it should avoid encumbering productive learning with nonproductive, unnecessary activity.

In addition to increased learning requirements, variety in design has a number of other prerequisites and by-products, including:

* more specialization by system users,
* greater demand for higher skills,
* more preparation time and less production time,
* more frequent changes in procedures,
* more error-tolerant systems (because errors are more likely),
* more kinds of documentation,
* more time to find information in documents,
* more unlearning and learning when systems are changed,
* more demands on supervisors and managers,
* more things to go wrong.

Inconsistencies in design are caused by differences in people—several designers might each design the same system differently. Inconsistencies also occur when design activities are pressured by time constraints. All too often the solutions in those cases are exceptions that the user must learn to handle.

Users, however, perceive a system as a single entity. To them, it should look, act, and feel similarly throughout. Excess learning requirements become a barrier to their achieving and maintaining high performance and can ultimately influence user acceptance of the system.

Can consistency make a big difference? One study found that user thinking time nearly doubled when the position of screen elements, such as titles and field captions, was varied on a series of menu screens (Teitelbaum and Granda, 1983).

Standards and guidelines. Design consistency is achieved by developing and applying design standards. The designer creativity that this stifles (if indeed it does) would seem a small price to pay for an effective design.

Two questions often asked are, "Is it too late to develop and implement standards?" and "What will be the impact on systems and screens now being used?" To address these questions, Burns and Watson (1986) reformatted several alphanumeric inquiry screens to improve their comprehensibility and readability. When these reformatted screens were presented to expert system users, decision-making time remained the same but errors were reduced. For novice system users, the reformatted screens brought large improvements in speed and accuracy. Therefore, it appears, changes enhancing screens will benefit novice as well as expert users already familiar with the current screens. It is never too late to change.

Design Tradeoffs

Human requirements must always take precedence over machine processing requirements.

Design guidelines often cover a great deal of territory and occasionally conflict with one another or with machine processing requirements. In such conflicts the designer must weigh alternatives and reach a decision based on accuracy, time, cost, and ease-of-use requirements. The ultimate solution will be a blend of experimental data, good judgment, and the user needs of most importance.

This leads to the second cardinal rule of system development: *Human requirements always take precedence over machine processing requirements*. It might be easier for the designer to write a program or build a device that neglects user ease, but this should not be tolerated.

Log-On

Only one simple action should be necessary to initiate a log-on.

Access to a system must be easy. Like the cover of a book, the log-on process should encourage, not discourage, the desire to go inside. It should be a separate procedure before the operational options are encountered, since having to anticipate additional steps and commands can be distracting and confusing. And it should be nothing more than the depression of a log-on or start key. If more actions are required, the system must lead a person through the necessary steps. A difficult or cumbersome log-on process can discourage a system's use before its benefits can be demonstrated. If for some reason the log-on is delayed, the user should receive an advisory message stating when the system will be ready.

Initiative

Initiative should be commensurate with the capabilities of the system users:

- for new and inexperienced people, provide a computer-initiated dialogue;
- for the experienced, permit a human-initiated dialogue.

Initiative is a system characteristic defining who leads the dialogue between the user and the computer. In a *computer-initiated dialogue,* the system leads the dialogue and a person responds to various prompts. These prompts may take the form of questions, directions, menus of alternatives, or forms to fill in. Computer-initiated dialogues are usually preferred by new users of systems because they rely on our powerful passive vocabulary (words that can be recognized and understood) and they are a learning vehicle, implicitly teaching a system model as one works.

Human-initiated dialogue puts the lead in the hands of the system's user. The computer becomes a blackboard waiting to be drawn upon. The user provides free-form instructions from memory—either commands or information—and the system responds accordingly. Human-initiated dialogues are often preferred by experienced system users, since they permit faster and more efficient interaction. A computer-initiated dialogue tends to slow down and disrupt the more experienced user.

Mixed-initiative dialogues have also been designed. An example is labeled function keys on display terminals. The label itself provides a prompt or memory aid, but the user must remember when it can be used.

Most of the earlier-generation computer systems used human-initiated dialogue, since this was the style designers were most comfortable with. However, because of problems encountered, and because of exposure of computer technology to more nonspecialists, emphasis has shifted in recent years to computer-initiated methods. This new emphasis has brought into focus more clearly the problems of this approach for a person who becomes experienced with a system. So, today we are beginning to see systems that combine both initiative styles. The needs of new and experienced system users can thus be simultaneously satisfied.

A question that has repeatedly been asked is at what point a person is ready to make the transition from computer- to human-initiated dialogue. In a study by Gilfoil (1982) novice system users were given a choice of a menu-driven dialogue (computer-initiated) or a command-driven dialogue (human-initiated). They chose the menu approach to start with and moved to the command approach after 16 to 20 hours of experience. At this point they were found to perform better and to be more satisfied with the command dialogue. A similar study (Chafin and Martin, 1980) found the transition occurring at about 25 to 50 hours.

Of course, these numbers should not be interpreted literally. Many characteristics of the system, task, and user population would substantially influence the results. What is important is the direction these numbers take. They show that it does not take long for new users of a system to start moving from dependent to independent status. To be truly effective, an office system must provide a dual-initiation capability.

Flexibility

A system must be sensitive to the differing needs of its users.

Flexibility is a measure of the system's capability to respond to individual differences in people. A truly flexible system will permit a person to interact with it in a manner commensurate with his knowledge, skills, and experience. One kind of flexibility, which has already been described, is initiation. A system that permits both human- and computer-initiated dialogues is flexible in that regard. Other examples are the display or nondisplay of prompts, permitting defaults and the creation of special vocabularies. An electronic mail system is flexible in that it permits its users to receive their messages in three ways:

- when a message is there, the system sends it (*assertive*);
- the system calls to indicate a message is there, but the message must be asked for (*interrogative*);
- the system never calls, all messages must be asked for (*passive*).

Each person working with such a system can choose the method most comfortable to himself or herself.

Flexibility can have differing levels. At one extreme the user can choose the preferred method and the system will respond accordingly. At the other extreme the system constantly monitors a person's performance (errors, speed, frequency of use of components, and so on) and modifies itself accordingly. The latter might more appropriately be called an *adaptive system*.

Flexibility is not without dangers. Highly flexible dialogues can confuse inexperienced users, causing them to make more errors. For this reason, such dialogues appear desirable only for experienced or expert users. The novice user should not be exposed to system flexibility at the start, but only as experience is gained. The concept of "progressive disclosure," to be discussed in the *complexity* guideline to follow is also applicable here.

Another problem with flexibility is that it may not always be used, people preferring to continue doing things in the way they were first learned. A variety of factors may account for this, including an unwillingness to invest in additional learning, or, perhaps, new ways may just not be obvious. The former problem may be addressed by making the new ways as easy and safe to learn as possible, the latter by including in training and reference materials not only information about how to do things, but when they are likely to be useful.

Complexity

Complexity should be commensurate with the capabilities of the system users.

Three ways to minimize complexity

* Use progressive disclosure, hiding things until they are needed.
* Make common actions simple at the expense of uncommon actions made harder.
* Provide uniformity and consistency.

Complexity is a measure of the number of alternatives available to the office worker. It is the number of ways something can be done or the number of choices one has at any given point. A highly complex system is difficult to learn. For inexperienced users, complexity frequently degrades performance, especially by increasing error rates. Complex systems are often not fully used, or used ineffectively, because a person may follow known but more cumbersome methods instead of easier but unfamiliar methods. A system lacking complexity may have a different set of faults: it may be tedious to use or may not accomplish much.

Complexity, then, is a two-edged sword. To effectively solve office problems it must exist, but it must not be apparent for the tool to be effectively utilized by the office worker.

There are three specific ways to minimize complexity.

Progressive disclosure. Introduce system components gradually, only when people see a need to do something they do not know how to do, or when they see they can do something faster or in fewer steps. This is also called the layered, or spiral, approach to learning. Such an approach was taken by Carroll and Carrithers (1984), who called it the "Training-Wheels System." They found that by disabling portions of the system that were not needed and that could lead to errors or confusions, improved system learning efficiency was achieved.

Make common actions simple. Make common actions within a system easier to accomplish than uncommon actions. Greater overall system efficiency results.

Provide uniformity and consistency. Inconsistency is a foolish form of complexity. A person has to learn that things that appear different really are not.

Closure

- To provide closure, organize sequences of actions into groups with a beginning, middle, and an end.
- Provide informative feedback at the conclusion of each group of actions.

Closure means to complete, to achieve a satisfactory ending. Closure with its necessary informative feedback provides the user the satisfaction of accomplishment and a sense of relief. It indicates that contingency plans and options are not necessary and the way is clear to move ahead (Shneiderman, 1987).

Power

Dialogue power should be commensurate with the capabilities of the system users.

Power is a measure of the amount of work accomplished by a given instruction to a system. A very powerful instruction can evoke a string of system operations doing many things. This same string of operations can also be evoked by a series of instructions, each directed toward one specific aspect. But each individual instruction is then less powerful because it accomplishes less.

High power is usually associated with high dialogue complexity and reduced system generality. Therefore, while a powerful system can be effectively utilized in the hands of a well-trained person, the untrained may be unable or unwilling to cope. The result is often system rejection. Goodwin (1982) provides an interesting analysis of an electronic mail system whose utility was diminished because of the dialogue power it possessed.

Power, then, is another dialogue property whose effectiveness is directly related to the experience level of people working with a system, and whose optimum level varies along a sliding scale that changes with user needs.

Information Load

Information load should be commensurate with the capabilities of the system user.

Six ways to reduce information load

- Provide graphic rather than alphanumeric displays.
- Format displays to correspond to users' immediate information requirements.
- Use natural languages.
- Move clerical operations into the system.

- Provide less powerful commands.
- Provide less complex dialogues.

Two ways to increase information load

- Permit more powerful commands.
- Permit more complex dialogues.

Information load is a measure of the degree to which a user's memory is being utilized and/or processing resources are absorbed by the design. It is a function of the task being performed, a person's familiarity with the task, and the design of the dialogue itself. Like other dialogue properties, the optimum level can change with a user's experience.

Information loads that are too high or too low can affect performance. High loads strain a person's capabilities and may cause an inability or unwillingness to cope. Low levels create boredom and inattentiveness, fostering errors.

Human memory is a weak link in the human–machine interface and should be supported whenever possible. Information load can be reduced by the actions listed above. As a user becomes more knowledgeable and the information load can be expanded, the direction should be toward greater dialogue power and complexity. These are positive steps toward greater system effectiveness.

Control

General

- The user must control the interaction:
    - actions should result from explicit user inputs;
    - actions should be capable of interruption or termination;
    - the user should never be interrupted for errors.
- The context maintained must be that of the user.
- The means to achieve goals must be compatible with the user's skills and the desired end result.

Paths

- The capability to go from/to any point or step must exist.
- Input stacking must be possible.
- A home position must always be available.

Options

- Options or actions available at any time must be accessible either on a display or through a help function.
- Only relevant options should be available.

Control is feeling in charge, feeling that the system is responding to your actions. It is achieved when the user, working at his own pace, is responsible for determining what to do, selecting how to do it, entering information into the system, processing that information in conjunction with the system, correcting errors, and later retrieving information from the system. Lack of control is shown by unavailable systems, surprising system actions or responses, tedious and long procedures that cannot be circumvented, difficulties in obtaining necessary information, and an inability to achieve the desired results.

The feeling of control has been found to be an excellent mitigator of the work stress associated with many automated systems (Gardell, 1979; Johansson et al., 1978; Karasek, 1979; Karasek et al., 1981; and Frankenhaeuser, 1979).

General. Control must always be in the hands of the user. Actions must result from explicit human inputs and requests, and should be capable of being interrupted or terminated by the user. User actions should never be interrupted by errors. There should be no delays or paced delays beyond a user's expectancies.

The context maintained must always be the user's perspective. The knowledge carried forward by the system must be that which represents the user's level of understanding. To help the user remember status or context, prior user entries should be available for review as needed. While processing modes are not desirable, if used, a facility should be available to remind the user of which one is current.

The means to accomplish actions should be compatible with the user's skills, either novice, expert, or somewhere in between. Frequent or common actions should be made very easy.

Paths. Users should, at their option, be able to move from any one point or step in an interaction to any other step or point within the context of the job. In a series of menus, for example, the capability should exist for going from one menu to any other menu in the string. This kind of action is illustrative of a human-initiated dialogue overriding a computer-initiated dialogue.

Stacking of inputs or requests must be possible. Stacking is the process of stringing together a series of discrete requests or commands so that they comprise one input. The system will then perform each action consecutively while the user awaits the result. The order of stacked commands should be the same as if they were discrete commands. Command separators should be standard symbols, preferably a slash (/). No concern with blanks should be required. If the system is unable to complete a series of stacked commands, it should stop and present the next appropriate step or menu. The user should be able to assign a single name to command strings that are frequently used together. This more powerful command should then be recognizable by the system and in the future elicit the discrete actions it refers to.

A home position, such as a primary or main system menu, should always be achievable by a simple user action.

Options.   Options or actions available at any given time must be available on a display or through a help function. All relevant options should be displayed except those that are always available systemwide. Only relevant options should be displayed. Options not currently available to a person should not be provided. If options are designated by codes, these codes must also be provided.

Feedback

A system should acknowledge all actions by:

- immediate execution,
- change in state or value,
- correction message,
- confirmation message,
- IN-PROGRESS message.

Knowledge of results, or *feedback,* is a necessary learning ingredient. It shapes human performance and instills confidence. All requests to the system must be acknowledged in some way. This acknowledgment is normally provided when the system completes the request, and may be implicit—a change in state—or it may be explicit—a message of the kind described above. The screen should not be blank for more than a few moments, as the user may think the system has failed.

If a request requires a longer processing period than is normally associated with the action requested (see the guidelines on response times), the system should acknowledge its receipt and provide an interim IN-PROGRESS message.

Substantial and more informative feedback is most important for the novice or casual system user. Expert users are often content to receive more modest feedback.

Recovery

A system should permit:

- commands or actions to be abolished or reversed,
- immediate return to a certain point if difficulties arise.

People should be able to retract an action by issuing what Miller and Thomas (1977) call an *undo* command. Knowing they can withdraw a command reduces much of the distress of new users, who often worry about doing something wrong. The return point could be the previous screen, a recent closure point, or the beginning of some predetermined period, such as back ten screens or some number of minutes. Reversing or abolishing an action is analogous to using an eraser to eliminate a pencil mark on a piece of paper.

The goal, as Martin (1973) says, is stability—returning easily to the right track when a wrong track has been taken. Recovery should be obvious, automatic, and easy and natural to perform. In short, it should be hard to get into deep water or go too far astray. Easy recovery from an action greatly facilitates learning by trial-and-error and exploration. If an action is not reversible, and its consequences are critical, it should be made difficult to accomplish.

Function Keys

Uses

- Use for frequent and basic control inputs.

Operation

- Require single action only.
- Disable keys when not applicable.

Labels

- Provide informative descriptions.
- If multifunctional, describe the current function.

Location

- Arrange in logical groupings.
- Make location compatible with importance.

Consistency

- Use a common meaning and location discipline across modes and applications.

Function keys are advantageous because they reduce memory requirements, permit faster entry (fewer keystrokes), and reduce errors. Therefore, they are integral parts of almost all office system keyboards.

Uses. Function keys are ideal for inputs that are frequent and basic. The control functions described in the next section are ideal candidates for inclusion as function keys.

Operation. Require only single actions to activate function keys. Shift key operations are especially prone to error. Hammond et al. (1980B) found that about one-third of the errors in a computer system were the result of mistyping, and half of these were due to using the correct key with the wrong shift. If a function key is not being used, it should be disabled.

Labels. Provide informative descriptions that clearly describe the key's purpose. If multifunctional, describe the key's current function through an overlay or on the display screen itself.

Location. Provide logical groupings of keys based upon an analysis of their sequence of use, frequency of use, function, and importance. In establishing function key meanings and locations, keep eye–hand movements to a minimum and position the most frequently used keys in the most prominent locations. The most accessible locations for two common keyboard function key arrangements are shown in figure 3.1.

Consistency. Be consistent in labeling and usage between modes and across applications.

Control Functions

Desirable control functions include:

- page forward
- page backward
- hold/store
- abort/cancel
- end/stop
- retrieve

Figure 3.1 Most accessible function key locations.

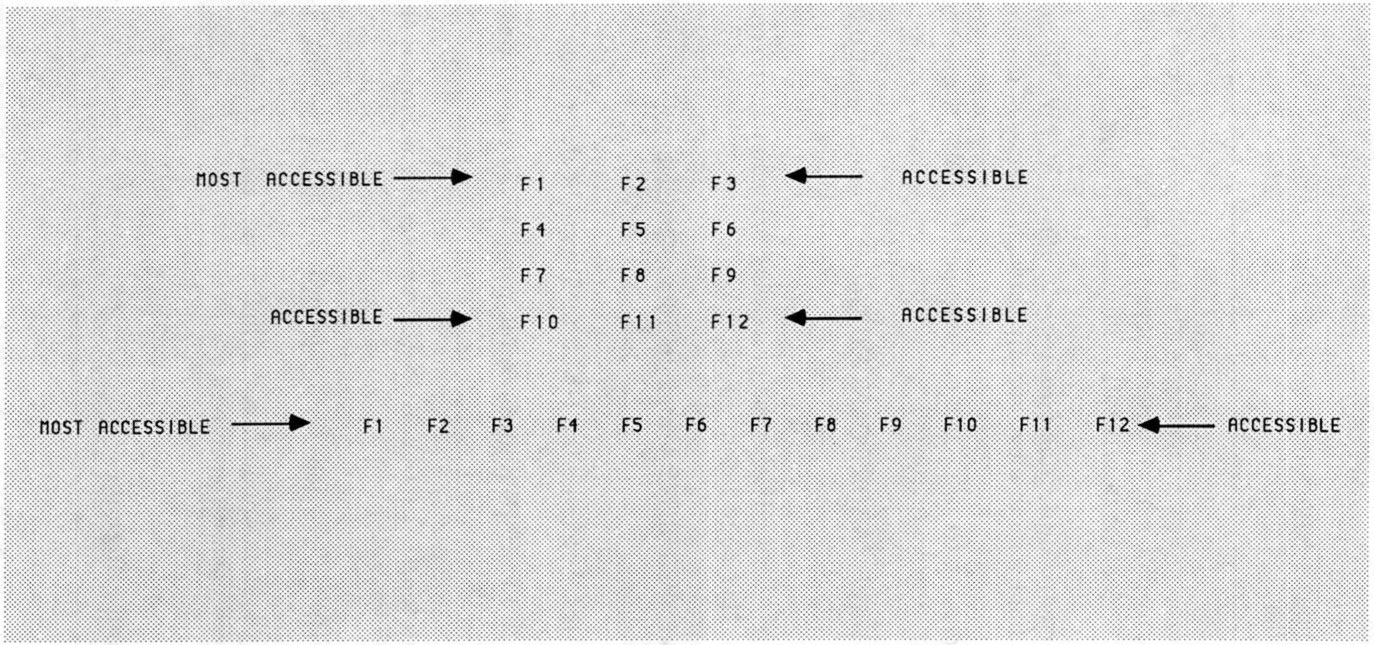

41

- help
- resume
- undo/back-up
- print

Interacting with an office system requires that some basic control operations be available at all times. Logical candidates are the following functions, which are ideal for incorporation into function keys.

Page forward and Page backward. PAGE FORWARD and PAGE BACKWARD enable one to move rapidly through a series of display screens.

Hold/store. HOLD/STORE stores something being worked on in a file facility that may later be retrieved.

Abort/cancel. ABORT/CANCEL cancels or erases what the user is working on.

End/stop. END/STOP stops processing immediately; processing may be resumed at that point later.

Retrieve. RETRIEVE brings up from a file facility what has previously been stored.

Help. HELP accesses the HELP facility, to be described.

Resume. RESUME returns to the point where one is working after HELP or END/STOP.

Undo/back-up. UNDO/BACK-UP reverses the action just performed, as previously described.

Print. PRINT provides hard-copy printout of the current display.

Any system application may, of course, require additional control functions based upon its objectives.

Command Languages

Content

- Use words that are familiar, highly suggestible, and discriminating.

Structure

- Use words that are perceptually dissimilar.
- Permit abbreviations but train with full words.

Organization

- Provide a structuring rule.
- Provide customized subsets.
- Permit naming flexibility.

Consistency

- Use a common command discipline throughout all applications.

Defaults

- Within a command, the system should supply missing arguments. Between commands, the system should supply missing commands if a predefined sequence is initiated; supply missing arguments based on previously supplied arguments; supply a missing command based on arguments.

Edits

- Only incorrectly entered command data should be reentered.

Command languages must be logical, consistent, and flexible. A logical and consistent language will expedite the learning process and slow the forgetting that results from language disuse. Flexibility allows users to adapt the command language to themselves instead of the other way around. The following guidelines highlight the more important features of a command language. Engel and Granda (1975) and Watson (1976) also provide detailed discussions.

Content. Command languages must be familiar and reflect the user's viewpoint, not the system designer's. Users must be able to express their needs with command constructions similar to their own language, thought processes, and natural problem-solving vocabularies. Ledgard et al. (1980) found far better performance after redesigning a commercial text editor so that the commands more closely resembled English phrases. Black and Moran (1982) found words always better than nonwords in free recall.

All too often a command language has been created by the system's designer. Jones (1978) pointed out the discrepancies between designers' assumptions and the realities of the users' language that have made many command languages difficult to use. He concluded that:

- Designers tend to assume a one-to-one correspondence between newly formed command statements and their meanings. Users see many of the commands as having the same meaning.
- Designers presume nothing is assumed by users except what is expressly stated about a command. Actually, users possess innumerable unstated assumptions that are applied to the interpretation process.
- Designers assume that users' deductions are made from absolutely unvarying frames of reference. In fact, users often establish meaning based upon immediate context.

Is the user the best creator of a command language for an office automation system? The evidence here is contradictory. Black and Moran (1982) conclude that computer naive people are not good command language designers. They tend to create frequent and general words for commands when the best performance is achieved with infrequent, discriminating words. Furnas et al. (1982) found great diversity in people's descriptions of even the most common objects. The average likelihood of any two people using the same main content word in their description of the same object ranged from 7 to 18 percent. Therefore a common word acceptable to all is difficult to achieve. Similar conclusions have been reached by Barnard et al. (1981) and Carroll (1980).

However, Scapin (1982) found that people performed better with their own command language. Perhaps the best solution is a joint effort between users and designers with the final solution derived from testing and refinement.

Command names should be highly suggestible. A command name is good to the degree that it suggests directly what the command does (PRINT is better than LIST), and that it suggests directly the relationship (whether similar, opposite, or unrelated) of that command to other commands in the system (Rosenberg, 1982). Hammond et al. (1980a) found that the pattern of errors in a dialogue correlates with the extent to which command names are ambiguous about their underlying operations.

Command names should be discriminating. Avoid small and subtle differences such as PRINT versus WRITE. Use specific instead of general words (SUBSTITUTE instead of CHANGE). As described above, both Barnard et al. (1982) and Black and Moran (1982) found that specific words resulted in better performance than general words.

Structure. Choose command words that are perceptually dissimilar to avoid confusion errors. While command languages must be meaningful and not highly coded, abbreviations and concise notation will support differing user proficiencies, from expert to novice. Advanced vocabularies and short, concise control notations and conventions maximize the performance of expert users.

Inability to abbreviate can contribute to user dissatisfaction, since forcing people to enter long words increases keying time, error frequency, and associated time-consuming recovery procedures.

When abbreviations are permitted, however, as discussed in chapter 5-1, truncation is the recommended method (Ehrenreich, 1985), and training should always be with the full command word to aid the learning and retaining of command meaning (Barnard and Grudin, 1985).

Organization. Provide a structuring rule for the population of commands. Scapin (1982) found that providing structure to a family of commands by breaking them into logical groupings was an important factor in aiding learning.

Provide subsets of the command language and features. This is particularly advantageous when the technology is first introduced, since it permits phased learning of system components.

Provide flexibility by permitting users to assign their own names to frequent command sequences. The result, as mentioned earlier, will be a more powerful dialogue.

Consistency. Consistency in command languages is mandatory if a collection of office systems with which a worker interacts is considered as one system. Table 3.1 illustrates some command words from current systems that are used to accomplish the same purpose. People must be able to learn additional functions by increasing their vocabulary, not by learning separate foreign languages.

Defaults. If a person fails to specify a command, the system may prompt him to supply the missing information by listing potential values. This approach is acceptable if the alternatives are limited, but it is less desirable when the list becomes complicated or time consuming. A second alternative is to ask users to supply the missing information from memory, but this is not an optimal approach.

A third option is for the system to supply a default value for the missing information. A *default* is an agreement between the user and the system con-

Table 3.1 Different command words often having the same meaning.

To begin an interaction:	*To create a hard copy:*
LOGIN	WRITE
LOGON	OUTPUT
HELLO	PRINT
SIGNIN	LIST
SIGNON	DISPLAY

Figure 3.2 Command argument methods.

```
Command:

        PRINT INCOMPLETE NEW BUSINESS
        (----------Command-----------)

        PRINT COMPLETE NEW BUSINESS
        (----------Command---------)


Command and argument:

    PRINT                           INCOMPLETE NEW BUSINESS

    (command)                       (------Arguments------)

    PRINT                           COMPLETE NEW BUSINESS

    (command)                       (------Arguments------)
```

cerning the normal or usual working environment. Defaults are a powerful aid in achieving a user-oriented language, but they are not without problems. The user may not know or understand the default or may not have a convenient way of changing it. For these reasons, perhaps default usage should be optional.

A *command argument* is an option that qualifies a general command. Figure 3.2 shows two command methods for obtaining a printout of two kinds of insurance transactions—incomplete and complete new business. The first method uses two separate commands, while the second has one command, used with two arguments.

Edits. A person should never have to reenter an entire command, especially if only one item on a line is incorrect. An appropriate mechanism such as cursor positioning should also exist to help the user by setting up the appropriate spot for reentry.

Command Language Arguments

Organization

- Few commands with many arguments is a better organization than many commands with a few arguments.

Format

* Keyword argument formats are superior to positional formats.

Organization. Boies (1974) found that a majority of users in a large time-sharing system used only a few of the many system commands available and frequently employed commands in their simplest and least powerful form. He speculated that this could result from command structures that were difficult for users to recall when needed. Boies subsequently compared the use of a small number of commands and a large number of arguments with the use of many specific commands and few arguments. He found the former more useful. More study is needed to find an optimal command language strategy.

Format. In a positional command language format, arguments are assigned a relative or absolute position in the argument string. With a keyword format, arguments may be in permutable strings, indicating the argument type and its value. The value of arguments must be remembered in both cases. Positional formats appear to impose greater memory requirements on users, since remembering positions is an additional burden. In an informal study Weinberg (1971) found high error rates in positional format use.

Error Management

Prevention

* Handle common misspellings.
* Permit review of message about to be sent.
* Permit editing of message about to be sent.
* Provide common send mechanism.
* Advise of nonreversible changes.

Detection

* Immediately detect all errors.
* Maintain the item in error.
* Visually highlight the item in error.
* Identify fields requiring missing data.
* Display an error message on the entry screen.
* Position cursor at first error.
* Use auditory signals conservatively.
* Prevent errors from causing the system to abort.

Correction

- Provide constructive error messages.
  - What error was detected.
  - Which field was in error.
  - What corrective action is necessary.
- Initiate clarification dialogue, if necessary.
- Resend only erroneous information back to system.

The magnitude of errors in computer systems is astounding. Shneiderman (1987) describes studies reporting error rates in commands, tasks, or transactions as high as 46 percent. In addition to stranding the user and wasting time, mistakes and errors interrupt planning and cause deep frustrations.

Some experts have argued that there are no "errors" as such; they are simply "iterations" toward a goal. There is much truth to that statement. It is also often said that "to err is human." The corollary to that statement, at least in computer systems, might be, " . . . to forgive, good design."

Whatever we call them, errors will occur. People should be able to correct them as soon as they pop up, as simply and easily as they are made. One objective of this book is to reduce or eliminate errors in computer systems. The focus here is on the mechanics of error prevention, detection, and correction.

Prevention. Where possible, human misspellings of commands and requests should be accepted by the system. Person-to-person communication does not require perfection. Person-to-computer communication should impose no more rigor. Inappropriate use of shift keys should also be distinguished, where possible, since they are such a large cause of keying errors. Entries made into a system should be reviewable and editable by the person who made them. Human memory is poor and keying errors will occur.

A common *send* mechanism should be provided to transmit an entry to the system. Two or more keys to accomplish the same purpose, especially if their use is mandated by different conditions, can be confusing and more prone to errors. If an action causes a nonreversible change, and the change is critical, the user should be requested to confirm the change. A separate key should be used for this purpose, not the send key.

Detection. All errors should be immediately detected and communicated to the user through a highlighting display technique (for example, high intensity or contrasting color). This does not mean the user should be interrupted for each error that occurs. It is preferable to wait for a closure point, such as the end of a screen. Identify missing information in fields with question marks (?).

The items in error, and error messages, should be displayed on the entry screen being viewed. If multiple error messages occur, and it is impossible to display all of them at one time, provide an indication that there are additional messages. Say, for example, " + 2 other errors." Also, provide with a distinct difference the same error message displayed more than once because the first attempt to correct failed.

For ease in correcting, position the cursor in the first field in error when the error message is displayed. Be cautious in using auditory signals to notify of an error. Many users, especially those with status or position, do not want their mistakes advertised.

Correction. Explicit and constructive error messages should be provided. These messages should describe what error occurred, what field was in error, and how it should be corrected. Corrective actions will be clearer if phrased with words like "must be" or "must have." Shneiderman (1982), in restructuring messages following guidelines such as this, and others to be described in chapter 4, found improved success rates in fixing errors, lower error rates, and improved user satisfaction.

All error ambiguities should be resolved by having the system query the user. Errors should be corrected with minimal typing. Only erroneous information should be sent back to the system.

Another important error control measure is to have the system identify and store errors. This will allow tracking of common errors, so that appropriate prevention programs can be implemented.

Response Time

System responsiveness should match the speed and flow of human thought processes:

- if continuity of thinking is required and information must be remembered throughout several responses, response time should be less than two seconds;
- if human task closures exist, high levels of concentration are not necessary and moderate short-term memory requirements are imposed; response times of two to four seconds are acceptable;
- if major task closures exist, minimal short-term memory requirements are imposed; responses within four to fifteen seconds are acceptable;
- when the user is free to do other things and return when convenient response time can be greater than fifteen seconds.

Constant delays are preferable to variable delays.

What the ideal system response time is has been the subject of numerous studies. Unfortunately, there still does not exist a definitive time, or times, that is acceptable under all conditions. What is clear is that dissatisfaction with response time is dependent on user expectations. It is also clear that expectations can vary, depending on the task as well as the situation. The ideal condition is one in which a person "perceives" no delays. A response time is too long when one "notices" that the system is taking too long. The following paragraphs summarize some study conclusions, and some tentative findings.

The optimum response time is dependent upon the task. There is an optimum work pace that depends on the task being performed. Longer or shorter response times than the optimum lead to more errors. (Barber and Lucas, 1983). In general, response times should be geared to the user's short-term memory load and to how he has grouped the activities being performed. Intense short-term memory loads necessitate short response times. While completing chunks of work at task closures, users can withstand longer response delays.

The human *now*, or psychological present, is two to three seconds. This is why continuity of thinking requires a response time within this limit. Recent research indicates that for creative tasks, response times in the range of four-tenths to nine-tenths of a second can yield dramatic increases in productivity, even greater in proportion to the increase in response time (Smith, 1983). The probable reason is the elimination of restrictions caused by short-term memory limitations.

As the response-time interval increases beyond ten to fifteen seconds, continuity of thought becomes increasingly difficult to maintain. Doherty (1979) suggests that this happens because the sequence of actions stored in short-term memory beyond that time is badly disrupted and must be reloaded.

The response time guidelines above, then, relate to the general tasks being performed. Their applicability to every situation is not guaranteed.

Satisfaction with response time is a function of expectations. Expectations are based, in part, on past experiences. These experiences may be derived from working with a computer, or from the world in general, and they vary enormously across individuals and tasks.

Dissatisfaction with response time is a function of one's uncertainty about delay. The degree of frustration with delay may depend on such psychological factors as a person's uncertainty concerning how long the delay will be, the extent to which the actual delay contradicts those expectations, and what the person thinks is causing the delay. Such uncertainty concerning how long a wait there will be for a computer's response may in some cases be a greater source of frustration than the delay itself (Nickerson, 1969).

People will change work habits to conform to response time. As response time increases, so does think time (Cotton, 1978; Boies, 1974; and Butler, 1983). People also work more carefully with longer response times (Bergman et al., 1981). In some cases more errors have been found with very short response times. This may not be necessarily bad if the errors are the result of trial-and-error learning that is enhanced by very fast response times.

Constant delays are preferable to variable delays. Carbonell et al. (1969) point out that it is the variability of delays, not their length, that most frequently distresses people. From a consistency standpoint, a good rule of thumb is that response-time deviations should never exceed half the mean response time. For example, if the mean response time is four seconds, a two-second deviation is permissible. Variations should range from three to five seconds. Shneiderman (1987) suggests, however, that response time variation should not exceed 20 percent. Lower response time variability has been found to yield better performance (Miller, 1977), but small variations may be tolerated (Bergman et al., 1981; Weiss et al., 1982).

More experienced people prefer shorter response times. People work faster as they gain experience, a fact that leads Shneiderman (1987) to conclude that it may be useful to let people set their own pace of interaction. He also suggests that in the absence of cost or technical feasibility constraints, people will eventually force response time to well under one second.

Very fast or slow response times can lead to symptoms of stress. There is a point at which a person can be overwhelmed by information presented more quickly than it can be comprehended. There is also some evidence indicating that when a system responds too quickly, there is subconscious pressure on users to also respond quickly, possibly threatening their overall comfort (Elam, 1978), increasing their blood pressure, or causing them to exhibit other signs of anxious behavior (Brod, 1984). Symptoms of job burnout have been reported after substantial reductions in response time (Turner, 1984).

Slow and variable response times have also been shown to lead to a significant build-up of mood disturbances and somatic discomfort over time, culminating in symptoms of work stress, including frustration, impatience, and irritation (Schleifer, 1986).

Specific Response Times

- *Log-on/initialization:* up to thirty seconds, with immediate interim acknowledgment.
- *Error messages:* a brief pause after a closure.
- *Inquiry:* one to fifteen seconds.
- *Browsing/scrolling:* one second or less.
- *Data entry:* within a transaction, four to six seconds; after completing a transaction, up to fifteen seconds.

Acceptable response times for certain office system activities have been put forth. Delays in completing system log-on while the computer reorganizes resources and facilities are not as annoying as long delays during interactions. Therefore, delays of up to 30 seconds for log-on are acceptable, but a fairly quick acknowledgment that log-on is occurring should be given when the process begins.

Interruptions in concentration can be frustrating, so people should be able to finish what they are doing before being told of an error. At task closures, the system should pause briefly to allow a person to change mental modes before having to attend to an error message.

Inquiry response times depend on urgency. They may range from 1 to 15 seconds.

Browsing or scrolling usually involves rapid search for information. Additional information to be searched must maintain the visual searching pace established. A 1-second response time should be expected.

Manual paper shuffling during data entry provides a good closure point. Longer response delays between screens can then be tolerated.

Guidance and Assistance

A system should provide:

- On-line documentation that supplements hard copy documentation.
- User-selectable prompting.
- A HELP facility.

New system users must go through a learning process that involves developing a conceptual or mental model to explain the system's behavior and the task being performed. HELP displays and prompting serve as cognitive development tools to aid this process.

Technical information, unlike works of fiction, is seldom read for pleasure. People turn to it only when a question has to be answered. Failure to provide the support needed in learning, answering questions, and problem solving makes it very difficult for the user to recover from trouble on his own and to avoid future trouble by learning from his mistakes. The result is most often more errors and great frustration.

While it is desirable that the human-computer interface be so "self-evident" and "intelligent" that people never experience difficulties, this lofty goal will not be achieved in the forseeable future (Quinn and Russell, 1986). So, great emphasis should be placed on minimizing references to documentation and managing the trouble that does occur.

Hard copy versus on-line documentation. A question frequently asked is whether the system documentation should be hard copy, on-line, or both. Advantages exist for each. On-line documentation is always there and available when needed, can be rapidly accessed, and is difficult to misplace. It is easy to update and guarantees that all users possess the same version. It also does not require workspace for storage.

Its disadvantages include a less familiar format than the traditional manual. It is not as "readable" and is less easy to "browse" in. Less information can be displayed on a "page" at one time. It is not portable and cannot be annotated, written on, or marked in any way. Illustrations may be difficult to include. If the screen is filled with other work, it may require erasing what is being questioned in order to find answers. On-line documentation also requires learning additional commands in order to be effective.

Is on-line documentation or help better than a hard copy manual? The evidence does not always indicate that it is. Several studies have found manuals, or manuals in conjunction with on-line materials, superior to on-line help or documentation alone (Dunsmore, 1980; Watley and Mulford, 1983; and Cohill and Williges, 1985). It appears that the advantages associated with a paper format outweigh those associated with an on-line format.

Is on-line documentation or help better than no hard copy manual? Yes, concluded Cohill and Williges (1985). Task time and errors were reduced when a system version with a help facility was compared to the same system without one.

Is a well designed help facility better than a poorly designed one? Magers (1983) found that a well designed one was better. Good writing, task orientation, context sensitivity, and good examples all contribute to a good on-line help.

In conclusion, the evidence indicates that some kind of on-line help or documentation is necessary. The style, structure, and writing of the materials are crucial to its effectiveness, and on-line and hard copy documentation should supplement, not duplicate, each other.

Selective prompting. Prompting is instructional information. It takes the form of messages or other advice, such as the values to be keyed into a field. Prompting is also the system's way of requesting additional or corrected information, or of guiding users step by step through tasks.

Inexperienced users find prompting a valuable aid in learning a system. Experienced users, however, often find prompting undesirable. It slows them down, then adds "noise" to the screen, and reduces the amount of working information that can be displayed at one time.

Ideally, prompting should be available only as needed. People should be able to selectively or completely turn prompting on or off as needed. As an alternative, two separate sets of screens could be made available, one with prompts, the other without.

Help Facility

A help facility should:

- Be easily accessible.
- Possess a hierarchical or multilevel structure:
  - brief operational definitions or input rules,
  - summary explanations in text,
  - typical task-oriented examples.
- Be specific to the situation.
- Be concise.
- Be easily browsed, having a distinctive format:
  - contents screens and indexes,
  - screen headings, sub-headings, and location indicators,
  - descriptive words in the margin,
  - visual differentiation of screen components,
  - bulleted outline style for nontext displays,
  - listings displayed alphabetically,
  - highlighted critical information.
- Maintain context.

An on-line help facility may consist of the following:

- a user manual, an electronic version of the traditional paper document;
- tutorials providing information about the system's operation, and possibly including exercises and practice sessions;
- status information describing the current system or screen purpose, the current system state, or functions available;
- command information describing the kinds of actions or commands available, or function key assignments;
- problem-solving information, including error correction guidance, examples of correct procedures or actions, descriptions of required inputs or displayed outputs, and meanings of codes or abbreviations.

Easy accessibility. A help facility should be retrievable simply, quickly, and consistently, either by a key action or a command.

Hierarchical or multilevel structure. A help facility should be multilevel, proceeding from very general to successively more detailed and specific explanations. The first level should have brief definitions and rules, simple reminders, and memory joggers. The second level should incorporate fuller explanations in a textual format. The final, and deepest, level should provide guidance in the form of examples. Wright (1984) suggests that when procedural steps are presented, consecutive numbering will make them easy to follow.

Specific to the situation. The help response should be tailored to the task and the user's current position. When accessed, the HELP facility should be aware of the kind of difficulties a person is having and respond with relevant information. Only the information necessary to solve the immediate problem or to answer the immediate question should be presented. If the HELP facility is unsure of the reason for the request, it should work with the user through prompts and questions to resolve the problem.

Concise. Brevity is a virtue. Good writing using small words and short sentences will improve comprehension.

Easily browsed. Often, the exact location of information needed to answer questions cannot be definitely established. Providing information in a format that can be easily skimmed aids the search process and also helps the user become familiar with the information being presented. Techniques that enhance the skimming process are:

- contents pages and indexes,
- page headings and sub-headings,
- location indicators,
- descriptive words in the margins,
- differentiation of help screen components through consistent locations and various display techniques (see chapter 4, Screen Design Considerations),
- a bulleted outline style for nontext displays and listings (commands, error messages, etc.) displayed alphabetically rather than functionally,
- highlighted critical information.

Maintain context. Help should not disrupt processing. Easy return to the point of the problem should be permitted. Ideally, the problem or work should be retained on the screen when help is accessed, but this will not always be possible unless the system provides a windowing capability.

One potential danger the HELP facility, as Barnard et al. (1982) found, is that a person's recall of command operations is related to frequency of HELP facility access; fewer HELP requests were associated with better command recall. The researchers speculate that the availability of HELP may become a crutch and lead to less effective retention. People may implement a passive cognitive strategy. A HELP facility may influence performance in systematic and subtle ways and thus must be investigated further.

Considerations in Screen Design

4

A Well Designed Screen

- reflects the needs and idiosyncracies of its users
- is developed within the physical constraints imposed by the terminal
- effectively utilizes the capabilities of its software
- achieves the business objectives of the system for which it is designed

---

The considerations integral to screen design are: (1) human, (2) hardware, (3) software, and (4) application.

Human considerations in screen design are the needs and requirements of people. They are oriented toward clarity, meaningfulness, and ease of use. *Hardware and software considerations* reflect the physical constraints of the terminal on which the screen will be used and the characteristics of the controlling program. They provide a framework within which the screen design must occur and define the display techniques available to the designer. *Application considerations* reflect the objectives of the system for which the screen is being designed. They are the data or information building blocks that make up a screen.

A well designed screen will also be consistent within itself, within related screen formats, and with other screens within the application or organization. If it is used for data entry, it will also be consistent within constraints imposed by related source materials such as worksheets, forms, or manuals.

HUMAN CONSIDERATIONS

Human use of a screen is affected by a variety of design factors that include the format and content of the screen itself, the structure and content of the data or information contained on the screen, the organization of groups of screens, the format and content of related source documents, and the screen keying procedures.

In the following pages some general guidelines concerning the format and content of screens and screen data or information are presented. These broad guidelines are applicable to most kinds of screens. Discussions of source documents, screen groupings, and keying procedures are contained in the chapters detailing rules for specific types of screens, since they are more dependent on screen type. First, however, we will determine what people are looking for in a well designed screen, and present a test that may be applied to a screen to determine how easy it is to use.

Most Wanted Screen Features

What are people looking for in the design of screens? One organization asked a group of screen users, whose response is summarized as follows:

- an orderly, clean, clutter-free appearance,
- an obvious indication of what is being shown and what should be done with it,
- expected information where it should be,
- a clear indication of what relates to what (headings, field captions, data, instructions, options, and so forth),
- plain, simple English,
- a simple way of finding what is in the system and how to get it out,
- a clear indication of when an action could make a permanent change in the data or system operation.

The desired direction is toward simplicity, clarity, and understandability; these qualities are lacking in many of today's screens.

Screen Format and Content

Clarity, meaningfulness, and ease of use are achieved through the format and content of the screen itself and the information it contains. The format and content of the screen will be determined by where information is placed, how information is structured, and what information is included. The guidelines that follow provide general rules addressing these issues—where, what, and how. Subsequent chapters translate many of these broad guidelines into specific rules for the various types of screens that may be encountered. First, a simple test for good screen design is described.

The Test for a Good Design

Visual clarity is influenced by a number of factors, including information organization, grouping, legibility, and relevancy. Clarity is achieved when display elements are grouped in meaningful and understandable ways, rather than in random and confusing patterns. A simple test for good screen design does exist. A screen that passes this test will have surmounted the first obstacle to effectiveness.

The test. Can all screen elements (field captions, data, title, messages, command field, etc.) be identified without reading the words that make them up? That is, can a component of a screen be identified through cues independent of its content? If this is so, a person's attention can quickly be drawn to the part of the screen that is relevant at that moment. People often look at a screen for a particular reason, perhaps to locate a piece of information such as a customer name, to identify the name of the screen, or to find an instructional or error message. The signal at that moment is that element of interest on the screen. The noise is everything else on the screen. Cues independent of context that differentiate the components of the screen will reduce visual search times and minimize confusion.

Try this test on the front page of your morning newspaper. Where is the headline? A story heading? The weather report? How did you find them? The headline was identified probably by its visually large and bold type size; story headings, again by a type size visually different than other page components; the weather report, probably by its location (bottom right? top left?). Imagine finding the headline on the front page of the newspaper if the same type size and style was used for all components and their positions changed from day to day.

Unfortunately, many of today's screens cannot pass this simple test and are unnecessarily difficult to use. All the tools available to the creator of the newspaper's front page are not yet available to the screen designer. An effective solution can be achieved, however, with the equipment at hand. It simply involves the thoughtful application of the display techniques that exist, consistent locations, and the proper use of "white space."

WHERE TO PLACE INFORMATION ON A SCREEN

- Provide an obvious starting point in the upper left corner of the screen.
- Reserve specific areas of the screen for certain kinds of information, such as commands, error messages, title, and data fields, and maintain these areas consistently on all screens.
- Provide visually pleasing composition, including balance, regularity, symmetry, predictability, economy, sequentiality, unity, proportion, simplicity, and groupings.

Eyeball fixation studies indicate that in looking at displays of information, usually one's eyes move first to the upper left center of the display and then quickly move in a clockwise direction. During and following this movement people are influenced by the symmetrical balance and weight of the titles, graphics, and text of the display. The human perceptual mechanism seeks order and meaning and tries to impose structure when confronted with uncertainty. Whether a screen has meaningful and evident form or is cluttered and unclear is, therefore, immediately discerned. A cluttered or unclear screen requires that some effort be expended in learning and understanding what is presented. The screen user who must deal with the display is forced to spend time to learn and understand. The screen user who has an option concerning whether the screen will or will not be used may reject it at this point if the perceived effort is greater than the perceived gain.

All elements on a screen should be located in a unique and consistent position. The elements of a screen are:

- Title,
- Screen Identifier, or ID,
- Screen Body, including:
  - Captions
  - Data
  - Section Headings
  - Completion Aids
  - Prompting
- Status or Instructional Messages,
- Error Messages,
- Command Field or Command Area.

The recommended positioning for title, screen ID, captions, data, messages and command field/area are described on the pages to follow. Section headings, completion aids and prompting have considerations unique to the specific kinds of screens and are addressed later.

Upper left corner starting point. Provide an obvious starting point in the upper left corner of the screen. This is near where visual scanning begins and will permit a left-to-right, top-to-bottom reading as is common in Western cultures.

Consistent component locations. Reserving specific areas of the screen for specific screen elements will aid in memorizing their location. People do tend to have good location memories. Some recommended locations are:

Screen title

Upper center, to aid in creating symmetry.

Screen identifier or page number

Upper right-hand corner, a less frequently used position in most screens.

Status or error messages

The line above the command field line or function key description line. This line will be blank a good portion of the time and will provide a visual break between the screen body and the command field and/or function key descriptions. On a 24-line screen this will normally be line 23.

Command field and/or function key descriptions

The bottom line of the screen. The message line serves to break it from the body of the screen. Granda et al. (1982), comparing top and bottom lines of the screen for command field location in a data entry application, found a bottom line location yielded superior performance and a decrease in the number and magnitude of user head movements. The bottom line also maintains sequential top-to-bottom direction flow through the screen.

Screen body

The area of the screen between title and message line, usually lines 3 to 22. For captioned data fields the caption should precede the data for reasons to be described shortly. Instructional or prompting information contained within the body of the screen should occur at its logical position in a top-to-bottom progression. Instructions on how to use the screen should precede the data fields or text. Instructions concerning disposition of a completed screen should be at the bottom of the body.

A formatted screen body helps the viewer process information. Formatting guidelines are also described shortly.

Visually Pleasing Composition

A design aesthetic, or visually pleasing composition, is attractive to the eye. It draws attention subliminally, conveying a message clearly and quickly. A lack of visually pleasing composition is disorienting, obscures the intent and meaning, slows one down, and confuses.

The notion of what is artistic has evolved throughout history. Graphic design experts have, through perceptual research, derived a number of principles for what comprises a visually pleasing appearance (Taylor, 1960; Dondis, 1973). These include balance, regularity, symmetry, predictability, economy, sequentiality, unity, proportion simplicity and groupings. Keep in mind that this discussion of visually pleasing composition does not focus on the words on the screen but on the perception of structure created by such concepts as spacing, intensities, and color. It is as if the screen is viewed through "squinted eyes," causing the words themselves to become a blur.

Balance. Balance is a stabilization or equilibrium, a midway center of suspension. The design elements have an equal weight, left to right, top to bottom. The opposite of balance is instability, the design elements seeming ready to topple over. Our discomfort with instability, or imbalance, is reflected every time we straighten a picture hanging askew on the wall.

Dark colors, unusual shapes, and larger objects are "heavier," whereas light colors, regular shapes and small objects are "lighter." Balance on a screen is accomplished through centering the display itself, maintaining an equal weighting of components on each side of the horizontal and vertical axis, and centering titles and illustrations.

Regularity. Regularity is a uniformity of elements based on some principle or plan. Regularity in screen design is achieved by establishing standard and consistently spaced column and row starting points for display fields. The opposite, irregularity, exists when no such plan or principle is apparent.

Symmetry. Symmetry is axial duplication: a unit on one side of the center line is exactly replicated on the other side. This exact replication also creates balance, but the difference is that balance can be achieved without symmetry. Symmetry's opposite is asymmetry.

Predictability. Predictability suggests a highly conventional order or plan. Viewing one display enables one to predict how another display will look. Viewing part of a display enables one to predict how the remainder of the display will look. The opposite of predictability—spontaneity—suggests no plan and thus an inability to predict the structure of the remainder of a display or the structure of other displays. In screen design predictability is enhanced through design consistency.

Economy. Economy is the frugal and judicious use of display elements to get the message across as simply as possible. The opposite is intricacy, the use of many elements just because they exist. Intricacy is ornamentation, which often detracts from clarity. Economy in screen design means mobilizing just enough display elements and techniques to communicate the desired message, and no more. The use of color in screens often violates this principle, with displays sometimes taking on the appearance of Christmas trees.

Sequentiality. Sequentiality is a plan of presentation to guide the eye through the screen in a logical, rhythmic order, with the most important information significantly placed. The opposite of sequentiality is randomness, where a flow cannot be detected. The eye tends to move from brightly colored to uncolored objects, from dark to light areas, from big to little objects, and from unusual to usual shapes.

Unity.   Unity is coherence, a totality of elements that is visually all one piece. With unity the elements seem to belong together, to dovetail so completely that they are seen as one thing. The opposite of unity is fragmentation, each piece retaining its own character. In screen design similar sizes, shapes, and colors promote unity, as does "white space"—borders at the display boundary.

Proportion.   Displays of greater width than height appear to be more aesthetically pleasing. An old (5th century B.C.) rule is the Golden Section—the divine division of a line—whereby a length is divided such that the smaller part is to the greater part as the greater part is to the whole. This creates a "golden rectangle" with a ratio of 1:1.618. Several other shapes have also been described as having a mathematical property with aesthetic qualities. These shapes possess height to width ratios ranging from 1:1 to 1:2 (Tufte, 1983).

Simplicity (Complexity)

- Optimize the number of elements on a screen, within limits of clarity.
- Minimize the alignment points, especially horizontal or columnar.

Simplicity.   Simplicity is directness and singleness of form, a combination of elements that results in ease in comprehending the meaning of a pattern. The opposite pole on the continuum is complexity. The scale created may also be considered a scale of complexity, with extreme complexity at one end and minimal complexity at the other.

Tullis (1983) has derived a measure of screen complexity based on the work of Bonsiepe (1968), who proposed a method of measuring the complexity of typographically designed pages through the application of information theory (Shannon and Weaver, 1949). This measure involves the following steps:

1. draw a rectangle around each field on the screen, including captions, data, title, etc.;
2. count the number of fields and horizontal alignment points (the number of columns in which a field, inscribed by a rectangle, starts);
3. count the number of fields and vertical alignment points (the number of rows in which a field, inscribed by a rectangle, starts).

This has been done for the screens illustrated in figures 4.1 and 4.2.

Figure 4.1 Original screen, from Tullis (1981) with title, captions, and data inscribed by rectangles.

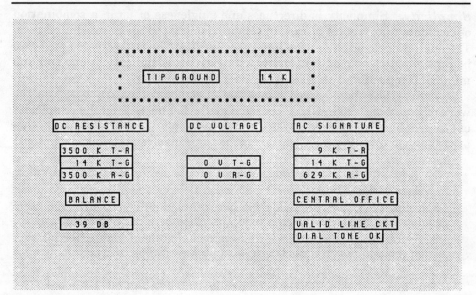

Figure 4.2 Redesigned screen, from Tullis (1981) with title, captions and data inscribed by rectangles.

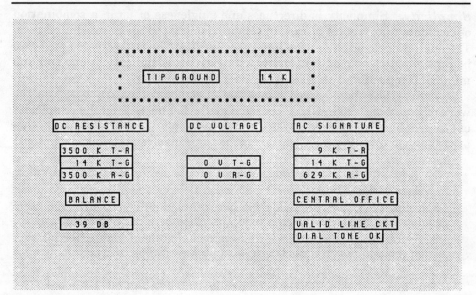

These screens are examples from the earlier study by Tullis (1981) described in the introduction. They are an original inquiry screen (figure 4.1) from the screens whose mean search time was 8.3 seconds, and a redesigned screen (figure 4.2) from the screens whose mean search time was 5.0 seconds. A complexity calculation using information-theory for each screen is as follows:

- figure 4.1 (original):
    - 22 fields with 6 horizontal (column) alignment points = 41 bits
    - 22 fields with 20 vertical (row) alignment points = 93 bits
    - Overall complexity = 134 bits
- figure 4.2 (redesigned):
    - 18 fields with 7 horizontal (column) alignment points = 43 bits
    - 18 fields with 8 vertical (row) alignment points = 53 bits
    - Overall complexity = 96 bits

The redesigned screen is thus about 28 percent simpler than the original screen.

An easier method of calculation, yielding similar results, is to count the following: 1) the number of fields on the screen, 2) the number of horizontal (column) alignment points, and 3) the number of vertical (row) alignment points. The sums for the original and redesigned screens are:

- figure 4.1 (original):
    22 fields,
      6 horizontal (column) alignment points,
    20 vertical (row) alignment points,
    48 = complexity.
- figure 4.2 (redesigned):
    18 fields,
      7 horizontal (column) alignment points,
      8 vertical (row) alignment points,
    33 = complexity.

By this calculation the redesigned screen is about 31 percent simpler than the original screen.

Complexity By both calculations the redesigned screen has a lower complexity measure than the original screen. In the Tullis (1981) study the redesigned and faster-to-use screens had lower complexity measures. This leads to the following complexity guidelines:

- Optimize the number of elements on a screen, within limits of clarity.
- Minimize the alignment points, especially horizontal or columnar.

Obviously, the way to minimize screen complexity is to reduce the number of fields displayed. Fewer fields will yield lower complexity measures. This is unrealistic, however, since ultimate simplicity means nothing is there, which obviously does not accomplish very much. Indeed, Vitz (1966) has found that people have subjective preferences for the right amount of information, and too little is as bad as too much. The practical answer, then, is to optimize the amount of information displayed, within limits of clarity. What is optimum must be considered in light of guidelines to follow, so a final judgment must be postponed.

What can be done, however, is to minimize alignment points, most importantly horizontal or columnar alignment points. Fewer alignment points will have a strong positive influence on the complexity calculation. Tullis (1983) has also found, in a follow-up study of some other screens, that fewer alignment points were among the strongest influences creating positive viewer feelings of visually pleasing composition.

Groupings

- Organize the screen into functional, semantic groups.
- Provide "spatial" groupings, conforming to visual "chunks":

  - leave space lines about every 5 rows, but not exceeding 7 rows;
  - confine line widths to about 11 to 15 characters;
  - the space between groups should be less than the margins.

Grouping. Grouping elements on a screen aids in establishing structure and meaningful form. In addition to providing aesthetic appeal, grouping has been found to aid recall (Card, 1982) and result in a faster screen search (Dodson and Shields, 1978; Haubner and Neumann, 1986; Tullis, 1983; Triesman, 1982).

The perceptual principles of proximity and closure foster visual groupings. But the search for a more objective definition of what constitutes a group has gone on for years. Tullis, in his 1981 study, described an objective method for establishing groups, based on the work of Zahn (1971) using the Gestalt psychologists' law of proximity. For the Tullis (1981) screens shown in figures 4.1 and 4.2:

1. compute the mean distance between each character and its nearest neighbor. Use a character distance of 1 between characters adjacent horizontally and 2 between characters adjacent vertically (between rows);
2. multiply the mean distance derived by 2;
3. connect with a line any character pair that is closer than the distance established in step 2.

This has been done for these inquiry screens, as illustrated in figures 4.3 and 4.4.

Figure 4.3 Original screen, from Tullis (1981) with grouping indicated.

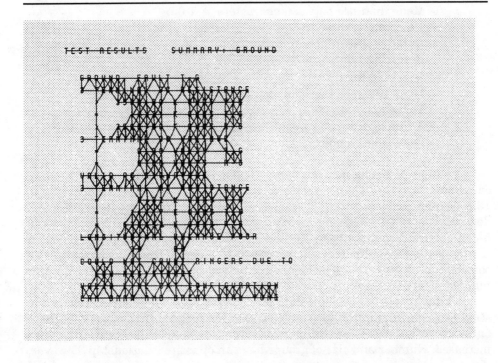

Figure 4.4 Redesigned screen, from Tullis (1981) with grouping indicated.

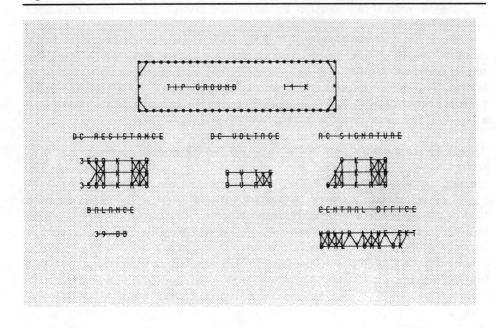

- figure 4.3 (original):
  - Mean distance between characters = 1.05,
  - Twice mean distance = 2.10,
  - A line is drawn between characters 1 or 2 apart, not 3 or more.
  - Resulting number of groups = 3,
- figure 4.4 (redesigned):
  - Mean distance between characters = 1.09,
  - Twice mean distance + 2.18,
  - A line is drawn between characters 1 or 2 apart, not 3 or more,
  - Resulting number of groups = 13.

Another grouping measure was calculated by Tullis: the average size of each screen's group. The average size of the 3 groups in the original screen is 13.3 degrees, whereas the 13 groups on the redesigned screen average 5.2 degrees. The redesigned screen group size, interestingly, closely matches the 5-degree visual acuity screen "chunk" described in chapter 3. So, in addition to complexity the Tullis redesigned screens differ from the original screens by some grouping measures. The more effective redesigned screens have a greater number of smaller size groups.

Tullis, in his 1983 follow-up study, also found that groupings were the strongest determinant of a screen's visual search time. If the size of a group on a screen increased, or the number of groups increased, search time also increased. Number and size of groups have an opposite relationship, however; if the number increases, size usually decreases. If the size increases, number usually decreases. What proves to be most effective is a middle-ground solution—a medium number of medium sized groups.

Based upon this and other research, the grouping guidelines described above are presented.

Functional, semantic groups are those that make sense to the user. Related information should be displayed together. A logical place to "break" a screen is between functional groups of information, but a massive grouping of information should be broken up into smaller groups. The most reasonable point is every five rows. A six- or seven-row grouping may be displayed without a break, if necessary, but do not exceed seven rows.

The 11- to 15-character width limitation must take into consideration the data to be displayed. Confining data to this width makes no sense if it thus suffers a reduction in legibility. Legibility and comprehension are most important.

To give unity to a display, the space between groups should be less than that of the margins. Fortunately, most cathode ray tubes have a fairly wide built-in margin. The most common and obvious way to achieve spacing is through white or blank space, but there are other ways. Alternatives include contrasting display features such as differing intensity levels, image reversals (dark characters on a light background versus light characters on a dark background), and color. Spacing, however, appears to be the strongest technique. Two studies (Haubner and Benz, 1983; Haubner and Neumann, 1986) found that adequate spacing, not color, is a more important determinant of ease of use for uncluttered, highly structured inquiry screens.

WHAT INFORMATION TO PLACE ON A SCREEN

- Provide only information that is essential to making a decision or performing an action. Do not flood a user with information.
- Provide all data related to one task on a single screen. The user should not have to remember data from one screen to the next.
- Maintain overall density levels of less than about 25 to 30 percent.

What information to place on a screen requires a determination of how much should be there.

Screens should provide only relevant information because the more information, the greater the competition among the screen components for a person's attention. Visual search times will be longer and meaningful patterns more difficult to perceive if the screens "flood" a viewer with too much information.

Providing all related data on a single screen will reduce the memory load on the user—an obvious benefit.

Density

An objective measure of "how much" is density. Density, by definition, is a calculation of the proportion of display character positions in the screen, or an area of the screen containing something.

Density is clearly related to complexity, for both measure "how much is there." Complexity looks at fields, density at characters, so they should rise and fall together.

In general, studies show that increasing the density of a display increases the time and errors in finding information (Callan et al., 1977; Dodson and Shields, 1978; Triesman, 1982). There are actually two types of density to be calculated on a screen: overall and local.

Overall density is a measure of the percentage of character positions on the entire screen containing data. Danchak (1976) stated that density (loading, as he called it) should not exceed 25 percent. Reporting the results of a qualitative judgment of "good" screens, he found their density was on the order of 15 percent. Tullis, in his 1981 study, reported that the density of screens from an up and running successful system ranged from 0.9 to 27.9 percent, with a mean of 14.2 percent. Using this and other research data, he concluded that the common upper density limit appears to be on the order of 25 percent.

Local density is a measure of how "tightly packed" the screen is. A measure of local density derived by Tullis is the percentage of characters in the 88-character visual acuity circle described in chapter 3, modified by the weighting factors illustrated below.

```
          0 1 2 2 2 2 2 1 0
        0 1 2 3 4 4 5 4 4 3 2 1 0
      0 2 3 4 5 6 7 7 7 6 5 4 3 2 0
      1 2 3 5 6 7 9 + 9 7 6 5 3 2 1
      0 2 3 4 5 6 7 7 7 6 5 4 3 2 0
        0 1 2 3 4 4 5 4 4 3 2 1 0
          0 1 2 2 2 2 2 1 0
```

For every character on the screen, a local density is calculated using the above weighting factors, and then an average for all characters on the screen is established.

Figures 4.5 and 4.6 are the original and redesigned screens from the 1981 Tullis study again. Density measures for these screens are:

- figure 4.5 (original):
  - overall density = 17.9 percent,
  - local density = 58.0 percent,

Figure 4.5 Original screen, from Tullis (1981).

```
TEST RESULTS    SUMMARY: GROUND

   GROUND, FAULT T-G
   3 TERMINAL DC RESISTANCE
      >    3500.00 K OHMS T-R
      =      14.21 K OHMS T-G
      >    3500.00 K OHMS R-G
   3 TERMINAL DC VOLTAGE
      =       0.00 VOLTS  T-G
      =       0.00 VOLTS  R-G
   VALID AC SIGNATURE
   3 TERMINAL AC RESISTANCE
      =       8.82 K OHMS T-R
      =      14.17 K OHMS T-G
      =     628.52 K OHMS R-G
   LONGITUDINAL BALANCE POOR
      =      39     DB
   COULD NOT COUNT RINGERS DUE TO
      LOW RESISTANCE
   VALID LINE CKT CONFIGURATION
   CAN DRAW AND BREAK DIAL TONE
```

Figure 4.6 Redesigned screen, from Tullis (1981).

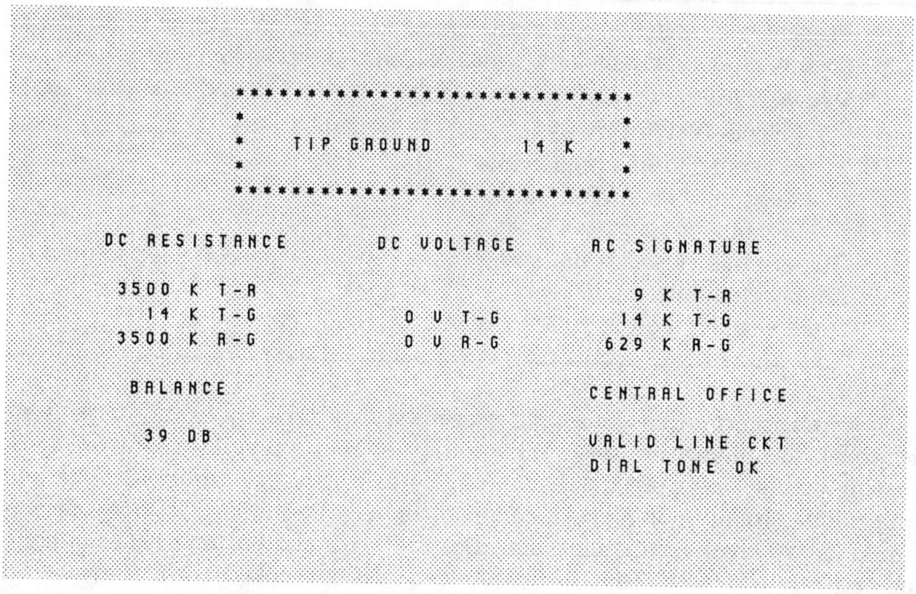

```
              • • • • • • • • • • • • • • • • • • • • • • • • •
              •                                             •
              •       TIP  GROUND            14  K          •
              •                                             •
              • • • • • • • • • • • • • • • • • • • • • • • • •

   DC  RESISTANCE          DC  VOLTAGE          AC  SIGNATURE

     3500  K  T-R                                  9  K  T-R
       14  K  T-G          0  V  T-G              14  K  T-G
     3500  K  R-G          0  V  R-G             629  K  R-G

     BALANCE                                   CENTRAL  OFFICE

       39  DB                                  VALID  LINE  CKT
                                               DIAL  TONE  OK
```

- figure 4.6 (redesigned):
  - overall density = 10.8 percent,
  - local density = 35.6 percent.

In both cases the more effective redesigned screen had lower density measures. In his 1983 follow-up study, Tullis found a lower local density to be the most important characteristic creating a positive "visually pleasing" feeling.

The research does suggest some density guidelines for screens. Maintain overall density levels no higher than 25 to 30 percent. This upper overall density recommendation should be interpreted with extreme care. Density, by itself, does not affect whether or not what is displayed "makes sense." This is a completely different question. Density can always be reduced through substituting abbreviations for whole words. The cost of low density may be illegibility and poorer comprehension. Indeed, poorly designed screens have been redesigned to achieve greater clarity and have actually ended up with higher density measures than the original versions. How it all "hangs together" can never be divorced from how much is there.

HOW TO PLACE INFORMATION ON A SCREEN

The following guidelines for determining how to put data on screens address general considerations, fonts, word and text arrangement, illustrations, field captions, and data fields.

General

- Present information in a directly usable form. Do not require reference to documentation, translations, transpositions, interpolations, etc.
- Use contrasting display features (different intensities and character sizes, underlining, reverse images, etc.) to call attention to:
  - different screen components,
  - items being operated upon,
  - urgent items.
- Guide a user through the screen with implicit or explicit lines formed by display elements.
- Make visual appearance and procedural usage consistent.

Screen information should be presented in a directly usable form. Reference to documentation for interpretation should never be required. Contrasting display features should be used to call attention to different screen components, items being operated upon, or urgent items. Features chosen should aid in screen component identification so that attention may be quickly and accurately focused. Some recommended uses of display features are found in the following section on software considerations.

The eye should be guided horizontally or vertically through the screen, with lines formed through use of white space and display elements. More complex movements may require the aid of display contrasts. Eye movement direction may also be communicated to the viewer through the actual drawing of horizontal and vertical lines. This is an effective technique in situations where a great deal of information must be displayed on a single screen. Display methods chosen should be consistent in visual appearance and procedural usage.

Fonts

- For text, use lower case with the initial sentence letter in upper case.
- For captions, labels, and visual search tasks, use upper case.

Tinker (1955), in a study of reading from hard copy materials, found that mixed font (upper/lowercase) text is read significantly faster than all uppercase text. Rehe (1974) found a 13 percent advantage in reading speed for lowercase text. Moskel et al. (1984) found even larger advantages of lowercase text compared to uppercase in comprehension and proofreading of screen materials. The advantage of lowercase text is that it gives a word a more distinctive shape, which aids comprehension. Vartabedian (1971) established that screens with labels containing uppercase characters are visually searched faster than those using lowercase characters.

Comparing paper to screen reading. Printing technology has been evolving for several centuries. Factors such as type size and style, character and line spacings, and column and margin widths have been the focus of research for a good part of that time. The product of this research is highly readable and attractive printed materials. Conversely, CRT-based characters are a relatively new innovation, with many technical limitations. The result is a displayed character that often lacks the high quality a paper medium can provide. This disparity in quality has resulted in performance differences when paper and screen reading of materials have been compared. Various researchers have found slower screen reading speeds, as much as 40 percent (Gould and Grischkowsky, 1984; Kruk and Muter, 1984; Muter et al., 1982; and Wright and Lickorish, 1983), and more errors (Gould and Grischkowsy, 1984; and Wright and Lickorish, 1983). For extended reading hard copy display of materials still has significant advantages.

Words

- Do not use jargon, words or terms:
  - unique to the computer profession
  - with different meanings outside of the computer profession
  - made up to describe special functions or conditions
- Use:
  - standard alphabetic characters to form words or captions.
  - short, familiar words.
  - complete words; avoid contractions,
    short forms, suffixes, and prefixes.
  - positive terms; avoid negative terms.
  - simple action words; avoid noun strings.
  - the "more" dimension when comparing.
- Do not:
  - stack words.
  - hyphenate words.
  - include punctuation for abbreviations, mnemonics, and acronyms.

Words displayed on screens should be easily comprehended, with minimum ambiguity and confusion. Some ways to achieve this are given below.

Do not use jargon. Jargon consists of several forms. It may be words or terms that are unique to the computer profession such as Filespec or Abend; words with different meaning outside of data processing such as Boot or Abort;

or made-up words to describe special functions or actions such as Ungroup or Dearchive.

Use standard alphabetic characters. Standard alphabetic characters are most familiar to screen viewers. Never use restricted alphabetic sets. Symbols should be used only if they are familiar to all who are using the screen. Common symbols that may be considered as substitutes for alphabetic characters are
for number,
% for percent,
$ for dollar.
Again, all potential screen users must be familiar with a symbol if it is used as a substitute for alphabetic characters.

Use short, familiar words. Shorter words tend to be used more often in everyday conversation, and so they are more familiar and easier to understand (Of course, there are exceptions). The most important factor is familiarization, not length. A longer but familiar word is better than a short, unfamiliar word.

Use complete words. A complete word is better understood than a contraction or short form. Thus, "will not" is better than "won't," "not valid" is better than "invalid."*

Words can also be more difficult to understand if they contain suffixes and prefixes, like "un-," or "-ness." Comprehension often involves decomposing such complex terms to establish their basic root meaning and then modifying the meaning to account for the various suffixes and prefixes (Wright, 1984). Structural complexity hinders comprehension.

Use positive terms. It is generally easier to understand positive, affirmative information than the same information expressed in a negative way. Therefore, avoid the prefixes "ir-," "in-," "dis-," and "un-." Implicitly negative terms, such as "decrease," should be replaced with positive terms, such as "increase."

Use Simple Action Words. Substitute noun strings with simple action words. Instead of saying, for example, PROJECT STATUS LISTING, say LIST PROJECT STATUS.

Use the "more" dimension when comparing. When using comparative terms, the "more" dimension is easier to deal with. The opposite of the "more" is usually considered the "negative." So, use "longer" rather than "shorter," "bigger" rather than "smaller."

*"Invalid" has come into such widespread usage in computer systems that one may ask whether this should be an exception to this rule. Maybe, but what happens in a medical system where screens are developed for use about, or by, invalids?

Do not stack words. Text is more readable if the entire statement is on one line.

Do not hyphenate words. Again, for better readability, never break a word between two lines.

Abbreviations, mnemonics, and acronyms should not include punctuation. This permits better readability and avoids confusion between the punctuation and data fields.

Text and Special Symbols

Text

- Use short sentences composed of familiar, personal words.
- Place a period at the end of each sentence.
- Include no more than 40 to 60 characters on each line. A double column of 30 to 35 characters separated by five spaces is also acceptable.
- Do not right-justify.
- Separate paragraphs by at least one blank line.
- Use paging (not scrolling).

Special Symbols

- Consider special symbols for emphasis.
- Separate symbols from words by a space.

Text. Extensive guidelines for constructing meaningful messages are described shortly. The above guidelines are intended to describe the mechanics of displaying the selected text. Rehe (1974) recommends that a text line should contain no more than 40 to 60 characters. An 80-character line of text makes it difficult for the eye to keep its place as it moves from the end of one line of text to the beginning of the next line. He has also found that unjustified (unequal length) text lines are just as legible as justified text lines. Large spaces in justified text interrupt eye movement and impede reading.

Another study found the reading speed of right-justified text was 8 to 10 percent slower than non-right-justified text (Trollip and Sales, 1986). For greater screen efficiency, it may be desirable to consider two columns of text, each about 30 to 35 characters wide.

Separating paragraphs by a blank line will result in more cohesive groupings and alleviate the impression of a dense screen.

Paging through screens, rather than scrolling, has been found to yield better performance and to be preferred by novice system users (Schwarz et al., 1983). Expert users were found to perform satisfactorily with either paging or scrolling. A severe disadvantage of scrolling for novices is loss of orientation. While experts can handle scrolling, the best choice if all users are considered is paging.

If scrolling is going to be used, the preferred approach is "telescoping" in which the viewing window moves around the data. This method is more natural and causes fewer errors than the "microscope" approach, in which the data appears to move under a fixed viewing window (Bury et al., 1982).

Special symbols. Special symbols should be considered to emphasize or call attention to elements on a screen. An error message, for example, can be preceded by asterisks (**), or the "greater than" sign can be used to direct attention (AMOUNT >>). Symbols should be separated from words by one space.

Field Captions/Data Fields

- Identify fields with captions or labels.
- Choose distinct and meaningful captions that can be easily distinguished from other captions. Minimal differences (one letter or word) cause confusion.
- Differentiate field captions from field data by using:
  - contrasting features, such as different intensities, separating colons, etc.:

~~SEX FEMALE~~   SEX: FEMALE
~~RELATION DAUGHTER~~   RELATION: DAUGHTER

  - consistent physical relationships:

~~SEX:~~
~~FEMALE~~   SEX: FEMALE
~~RELATION: DAUGHTER~~   RELATION: DAUGHTER

- For single data fields, place the caption to the left of the data field:

~~PRODUCER~~
                                             PRODUCER: 770117
~~770117~~

- For repeating data fields, place the caption above the data fields:

~~PRODUCERS: 770117~~   PRODUCERS
~~   589136~~   770117
~~   642210~~   589136
                                             642210

- Separate captions from data fields by at least one blank space:

CITY:CHICAGO   CITY: CHICAGO

Many screens contain information that must be identified by a caption or label. Captions must be complete, clear, easy to identify, and distinguishable from other captions and data fields.

Identify fields with captions. All screen data fields should be identified by captions. The context in which data is found in the world at large provides cues as to the data's meaning. A number on a telephone dial is readily identifiable as a telephone number; the number on a metal plate affixed to the back of an automobile is readily identified as a license number. The same data displayed on a screen, being out of context, may not be readily identifiable.

There are, however, some exceptions to this rule on inquiry screens. The structure of the data itself in some cases may be enough to identify its meaning. The most obvious example is name, street, city, state, and zip code. Date may be another possibility. Elimination of these common captions will serve to further clean up inquiry screens. Before eliminating them, however, it should be determined that all screen users will be able to identify these fields all the time.

Choose distinct and meaningful captions. Captions that are similar often repeat the same word or words over and over again. This increases the potential for confusion and often adds to screen clutter. A better solution is to incorporate common words into group identifiers. Techniques to accomplish this are described in the chapters addressing specific kinds of screens. Captions chosen should be distinct from one another. One or two letter differences between captions can also create confusion.

Differentiate field captions from data. Captions and data should be distinguishable in some manner so that they do not have to be read in context to determine which is which. Another common failing of many screens is that captions and data have the same appearance and blend into one another when the screen is filled. This makes differentiation difficult and increases caption and field data search time. Vehicles to accomplish differentiation include using contrasting display features and consistent positional relationships.

For single data fields, place the caption to the left of the data field. There are two practical ways to establish a positional relationship between a caption and its associated data field. As figure 4.7 shows, the caption may immediately precede the associated data field (A), or it may be above the associated field (B). The horizontal approach (A) is recommended for the following reasons:

- It conforms to the normal left-to-right reading pattern.
- It permits easier field alignment, facilitating visual scanning and field location, and reducing the screen complexity measure. The scanning advantage will be addressed more fully in the discussion on inquiry screens.
- It provides the best compromise between caption clarity and screen space utilization. The horizontal example (A) in figure 4.7 consumes 59 character positions, while the caption-above approach (B) consumes 74 positions. The B approach allows only 12 lines of data on a 24-line screen, while the A approach accommodates 24 lines of data. An approach screen designers often take to make B more efficient is to reduce the length of the caption to equal that of the data field below it. The result is often screens that look like that illustrated in figure 4.8. Captions become very cryptic, and it is frequently difficult to tell where one caption stops and the next starts. The horizontal (A) approach requires that neither caption nor data be dependent on the other in the screen design process. Figure 4.9 is an example of the fields in figure 4.8 restructured into the caption-preceding-data-field approach. While consuming five lines on the screen, caption lengths have been greatly expanded. To increase slightly the size of just a few of the captions in figure 4.8 would have necessitated going to at least six lines. The caption-preceding approach (A) often permits longer caption sizes within the same space on the screen.
- Viewed in relationship to source document design, the best fit between a form and a screen created in the form's image is the horizontal (A) approach. Following good form design principles, an 8½ by 11 source document line of fields is usually filled up before the screen line. That is, a line on paper 8½ inches wide holds fewer characters than an 80-

Figure 4.7 Caption/data field relationship.

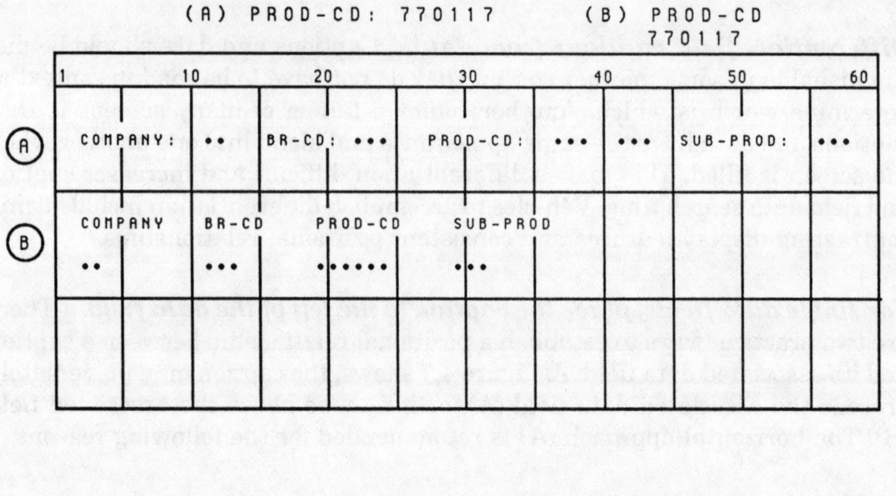

Figure 4.8 Example of screen fields using caption-above-data style (Approach B).

```
BEN  FROM      TO DATE   OCC  BILLED   N/C AMT  CD  MDCR PD   B/DED   B/PAID
---  --/--/--  --/--/--  ---  -------  -------  --  -------   -----   ------

INS  EXA  MAT DED  MM ELIG  MM DER  COI  MM PAID  PROV  DCN     O  P  E
---  ---  -------  -------  ------  ---  -------  ----  ------  -  -  -
```

Figure 4.9 Fields from figure 4.8 restructured into the caption-preceding-data style (Approach B).

```
BEN-CD: -----     FR-DATE: --/--/--   TO-DATE: --/--/--   OCC: ---
BILLED: -------   N/C-AMT: -------    N/C-CD: --          MDCR-PD: -------
BASE-DED: ------  BASE-PD: -------    INS-EXA: ------     MT-DED: ------
MM-ELIG: ------   MM-DED: ------      COINS: ------       MM-PD: ------
PROV: ---------   DCN: ----------     OU-CD: ---          POOL: ------   EOB: --
```

Figure 4.10 Visual discrimination of captions/data fields.

```
(A)    EMPLOYER: CNA       DEPARTMENT: SERVICES      JOB: ANALYST
              SEX: M          EMPLOYEE#: A65449      DATE: 07/21/80


(B)    EMPLOYER            DEPARTMENT            JOB
       CNA                 SERVICES              ANALYST
       SEX                 EMPLOYEE#             DATE
       M                   A65449                07/21/80
```

character screen line with appropriate spacing. (Galitz, 1975). This means that the horizontal (A) approach results in more efficient screen utilization than the caption-above (B) approach, since the latter tends to fill in less of each line, while using more lines.

- On a completely filled screen, the horizontal format (with colons) provides better visual discrimination between captions and data, as shown in figure 4.10. On large or crowded screens, the caption-above format can cause captions and data to visually merge. This can be alleviated only by differentiating captions and data through a contrasting display technique. In the horizontal approach the colon serves as a flag allowing positional discrimination to be achieved.

For repeating fields, place the caption above the data field. Captions should be placed above a stack of data fields that are repeated two or more times. Using horizontal caption formats for single fields and a columnar caption orientation for repeating fields will also provide better discrimination between single and repeating fields. The single-field caption will always precede the data, and captions for repeating columnar fields will always be above the top data field.

Field Caption/Data Field Justification

1. First Approach

- Left-justify both captions and data fields.
- Leave one space between the longest caption and the data field column.

```
            DIVISION:       _____
            DEPARTMENT:x_____
            TITLE:          _____
```

2. Second Approach

- Left-justify data fields and right-justify captions to data fields.
- Leave one space between each.

```
 D I V I S I O N : x _ _ _ _ _ _ _ _ _ _ _
DEPARTMENT:  _ _ _ _ _ _
    T I T L E :  _ _ _ _ _ _ _ _ _ _ _ _ _ _
```

Justification of single captions and data fields can be accomplished in several ways. These include:

A. Left-justifying captions; data field immediately follows caption.

```
BUILDING:  _ _ _ _ _ _ _ _ _ _
FLOOR:  _ _ _
ROOM:  _ _ _ _ _
```

B. Left-justifying captions; left-justified data fields; colon (:) associated with captions.

```
BUILDING:  _ _ _ _ _ _ _ _ _ _
FLOOR:  _ _ _
ROOM:  _ _ _ _ _
```

C. Left-justifying captions; left-justifying data fields; colon (:) associated with data field.

```
BUILDING :  _ _ _ _ _ _ _ _ _ _
FLOOR  :  _ _ _
ROOM  :  _ _ _ _ _
```

D. Right-justifying captions; left-justifying data fields.

```
BUILDING:  _ _ _ _ _ _ _ _ _ _
FLOOR:  _ _ _
ROOM:  _ _ _ _ _
```

Alternatives A and C are not recommended. Alternative A, left-justified aligned captions with data fields immediately following, results in poor alignment of data fields and increases the screens' complexity. It is more difficult to find data when searching data fields. Alternative C, while structurally sound, associates the colon (:) primarily with the data field. The strongest association of the colon should be with the caption.

The two most desirable alternatives are B and D. Alternative B, left-justified captions and data fields, is the first approach illustrated in the guideline. Alternative D, right-justified captions and left-justified data fields, is the second approach illustrated in the guideline.

Left-justified captions and data (1). A disadvantage to this approach is that the caption beginning point is usually farther from the entry field than the right-justified caption approach. A large mix in caption sizes can cause some captions to be far removed from their corresponding data field, greatly increasing eye movements between the two and possibly making it difficult to accurately tie caption to data field. Tying the caption to the data field by a line of dots (. . . . .) solves the association problem but adds a great deal of noise to the screen. This does not solve the eye movement problem. Eye movement inefficiencies can be addressed by abbreviating the longer captions. The cost is reduced caption clarity.

An advantage to this approach is that section headings using location positioning as the key element in their identification do stand out nicely from the crisp left-justified captions.

Right-justified captions and left-justified entry fields (2). A disadvantage here is that section headings using location positioning as the identification element do not stand out as well. They tend to get lost in the ragged left edge of the captions.

Advantages are that captions are always positioned close to their related data fields, thereby minimizing eye movements between the two, and that the screen takes on a more balanced look.

There is no universal agreement as to which is the better approach. Experimental studies have not provided any answers.

Examples to follow in this and succeeding chapters reflect both styles. This is done to enable the reader to see and evaluate each. Whichever the method chosen, however, should be consistently followed in a system's screen design.

MESSAGES

Sentences

- Sentences must be:
    - brief, simple, and clear,
    - directly and immediately usable,
    - affirmative,
    - in an active voice,
    - nonauthoritarian,
    - nonthreatening,
    - nonanthropomorphic,
    - nonpatronizing,
    - in the temporal sequence of events,
    - structured so that the main topic is near the beginning,
    - cautious in the use of humor,
    - nonpunishing.

Other Considerations

- Abbreviated, more concise versions of messages should be available.
- Something that must be remembered should be at the beginning of the text.

A system communicates with people through many kinds of messages: prompts, diagnostic messages generated by error, information messages, and status messages. A message must minimize ambiguity and confusion, allowing easy, correct, and fast interpretation. It must also have the proper tone; threatening, rude, or impolite messages can evoke negative response.

The following guidelines will lead to easy, correct, and fast message interpretation and acceptance.

Schneiderman (1982B), in restructuring messages along such guidelines, found higher success rates in fixing problems, lower error rates, and improved user satisfaction.

Sentences

Use brief, simple sentences. A message that has to be explained does not communicate. It fails as a message. Brief, simple sentences are more readily understood than longer sentences containing multiple clauses. Break long sentences into two or more simple sentences if this can be done without changing the meaning.

Roemer and Chapanis (1982) created messages at three levels of reading ability (fifth, tenth, and fifteenth grade) and tested them on people of varying verbal abilities. The fifth grade version was found to be best for all levels. People of high verbal ability did not perceive the fifth grade version as insulting as some have feared.

Provide directly and immediately usable sentences. Searching through reference material to translate a message is unacceptable, as are requirements for transposing, computing, interpolating, or mentally translating messages into other units.

Use affirmative statements. Affirmative statements are easier to understand than negative statements. For example, "Complete entry before returning to menu" is easier to grasp than "Do not return to menu before completing entry" (Herriot, 1970; Greene, 1972).

Use active voice. Active voice is usually easier to understand than passive voice. For example, "Send the message by depressing TRANSMIT" is more understandable than "The message is sent by depressing TRANSMIT" (Herriot, 1970; Greene, 1972; Barnard, 1974).

Be nonauthoritarian. Imply the system is awaiting the user's direction, not that the system is directing the user. For example, phrase a message "Ready for next command" not "Enter next command."

Nonthreatening. Negative tones or actions, or threats, are not very friendly. Since errors are often the result of a failure to understand, mistakes, or trial-and-error behavior, the user may feel confused, inadequate, or anxious (Shneiderman, 1987). Blaming the user for problems can heighten anxiety, making error correction more difficult and increasing the chance of more errors. Therefore, harsh words like "illegal," "bad," or "fatal" should be avoided. For example, instead of saying "Numbers are illegal," say, "Months must be entered by name." Since the computer does not have an ego to be bruised, an excellent design approach would be to have it to assume the blame for all miscommunications.

Be nonanthropomorphic. Having the computer "talk" like a person should be avoided for several reasons. An attribution of knowledge or intelligence will, first, imply a much higher level of computer "knowledge" than actually exists, creating user expectations soon shattered. Second, this attribution eliminates the distinction that actually exists between people and computers. People "control" computers; they "respect the desires" of other human beings. Third, many people express anxiety about using computers by saying things like "they make you feel dumb." The feeling of interacting with another person who is evaluating your proficiency can heighten this anxiety (Shneiderman, 1987). There is some research evidence that a nonanthropomorphic approach is best, being seen as more honest (Quintanar et al., 1982), more preferred (Spiliotopoulos and Shackel, 1981), and easier to use (Gay and Lindward, in Shneiderman, 1987).

So, do not give a human personality to a machine. Imply that the system is awaiting the user's direction, not vice versa. Say, for example, "What do you need?" not "How can I help you?".

Be nonpatronizing. Patronizing messages can be embarrassing. "Very good, you did it right" may thrill a fourth grader, but would be somewhat less than thrilling to an adult. Being told "You forgot again" once may be acceptable, but being told three or four times in one minute is another story. A commonly available video golf game, after a particularly bad hole, returns with the suggestion to "try another sport." A golf professional who played this game took great offense to this advice and walked away. A person may disagree with patronizing conclusions, so why risk the offense?

Order words chronologically. If a sentence describes a temporal sequence of events, the order of words should correspond to this sequence. A prompt should say, "Complete address and page forward" rather than "Page forward after completing address."

Messages that begin with a strange code number do not meet the user's needs. A code number, if needed at all, is only necessary after reading the message and should therefore be placed in parentheses at the end of the message.

Avoid humor and punishment. Until an optimal computer personality is designed, messages should remain factual and informative, and should not attempt humor or punishment. Humor is a transitory and changeable thing. What is funny today may not be funny tomorrow, and what is funny to some may not be to others. Punishment is not a desirable way to force a change in behavior, especially among adults.

Other Considerations

Display abbreviated versions of messages when requested. People are impatient with noninformative or redundant computer messages. A problem, however, is that the degree of computer-to-person message redundancy depends on the person's experience with the system. And it may vary with different parts of a system. So the availability of abbreviated or detailed messages allows tailoring of the system to the needs of each user. During system training and early implementation stages, detailed versions can be used. Individuals can switch to abbreviated versions as their familiarity increases, but they should always be able to receive detailed messages.

Place information that must be remembered at the beginning of text. One can remember something longer if it appears at the beginning of a message. Items in the middle of a message are hardest to remember.

Some words to forget. Words should be meaningful and common to all, not just to the designers. Language perceived as "computerese" may confuse or intimidate some users (Loftus et al., 1970; Wason and Johnson-Laird, 1972). The vocabulary of the designer often finds its way into messages or system documentation. While not always bad, some words have particularly harsh or vague meanings to many users. These words, which are summarized in Table 4.1, should be avoided whenever possible. Suggested alternative words are presented (derived from IBM, 1984).

HARDWARE CONSIDERATIONS

- Important hardware considerations include:
  - display screen size limits,
  - keyboard character population.

Table 4.1 Some words to forget.

AVOID	USE
Abend	End, Cancel, Stop
Abort	End, Cancel, Stop
Access	Get, Ready, Display
Available	Ready
Boot	Start, Run
Execute	Complete
Hit	Press, Depress
Implement	Do, Use, Put Into
Invalid	Not Correct, Not Good, Not Valid
Key	Type, Enter
Kill	End, Cancel
Output	Report, List, Display
Return Key	Enter, Transmit
Terminate	End, Exit

Screen design is limited by the physical characteristics of the display terminal itself. The two most important parameters are the display screen size and the characteristics of its associated keyboard.

Display screens come in a variety of sizes and shapes. One of the most common is the 24-line, 80-column display encompassing 1920 character positions. Larger and smaller display screens will also be found. Some systems may impose smaller limits than the display terminal is physically capable of supporting. The CNA Insurance data entry utility DEBUT II, for example, restricts a designer from using 5 of the available 24 lines, leaving only 19 lines (1520 characters) for development of screen bodies (Galitz, 1979). The restricted lines are used for displaying such things as error messages and keying transaction commands. Before beginning any screen design activity, absolute limits and working areas must be identified.

In appearance and layout most keyboards resemble a standard typewriter keyboard with alphabetic and numeric characters, symbols, and punctuation marks. Typical symbols and punctuation marks are illustrated in figure 4.11.

The keyboard character population is important because it defines the family of characters available for display on screen formats. Operator guides will generally provide this exact information. Before beginning any design activity, however, it should be ascertained whether all these symbols are available for general use. Certain symbols may have predefined functions or may be unavailable.

Figure 4.11   Typical Displayable Symbols and Punctuation Marks

	= logical OR, vertical bar	_ = underscore
! = exclamation point	+ = plus sign
@ = at sign	: = colon
# = number sign	" = quotation mark
$ = dollar sign	< = less than sign
% = percent sign	> = greater than sign
¢ = cent sign	? = question mark
− = minus sign	= = equals sign
& = ampersand	¬ = logical NOT sign
* = asterisk	; = semicolon
(= left parenthesis	' = apostrophe
) = right parenthesis	, = comma
. = period	/ = slash

SOFTWARE CONSIDERATIONS

Software considerations include how fields are defined on display terminals, the display techniques available to the screen designer, and concerns for edit and storage efficiency.

Field Characteristics

- A field is an area on the screen format possessing certain predefined characteristics.
- A field may encompass as little as one character position on the screen, or cover the entire screen.
- The predefined characteristics of a field are normally established by a:
  - control character that immediately precedes the field,
  - control character within the field.
- This control character is called an attribute character. The attribute is invisible to the user.

The basic building block of the screen format is the *field*. A screen may consist of only one field or upwards of two hundred. Most terminals define a field's characteristics through use of a control character. This control character, commonly called an *attribute* character, occupies one screen character position immediately preceding the field. It is invisible to the user, appearing as a blank space.

Some terminals define a field's characteristics by other methods, not imposing restrictions on how certain screen character positions must be used. The attribute character is actually embedded within the field. From a practical standpoint, however, most screen fields will always include one or more blank spaces preceding a field for visual clarity requirements. So this imposed software restriction to allow for attributes has no practical consequences. It is also prudent to leave an attribute position on all screens for reasons of flexibility. If the screen is designed for use on systems not imposing this requirement, and at some point it must be converted to one requiring attributes, screen redesign will not be necessary.

For purposes of this handbook, screens are considered to use the attribute method of field specifications. For simplicity we will illustrate a field definition terminology employed by many terminal vendors. The field concepts described, however, can be generalized to most other terminals, since they encompass the basic kinds of fields necessary to lay out screens.

Fields on a screen format, then, can be visualized as follows:

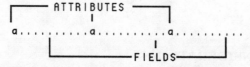

The letter *a* signifies an attribute character position.

Field Types

- Fields may be designed to contain the following types of data:
    - captions or nonchanging material,
    - variable and changeable keyed data,
    - variable but nonchangeable data.

Captions are descriptive identifiers of the information contained in an associated data field. Nonchanging materials are such things as titles or instructions. These kinds of fields are also often referred to as *literals*, *labels*, or *prompts*.

Variable and changeable keyed data fields are data entry screen fields into which data may be keyed. Variable but nonchangeable data fields frequently contain the contents of computer files. They are usually found on inquiry screen formats.

These field types are commonly related on screen formats, as illustrated below:

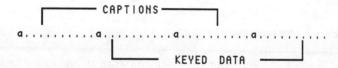

For example:

αEFF-DATE:α.....αEXP-DATE:α.....

Defining Field Characteristics

- The characteristics of a field's attribute specify the type of data contained in a field.
- An attribute's characteristics are determined by selecting one alternative condition in each of a series of conditions.
- Common alternative conditions are:
    1. Protected or Unprotected:
        - Protected—will not permit keying of data into field; field content is for viewing only;
        - Unprotected—permits keying of data into field.
    2. Numeric or Alphanumeric
        - Numeric—only permits keying of numeric data (0–9, decimal point,

and minus sign) into field, if used in conjunction with unprotected condition. If used with protected condition, activates "auto skip" cursor movement function over field;

– Alphanumeric—permits keying alphanumeric data into field, if used in conjunction with unprotected condition. If used with protected condition, requires operator manual tabbing to move cursor over the field.

3. Normal intensity, high intensity or nondisplay:

– Normal intensity—information in the field is displayed at a normal intensity;

– High intensity—information in the field is displayed at a brighter than normal intensity;

– Nondisplay—information in the field is not visible to the operator.

For each screen field one value must be selected from each of the alternative conditions 1, 2, and 3. The most common field definitions in screen layout follow.

Common Field Definitions

- *Data entry of alphanumeric data*—unprotected/alphanumeric/high intensity.
- *Data entry of numeric data*—unprotected/numeric/high intensity.
- *Caption (manual tabbing required)*—protected/alphanumeric/normal intensity.
- *Caption (auto skip required)*—protected/numeric/normal intensity.
- *Descriptive or nonchangeable information*—protected/alphanumeric/normal intensity.

Manual tabbing requires operator depression of the keyboard tab key to move the cursor over a protected field to the next unprotected field. Auto skip results in the cursor automatically moving over the protected to the next unprotected field if the previous unprotected field is fully completed. Nondisplay is typically reserved for "security" fields such as passwords.

Many terminals allow the designer much more flexibility than this, permitting such things as reverse video (dark characters on a light background), underlining, and blinking. These techniques and some recommended uses are described in the next section.

Because screen format layout is addressed in the following chapters, attribute specification is not a topic of discussion. Positions are allowed on the screen where the proper attribute can be specified. The screen designer must be aware of existing conventions and specifications methodologies for the terminals being used and see that all fields are defined as desired and in the required manner.

Monochromatic Display Features

High Brightness

- Good attention-getting capability.
- Least disturbing features.
- Provides two levels only.
- Suggested uses:
  - data fields,
  - items in error.

Lower Case

- Moderate attention-getting capability.
- Use for textual information.

Upper Case

- Moderate attention-getting capability.
- Use for captions, section headings, title, etc.

Reverse Video

- Good attention-getting capability.
- Can reduce legibility.
- Can increase eye fatigue.
- Use in moderation.
- Suggested uses:
  - error messages,
  - fields in error,
  - information being acted upon,
  - information of current relevance.

Underlining

- Poor attention-getting capability.
- May reduce legibility.
- Use to emphasize (e.g. title or headings).

Blinking

- Excellent attention-getting capability.
- Reduces legibility.
- Distracting.
- Provide two levels only (on and off).
- Blink rate should be 2–5 hz with minimum on interval of 50 percent.
- Suggested uses:
    - urgent situations,
    - situations where quick response required.
- Turn off when person has responded.

Multiple Fonts

- Moderate attention-getting capability.
- Use to differentiate screen components, with larger, bolder letters to designate higher-level pieces such as title and headings.

Thin/Thick/Double Rulings

- Suggested uses:
    - break screen into pieces,
    - guide eye through screen.

80/132 Columns

- 132 columns may reduce legibility.
- Avoid 80 and 132 columns for textual material.
- Confine text to 40 to 60 characters.
- Consider double and triple columns for displaying text.

Scrolling

- Not appropriate for novice users.
- Use "smooth" movement.

Phosphor Color

- At the standard viewing distance, white, orange, or green are acceptable colors.
- At a far viewing distance, white is the best choice.
- Over all viewing distances, from near to far, white is the best choice.

Today's monochromatic displays provide a wide range of techniques to aid the screen design process. Few terminals will have all the features described, but the more that do exist, the more flexibility the designer will have. Effective screen design can be accomplished, though, even with only a small number of features available.

Before beginning screen design, the designer must be aware of the capabilities existing on the terminal where the screen will be displayed. It is important to note whether the various features are available on an individual field basis, or whether they must be incorporated on a screen-wide basis. (For example, can any one caption be displayed at high intensity or must all captions be displayed at high intensity?). The latter will, of course, allow less flexibility in design.

Often these features will be used to call attention to various items on the display. The attraction capability of a mechanism is directly related to how well it stands out from its surroundings. Its maximum value is achieved when it is used in moderation. Overuse is self-defeating, as contrast with the surroundings is reduced and distraction may even begin to occur.

Not all display features are ideal for all situations. Following are some recommended uses and limitations that currently exist.

High brightness.   High brightness has a good attention-getting quality and no disturbing features. It is frequently used to indicate fields in error on data entry screens and is an excellent vehicle for calling attention to data fields on inquiry screens. It may be used for data fields on data entry screens if an alternative method such as reverse video is available to call attention to errors. If it has a fault, it is that terminals with improperly set manual screen contrast controls can diminish its effectiveness, even causing it to disappear. This can be a major problem for terminals placed in exceptionally bright viewing conditions.

Lower case.   Lower case should be used for textual information since it is read faster than upper case. However, use it only if the character set contains true descenders (the line dropping from a *g* or *p* that makes it lower than an *a* or *o*) or ascenders (the upward line on a *b* or *d*). Words composed of characters without true ascenders and descenders (the bottom of the *p* is not longer than the bottom of the *o*) are harder to read than upper case since the structure of the word fits no pattern we have memorized. Without true ascenders and descenders, it is better to use upper case exclusively.

Upper case.   Upper case is used for captions, headings, title, and data fields, unless the data fields are heavily text oriented.

Reverse video.   Reverse video is a display feature that permits a screen to resemble the normal printed page (dark letters on a light background). Rooms with overhead lighting can cause disturbing screen reflections, a problem that is significantly reduced by reverse video because the reflection is masked by the light screen background. However, reverse video should be used with caution. Some potential problems are:

- Excessively bright display caused by the large area of emitted light from the electron gun. The result is best described as "dazzle" to one's eyes that can be fatiguing. Paper viewing is accomplished by reflected light, which is not subject to this phenomenon (although a light source positioned close to a piece of paper can create reflected glare that also creates viewing problems).
- Light emitted by the display screen tends to bleed into the dark surrounding area, as perceived by the viewer's eyes. Therefore a display with a light background results in the background bleeding into the characters displayed. Light characters bleed into a dark background. Thus, a light character on a dark background will actually look larger to the viewer than do dark characters on a light background. If character size and resolution are not adequate, the reverse video characters may not be as legible as the light-on-dark characters.
- For a normal light character on dark background display, a display refresh rate of 60 cycles per second must be maintained so the viewer does not perceive a display flicker (which can be fatiguing to the eye). A full reverse video display is much more susceptible to the perception of flicker, and the refresh rate must be increased to 90 to 100 cycles per second to eliminate it. If reverse video is used on a display being refreshed at 60 cycles per second, flicker can become a problem.

Several studies comparing reverse video screens to the more prevalent light character on dark background screens have found no performance differences (Cushman, 1986; Kühne et al., 1986, and Zwahlen and Kothari, 1986) and no differences in eye-scanning behavior and feelings of visual fatigue (Zwahlen and Kothari, 1986). One study did find reverse video more visually fatiguing (Cushman, 1986), while another (Wichansky, 1986) found green and orange phosphor reverse video screens easier to read, but found no differences in white phosphor readability.

Given the above potential problems and conflicting study results reverse video should be used with discretion. Before implementing it on a full-screen basis, it is necessary to verify whether or not these problems do actually exist. Some terminals will be fully acceptable, others will not. The number of different display terminals in existence makes it impossible to specify any all-encompassing conclusions. The safest general conclusion is to use reverse video in moderation. Calling attention to fields in error or using in error messages are two practical uses. Another is to highlight actions such as program function key alternatives. If reverse video is used to identify certain fields or highlight certain kinds of information, some additional cautions are warranted:

- If reverse video is used to identify one kind of field such as data entry, avoid what can best be described as the crossword puzzle effect—the haphazard arrangement of fields on the screen creating an image that somewhat resembles a typical crossword puzzle. An arrangement of elements might be created that tries to lead the eye in directions that the designer has not intended. Alignment and columnization rules, to be described in the sections on designing specific kinds of screens, will minimize this effect.
- If reverse video is used to highlight information such as error messages or actions to be taken, allow an extra reversed character position on each side of the field. This will leave a margin around the information in the field, giving it a more pleasing look. This will also eliminate any degradation in information legibility caused by lines made up of wide characters being placed too close to the edge of the field.

Underlining. Underlining can reduce legibility, so it should be used with caution. One possibility is to emphasize titles or headings. Use underlining only if some space exists between the underlining and the word being underlined. On some terminals the underline is part of the character itself, thereby reducing word legibility.

Blinking. Blinking has a very high attention-getting capability, but it reduces character legibility and is disturbing to most people. It often causes visual fatigue if excessively used. Therefore, it should be reserved for urgent situations and when quick response is necessary. A user should be able to turn off the blinking once his attention has been captured. The recommended blink rate is 2–5 hz with a minimum "on" time of 50 percent. An alternative to consider is creating an "on" cycle considerably longer than the "off," a "wink" rather than a "blink."

Multiple Fonts. Multiple fonts have moderate attention-getting capability. Their varying sizes and shapes can be used to differentiate screen components. Use larger, bolder letters to designate higher-level screen pieces, such as titles and headings.

Thin/thick/double rulings. Use horizontal rulings as a substitute for spaces in breaking a screen into pieces. Use vertical rulings to convey to the screen viewer that a screen should be scanned from top to bottom.

80/132-column screens. A 132-column screen is an increasingly popular alternative to the traditional 80-column screen. Some terminals are capable of displaying either width. If the terminal is capable of both widths, verify that the 132-column screen does not degrade character legibility. This can happen because, in many cases, 132 columns are created by compressing the 132 characters into an 80-column width.

Avoid using the full 80 and 132 columns for display of textual material. Confine text to 40-60 characters per line.

Scrolling. Scrolling is a technique to move data across or through the screen. Scrolling is not appropriate for novice users (Schwarz et al., 1983). Scroll movement should be "smooth"; it should not use the "jump" method which is bothersome to most people.

Phosphor color. In a study by Hewlett-Packard (Wichansky, 1986), at the standard screen viewing distance (18-24 inches), no performance differences were found between white, orange, and green phosphor in either polarity (light characters on a dark background, or dark characters on a light background). Subjective ratings of ease of reading were highest for green and orange reverse video screens as compared to normal video (light character screens), while no differences in ease of reading were found for either polarity with white phosphor at this distance. At a far viewing distance (4-5 feet), orange and green phosphor reverse video screens could be seen more clearly than normal video screens, while white screens were equally legible in either polarity. More errors were found with green phosphor than the other two.

Green phosphor caused red or pink afterimages for 35 percent of the screen viewers; orange phosphor yielded blue afterimages for 20 percent; and white phosphor yielded afterimages for 5 percent. A 35-percent green phosphor afterimage for viewing was also found by Galitz (1968).

Some conclusions are:

- At standard viewing distances, no significant performance differences exist for white, orange, or green. All are acceptable. Subjective preferences may vary, however, so providing the viewer a choice of any of these colors is desirable.
- At far viewing distances, white is the more legible color and therefore the best choice.
- Over all viewing distances, white phospor is the best choice.
- White phosphor has the lowest probability for creating afterimages.

Windows

A window is a technique in which only a portion of the display screen is used for a particular interaction or task. In effect, two or more "mini-screens" are available to the viewer. A window may be small, a single message, or it may be large, consuming most of the display space available. Windows are a relatively recent innovation in the evolving human-computer interface. They were created to allow the "display workspace" to more closely mirror the "desk workspace."

The value of a window is that it reduces short-term memory loads. The ability to do mental calculations is limited by how well one keeps track of one's place, interim products, and results. The window acts as an external memory that is an extension of one's internal memory (Card, et al., 1984). Windows also provide access to more information than would normally be available on a single screen of the same size. This is done by overwriting or placing more important information on top of information that is less important at that moment. While all the advantages and disadvantages of windows are still not well understood, they do seem to be useful in the following ways.

Providing access to multiple sources of information.   Independent sources of information may have to be accessed at the same time. For example, information to solve a problem may be stored in a HELP function. This information may be presented on the screen alongside the problem, greatly facilitating its solution. Or, a writer may have to refer to several parts of text being written at the same time. Or, a travel agent may have to compare several travel destinations for a particularly demanding client.

Combining multiple sources of information.   Text from several documents may have to be reviewed and combined into one. Pertinent information is selected from one window and copied into another.

Performing more than one task.   More than one task can be performed at one time. While waiting for a long, complex procedure to finish, another can be performed. Tasks of higher priority can interrupt less important ones. The interrupted task can then be resumed with no "close down" and "restart" necessary.

Reminding.   Windows can be used to remind the viewer of things likely to be of use in the near future. Examples might be menus of choices available, a history of the path followed or command choices to that point, or the time of an important meeting.

Monitoring.   Changes, both internal and external, can be monitored. Data in one window can be modified and its effect on data in another window can be studied. External events, such as stock prices, out of normal range conditions, or system messages can be watched while another major activity is carried out.

Multiple representations of the same task.   The same thing can be looked at in several ways—for example, alternative drafts of a speech, different versions of a screen, or different graphical representations of the same data.

Although windows do offer significant advantages, they require additional learning by the user and pose some unique design considerations, as follows.

Tiled versus overlapping windows.   Two kinds of windows exist. A "tiled" window (Figure 4.12) is one whose contents are always visible. Since windows

Figure 4.12 Tiled windows.

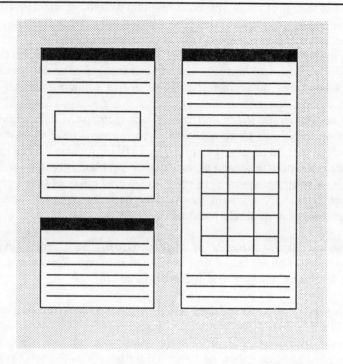

do not overlap one another, the user may not see much of the contents of a newly opened window, and the number of windows that may be simultaneously open is limited. When a new window is opened, other open windows are re-located and resized as needed, but never obscured. The size and location of tiled windows are usually managed by the system. "Overlapped" windows (Figure 4.13) may be placed on top of one another. When the location and/or size of a window changes, the contents of underlying windows will be obscured. The location and size of the underlying window does not change. When a new window is opened, its contents are usually fully visible. The size and location of overlapping windows are under user control.

Window manipulation. Manipulation requirements include specifying win-dow location and size, estimating the effect of adding or changing one window on the size and location of other displayed windows (tiled windows can become very small; overlapping windows can hide other information), and navigating between windows.

Some window problems. Window manipulation can be very time consuming and distracting. In a study comparing screens with overlapping windows and full screens (Davies, et al., 1985), task completion times were longer with the

Figure 4.13 Overlapping windows.

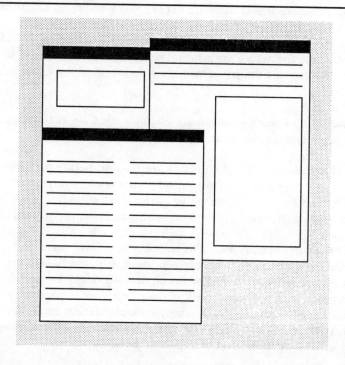

window screens, but the non-window screens method produced more errors. After eliminating screen arrangement time, however, task solution times were shorter with windows. The results suggest that advantages for windows do exist, but they can be negated by excessive manipulation requirements. Other window problems include the necessity for window borders to consume valuable screen space, and that small windows providing access to large amounts of information can lead to excessive, bothersome scrolling.

Window Guidelines

- Display no more than 6 or 7 windows at one time.
- Provide cues for closing windows.
- Use tiled windows for:
  - single task activities,
  - fewer window manipulation activities,
  - novice users.
- Use overlapping windows for:
  - switching between tasks,
  - situations in which window manipulation can be tolerated,
  - expert users.

Since windows are a relatively new concept, and research evidence is sparse, guidelines are based more on experience and "rules of thumb."

Display no more than 6 or 7 windows. It may be advantageous to save 25 to 30 windows, but the active working set seldom exceeds 7. One study (Gaylin, 1986) found the mean number of windows maintained for experienced users was 3.7.

Provide cues for closing windows. Explicit cues seem to be necessary to remind the user how to close windows.

Use of tiled windows. Tiled windows seem to be better for single task activities. Bly and Rosenberg (1986) found that tasks requiring little window manipulation can be carried out faster using tiled windows. They also found that novice users performed better with tiled windows, regardless of the task.

Use of overlapping windows. Overlapping windows seem to be better for situations that require switching between tasks. Bly and Rosenberg concluded that tasks requiring much window manipulation could be performed faster with overlapping windows, but only if user "window expertise" existed. For novice users tasks requiring much window manipulation could be carried out faster with tiled windows. Therefore, the advantage to overlapping windows comes only after a certain level of expertise is achieved.

Edit Requirements

- The three basic types of edits are:

  Field – verification that the data contained within a field is within predefined limits, or present when required;

  Cross-Field – verification that the data contained within two or more fields on one screen format is consistent;

  Cross-Screen – verification that the data contained within two or more fields on two or more screen formats is consistent.

- Field edits are performed faster and more efficiently than cross-field edits.
- Cross-field edits are performed faster and more efficiently than cross-screen edits.

Transaction processing time can be lessened to the extent that edits (validation or checking the correctness of the entered data by the computer) can be reduced to the lowest level, as follows: (1) field, (2) cross-field, (3) cross-screen.

For many years edits have been a technical consideration receiving much attention by screen designers. As a result, edits have been a major cause of the frequent mismatches between the computer subsystem and the manual subsystem. Whereas the organization of screens is weighted heavily toward screen edits, the organization of information as it flows through the manual subsystem has usually not reflected screen edit needs. Therefore, the data has often arrived at the display terminal organized differently than the system has structured it for entry. The organization of information in the manual subsystem should reflect the needs of the system edits. The system and screen, however, should not expect the data to be organized in a way that is not meaningful to the users of the system. So, screens should be organized for edit ease on the basis of what makes sense to the data provider.

Storage Capabilities

- Do not define identical screens as separate screen formats.
- For functions with similar requirements, try to utilize one screen format.

Identical screen formats should not be defined as separate screen formats. This is an unnecessary waste of screen format file storage space. Similarly, it may be possible to develop one screen format to handle two separate but similar functions. Again, screen format storage benefits accrue.

A point of caution, however. Storage should not be optimized at the expense of screen clarity and ease of use.

APPLICATION CONSIDERATIONS

- Screen design must reflect the objectives of the system for which the screens are designed.

Screens consist of data elements. These data elements must incorporate the requirements of the application for which this system is being developed, in order that the purpose of the system can be fulfilled. This last consideration can be stated briefly, but it is the cornerstone of all screen design activity.

Data Entry Screens 5

Data entry screens are those onto which data is keyed. Also called data collection screens, their purpose is to capture information quickly and accurately. Quite often this data is edited on-line so that errors can be corrected quickly.

This class of screens encompasses applications that frequently include large numbers of data elements. Several screens may be required to complete one transaction, and a system may comprise many transactions. The traditional definition given to this kind of application has been the term *data entry*. The definition of screens discussed on these pages, however, applies to all screens onto which data is keyed. This includes the newer office automation applications such as electronic mail, executive calendars, and so forth.

The design style of a data entry screen can also be characterized as "form fill-in." The screen itself should provide the cues necessary to permit an inexperienced user to easily and accurately determine what must be keyed, enter the required information, and then later review it if necessary. That the novice user of a computer performs better with, and prefers, this kind of screen to a command dialogue was experimentally ascertained by Ogden and Boyle (1982). Nevertheless, while helping the novice user, the design of the data entry screen should not inhibit the experienced person.

The most important variable in data entry screen design is the availability of a specially designed source document from which data is keyed. If such a document is used, and if it has been designed in conjunction with the screen, the primary visual focus of the user will be toward the document, with the screen assuming a secondary role in the keying process. If a special source document is not developed, the user's primary visual focus is usually the screen, and the data source assumes a less important role in the overall design.

This distinction is important because it determines whether keying aids are built into the screens or into source documents. With a dedicated source document, the document itself can include keying aids. But without a dedicated source document, the screen format must incorporate aids. The resulting screens will have fundamental conceptual differences in data organization, content, and structure.

Due to the fundamental differences in these kinds of screens, they are addressed in three separate sections in this chapter.

Section 5-1 reviews the guidelines that are common to both kinds of screens. These guidelines are not affected by screen type. Subjects include information grouping techniques, transaction organization rules, keying procedures, the structure of keyed data, and data editing guidelines. Section 5-2 is devoted to guidelines for screens used with a dedicated source document, and section 5-3 details screen guidelines for which a dedicated source document is not available.

SECTION 5-1

Data Entry Screens—General

INFORMATION GROUPING TECHNIQUES

- *Sequential*—grouping items of information in the order in which they are commonly received or transmitted, or by natural groupings.
- *Frequency of use*—grouping together items that are used most frequently.
- *Function*—grouping items according to the function they perform.
- *Importance*—grouping items of information according to how important they are to the task or transaction.

Screens will contain items of data that must be organized in some meaningful manner. This arrangement will be based on sequence and frequency of use, function, and importance.

Sequence of use. Sequence of use grouping involves arranging information items in the order in which they are commonly received or transmitted, or in natural groups. An address, for example, is normally given by street, city, state, and zip code. Another example of natural grouping is the league standings of football teams, appearing in order of best to worst records.

Frequency of use. Frequency of use is a design technique based on the principle that information items used most frequently should be grouped at the beginning, the second most frequently used items grouped next, and so forth.

Function. Function involves grouping information items according to their purpose. All items pertaining to insurance coverages, for example, may be placed in one location. Such grouping also allows convenient group identification for the user.

Importance. Importance grouping is based on the information's importance to the task being performed. Important items are placed in the most prominent positions.

Screen design normally reflects a combination of these techniques. Information may be organized functionally but, within each function, individual items may be arranged by sequence or importance. Numerous permutations are possible.

TRANSACTION ORGANIZATION

- Optimize system editing by grouping edit-related items on the same screen.
- Minimize cursor positioning movements by locating required elements toward the top of screens or at the beginning of lines.
- Structure the transaction to consist of as few screen formats as possible, but not at the expense of visual clarity.
- Break screens at logical or natural points, such as:
    - between different kinds of information,
    - between sections of a source document,
    - at the end of a source document page,
    - at breaking points between reference sources.

Availability of a dedicated source document will have little impact on overall organization of data entry transactions. The guiding concept here is to minimize the number of screens required to complete a transaction by incorporating required data elements (those always completed during data entry) in the earliest screens and in upper screen positions. This permits concluding transactions without displaying all transaction screens, and ending screens without having to tab through all screen elements. Incorporating on one screen items to be edited against one another will yield faster and more efficient transaction editing than placing such fields on different screens.

Structuring a transaction to consist of as few screens as possible will also reduce user "wait" periods between screens. For example, 100 fields split between two screen formats will yield a faster data entry rate (in terms of characters per second) than the same number of fields split between four screen formats. In the two-screen scenario, user inactivity occurs only once—between screens one and two. In the four-screen scenario, three inactive periods occur.

An important word of caution, however. Development of a transaction must be based on the logical order of data collection (especially if a source document is involved). Transaction organization rules should be implemented with the understanding that the organization must make sense to the person providing or collecting the data. Screen design must never dictate source document design. Form design must be the controlling factor.

KEYSTROKES

* Do not focus on minimizing keystrokes without considering other factors such as:
  – keying rhythm,
  – output evaluation requirements.

A sought-after goal in many data entry applications is to minimize keystrokes. Fewer keystrokes have been synonymous with faster keying speeds and greater productivity in the minds of many. But this is not always true. Fewer keystrokes may actually decrease keying speeds and reduce productivity in many cases.

One example is found in Galitz (1972), who compared auto skip with manual tabbing in a data entry application. Auto skip, while requiring fewer keystrokes, was found to result in longer keying times and more errors than manual tabbing because it disrupted keying rhythm. This study is described in more detail in the following section.

Another example is a study by Springer and Sorce (1984), who, in an information retrieval task, compared input keystrokes to resulting output evaluation time. They found that more keystrokes yielded more precise outputs, which resulted in faster problem solving.

So, the number of keystrokes must be considered in light of keying rhythms and the objectives to be achieved as a result of the keying. Fewer is not always better.

KEYING PROCEDURES
Manual Tab versus Auto Skip

* Define fields to permit manual tabbing.

Auto skip is a display terminal feature that causes a cursor to automatically move to the beginning of the next entry field once a field is completely filled. Auto skip obviates manual tabbing and requires fewer keystrokes to complete a screen. Theoretically, keying speeds should increase with auto skip. In practice, however, they do not always do so.

Rarely are many entry screen fields completely filled with data. When an entry field is not full, the user must still depress the tab key to move the cursor to the next entry field. Figure 5.1 illustrates the auto skip function.

Figure 5.1 Data entry using auto skip.

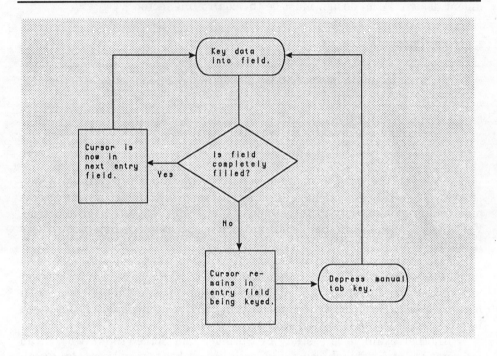

Auto skip, therefore, imposes decision-making and learning requirements. After keying data in each field, one must determine where the cursor
is and whether to depress the manual tab key. Only then can the next keying
action be performed. As illustrated in figure 5.2, manual tabbing requires extra
keystrokes, but no decisions need be made. The data entry task is rhythmic
and consistent. Galitz (1972) summarizes operator performance data from a
study of both auto skip and manual tabbing. In that study manual tabbing
resulted in faster performance and fewer keying errors.

Auto skip can delay detection of one particular human error. If an extra
character is inadvertently keyed into a field, the cursor will still move automatically to the next entry field and keying can continue. The error will not
be immediately detected and the spacing in subsequent fields may also be one
position off, at least until the tab key is depressed. Were this situation to occur
while using manual tabbing, the keyboard would lock as soon as the entry
field was full or when an attempt was made to key the extra character. The
error would be immediately obvious.

But auto skip, despite its limitations, can be useful if a system's screens
are easily learned or if all screen fields are always completely filled. Nevertheless, most large-volume data entry applications would not appear to meet
these criteria.

Figure 5.2 Data entry using manual tabbing.

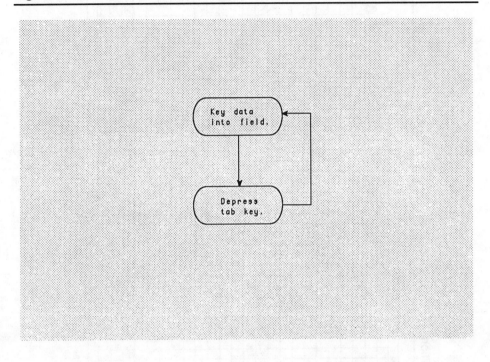

Cursor-Rest Position

- Maintain a cursor-rest position at the end of each display line.

While manual tab control is in use, and when an entry field is completely filled, the cursor will move to the first character position of the next protected field to await a manual tab command. This command will direct the cursor to the first character position of the next entry field. After a line of data is keyed, the user can also depress the return key to direct the cursor to the first entry field of the next line. If an entry field extends into the next-to-last or last column in a line, however, depression of the return key can put the cursor in the wrong location. Figure 5.3 illustrates how this happens. Restricting the endpoint of an entry field to the second-to-last column in a line will prevent the situation in example B, thus eliminating a potential error and establishing a consistent data entry procedure.

Figure 5.3 The need for a cursor-rest position.

```
              10                    60            70                80
  @ P O L I C Y : @ 6 5 4 3   @
  B R A N C H : @ • • @       @ P O L I C Y : @ 6 5 4 3 7 @
  R E G I O N : @ • • @
  B R A N C H : @ • • @       @ P O L I C Y : @ 6 5 4 3 7 @
  R E G I O N : @ • • @
  B R A N C H : @ • • @       @ P O L I C Y : @ 6 5 4 3 @
  R E G I O N : @ • • @
  B R A N C H : @ • • @       @ P O L I C Y : @ 6 5 4 3 7 @
  R E G I O N : @ • • @
  B R A N C H : @ • • @       @ P O L I C Y : @ 6 5 4 3 7 @
  R E G I O N : @ • • @
```

Example A
1. The cursor (a block) is positioned in column 78 awaiting the last key entry in the field.

2. A 7 is keyed and the cursor moves to column 80 awaiting a tab or return key depression.

3. A tab or return key depression moves the cursor to the first position of the next entry field.

Example B
1. The cursor is positioned in column 79 awaiting the last entry in the field.

2. A 7 is keyed, and the cursor moves to the next available position to await a tab or return key depression. It is now in column 1 of the next line.

3. The return key is depressed and the cursor moves down to the first entry position of the next line. A situation has thus been created that will allow an error to occur.

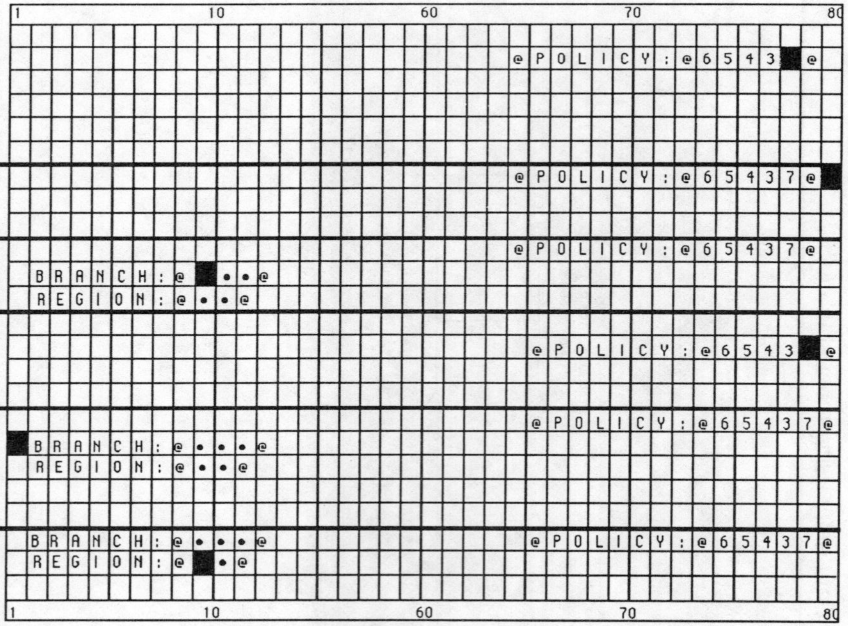

Note: The @ is an attribute character that defines the field's characteristics (protected, entry, etc.).

Keying Rules

---

* Do not require recoding, changing, omitting, or including data based on special rules or logical transformations.

Slower data entry keying speeds and increased error probability result if users must make such decisions as:

* should this data always be keyed?
* if that field is keyed, should this one be keyed?
* if the data is *X*, then should *I* be keyed in the field?
* If a *4* goes here, where should other figures be keyed?

Such keying decisions impose learning requirements on users. Except in the most simple systems, this learning will never reach a satisfactory level. The fewer rules and decisions involved in keying, the faster and more accurate data entry will be. Coding, omitting, changing, and including data by special rules or transformations as a group represent probably the greatest single decrement to data entry speed.

Cursor Positioning

---

* Position the cursor at the first character location of the first entry field upon initial presentation of a screen.

Upon presentation of a screen, the cursor should be positioned for quick and easy start of the keying process. Never require a user to move the cursor manually to the proper location before keying can start.

Character Entry

---

* Key entry should be accomplished by direct character replacement (of underscores, previous entries, default values, or blanks).
* Keyed entries should always appear on the display (except for passwords or other secure entries).
* Data should be keyed without separators or delimiters such as dashes (—) or slashes(/).
* Data should be keyed without dimensional units (such as "$," "mph," etc.).
* Right or left justification of keyed data for variable length fields should not be required.
* Key entry of leading zeros should not be required.

- Removal of unused underscores for variable length fields should not be required.
- Areas of the screen not containing entry fields (i.e., protected fields) should be inaccessible, not requiring repeated key depressions to step through.

The above guidelines will speed the key entry of data on the screen and minimize the potential for errors.

ENTRY FIELDS

- Identify the entire entry field by underscores.

                    C I T Y :   _ _ _ _ _ _ _ _ _ _ _ _ _ _

An entry field should possess the following qualities:

- it should draw a person's attention to the fact that information must be keyed into it;
- it should not detract from the legibility of the characters keyed into the field;
- it should provide some indication of the nature of the desired response;
- it should indicate the appropriate number of characters for the entry.

Savage (1980), in an opinion study comparing reverse video and underscore field indicators with no indicators at all, found that users overwhelmingly preferred indicators to no indicators in the entry field.

In a follow-up study, several entry field techniques, including broken line underscores, a reverse video box, pointed brackets (⟨⟨ ⟩⟩), and two column separation methods (a dot or a line between each character position), were compared by Savage et al. (1982). They found that while it was not superior in every quality, the best delimiter overall was the underscore. More details on this study are given in following chapters.

The underscore has an added advantage in that it visually resembles an entry field line on a paper form (as the reverse video box resembles a paper form box, though the underscore doesn't have the readability problems).

Entry Field Separators and Delimiters

If the attribute convention does not require a reserved character position on the screen:

- incorporate separators or delimiters (such as slashes (/) or dashes (—) within the entry field.

DATE: __ / __ / __

If the attribute convention requires a reserved character position on the screen:

- incorporate spaces where separator or delimiter characters would normally occur within the entry field.

DATE: __ __ __

Separators and delimiters are often included with common data elements such as date and telephone number. Incorporated within an entry field on the screen, they permit much easier visual checking of the data keyed within that field. On a screen whose conventions do not require attribute character positions to be reserved on the screen itself, these separators or delimiters should be included in the entry field, as illustrated in the first example above.

When the screen attribute convention requires that attribute character positions be reserved on the screen, incorporating separators or delimiters is wasteful of screen space and lacks visual closure, as illustrated below.

DATE: __ / __ / __

In this case the most reasonable alternative is to break the entry field into pieces by defining each component normally separated by a delimiter into separate unprotected fields. The attribute character positions will create spaces between data components, as illustrated in the second example above. The cursor will auto skip between the separate entry fields that have actually been created. To the user, however, what will visually appear is one field with the necessary structure to aid visual checking.

Default Values

- Current default values should be displayed in their appropriate entry fields upon transaction initiation. Do not rely on a user to remember them.
- Acceptance of a default value should be accomplished easily, such as by:
  - a single confirming key entry,
  - a tab past the default field.
- Replacement of a default value should be accomplished without changing the default's current definition.

Incorporation of default values can also speed the data keying process, as long as the above guidelines are followed.

Screen Transmission

- Transmission of screens containing multiple data entry fields should be accomplished by a single explicit action when all entries are completed. Separate entry of fields should not be required or performed.
- Transmission should be accomplished through an explicitly labeled ENTER or TRANSMIT key.
- An action requesting transmission of keyed data on a screen should result in transmission of all items on that screen, regardless of where the cursor is currently positioned on the screen.

Often the choice exists to transmit keyed data to the computer by either 1) a field-by-field basis, or 2) the entire screen at one time (commonly referred to as "block mode").

Full screen, or block mode, entry is thought to have these advantages:

- greater speed,
- easier review and correction of errors,
- more obvious logical groupings and more obvious relationships of elements,
- more efficient cross-field edits.

Field-by-field entry is thought to have these advantages:

- less dense screens because they do not have to display optional elements unless necessary,
- faster error correction,
- fewer errors due to early detection of errors that could trigger cross-field errors if detected later.

One study comparing these two modes of entry is Romano and Sonnio. They found that the full screen (block) mode was significantly faster, though no error differences existed between the two modes.

It would seem that in cases of large amounts of data and source document-oriented entry, the block mode advantages are substantial, and this is the recommended mode in these cases. In other cases—smaller volumes of data, where speed is not critical, and non-source document-oriented entry—either mode is satisfactory. For very casual system users, a field-by-field mode has the greatest advantages.

Abbreviations

- Truncation has been found to be the most consistent abbreviation method for encoding.
- No significant abbreviation methods exist for decoding.
- Teach users the abbreviation method to be used.
- Train users with full words, not abbreviations.
- Develop a standard dictionary of abbreviations.

Computer systems often require the creation of abbreviations, for field captions, data, or commands. A variety of studies have addressed optimum abbreviation strategies, good summaries being found in Ehrenreich (1985) and Grudin and Barnard (1985). A dozen or so abbreviation methods that have been described, the most common being:

- natural—subjective judgments of what is a good representation of the full word;
- contraction—the first and last letter of the word are retained, some letters in between are deleted;
- vowel deletion—all vowels in the word are deleted;
- truncation—the first few letters of the word are retained, the remainder deleted.

The studies have concluded that for encoding, or creating abbreviations, the truncation method has yielded the most consistent results. In general, it has been found that people have great difficulties in reconstructing consistent abbreviations for the same words. Word lengths and letter selection rules vary considerably. For decoding, understanding the abbreviation, no method has been found to be superior to any other.

Teaching users the abbreviation rule to be followed will result in more consistent abbreviations. Train them with the full word or words first to aid word–abbreviation association. Users who learn only abbreviations, it has been found, often do not know what they stand for. Because of the problems in creating and remembering abbreviations, a standard dictionary of abbreviations is a valuable aid in any screen design activity.

DATA EDITING

When

- Data should be edited as close to its source as possible.
- Data should be automatically edited after entry of all fields on a screen has been keyed, not on an item-by-item basis.

- Correction of errors should be permitted immediately after an error is detected.

How

- Computer data editing should always be performed. Never rely upon the operator to make correct entries.
- Inability to correct an error should not prevent initiation of another transaction. The capability should exist for the storage and later retrieval of the transaction with an error.

Data should always be edited as close as possible to its source. When errors occur, and they will, the correction process will thus be much more efficient. Data should also be edited on a screen basis, not an item basis. An experienced data entry operator will find stopping for errors disruptive to the keying rhythm.

DATA STRUCTURE

Data Size

- Restrict all alphabetic codes to four or fewer characters.
- Restrict all numeric codes to six or fewer characters.
- Keep code length and format constant throughout any single category.

As the length of a field increases, errors in using it also increase. Figure 5.4 shows mean error rates for various field lengths. Smaller data fields will pay dividends in lower error rates.

Figure 5.4 Error percentage for varying field lengths.

Average Number Characters per Field	Percent of Fields in Error
3	1.4
5	2.0
7	2.6
9	3.1
11	3.6

Data Content

- Do not intersperse letters with numbers.
- Use alpha combinations that are:
  - meaningful,
  - distinctive,
  - predictable.
- For alphabetical data entry, do not use restricted alphabetic sets.
- If special characters are selected for keying (e.g., =, /, @, etc.) choose those that will not require frequent shifts between upper and lower case.

Codes based on common English usage (words, contractions, abbreviations, acronyms, quantities, etc.) are the most easily used because they require minimum learning. Arbitrary codes require extensive learning and are seldom easy to use. Keying errors decrease when people learn familiar letter sequences and patterns. They can also detect and correct inconsistencies and inaccuracies more easily.

If abbreviated codes are chosen for entry, make sure they are as distinctive as possible. This will minimize potential confusions due to similarity. BAM vs. BAN, for example, is bad. BAM vs. PRV is good.

Codes containing predictable letter sequences can be keyed more rapidly. The letter combinations "TH" and "IN" are much more predictable than "YX" or "JS," and can be keyed faster.

Many keying errors are caused by incorrect SHIFT key usage. Shifts take longer to accomplish and can severely disrupt the keying rhythm.

Data Legibility

- Break long codes (seven or more characters) into three- or four-character groups.
- Present source data visually, not with auditory devices, such as telephones or dictating machines.
- Eliminate frequently confused characters and character pairs from code vocabularies.
  - Eliminate the letters *O* and *I* from alphanumeric code vocabularies.
  - Do not use the letters, *Y, N, V, Z, Q, U,* and *G* in hand printing.

Figure 5.5 shows the most frequent character substitutions.

About half of all coding errors could be eliminated if *O* and *I* were not in the alphanumeric code vocabulary. And about two-thirds of all errors could be eliminated if *I, O, 8, 0,* and *B* were not used as codes.

Figure 5.5 Frequency of character substitutions.

Characters:

Characters:	*Substitution Frequency*		
I	24%		
O	23%	} 47%	
8	9%		} 70%
0	5%		
Z	5%		
B	4%		

Character Pairs:

Characters:	*Cumulative Frequency*
I-1	25%
O-0	50%
B-8	60%
Z-2	70%

Figure 5.6 Illegibility of hand-printed characters.

(ranked from highest to lowest probability of being printed illegibly)

1.	Y	} 24%	} 50%				
2.	N						
3.	V						
4.	Z						
5.	Q						
6.	U						
7.	G						
8.	J			18.	5	28.	H
9.	C			19.	4	29.	Z
10.	X			20.	I	30.	R
11.	O			21.	A	31.	P
12.	T			22.	F	32.	0
13.	E			23.	6	33.	7
14.	D			24.	L	34.	3
15.	K			25.	W	35.	8
16.	S			26.	M	36.	1
17.	B			27.	9		

The two worst legibility offenders in hard hand printing, as shown in figure 5.6, are *Y* and *N*. Removal of the first 7 offending characters would delete about 50 percent of the characters causing legibility errors.

People prefer to handle codes in small chunks. A 6-character code may be perceived as two 3-character codes, and a 7-character code as a three-four pair. For example, the telephone number 2155847053 is commonly handled as 215 584 7053. Lengthy codes should be structured in 3- or 4-character groupings.

Legibility problems could be greatly reduced by training people to write big, closed loops; to use simple shapes; to connect lines; to block print rather than scrawl; and not to link characters together.

Data Entry Screens Used With a Dedicated Source Document

SCREEN ORGANIZATION

- The screen must be an image of its associated source document.

Skipping around a source document to locate data adds time to the data entry process. It also imposes learning requirements on users, since they must master the order and location of fields. Having the source document and screen in the same sequence can eliminate these problems. Cursor location on the screen is then always known because it corresponds with the user's position on the source document. Proper sequence also allows the user's eyes to move easily ahead of his hands—another design objective of data entry.

Ideally, keying should never require eye movement from the source document to the screen. Theoretically (and frequently, if the design is proper), the user should be able to key an entire screen without glancing at it. Often, however, eye movements between document and screen are necessary to check for possible keying errors and to correct edit-detected errors. This eye movement will be most efficient (and natural) if fields on the screen and the document are in the same relative position. These considerations lead to this cardinal rule for developing data entry systems: *Develop screens that are exact images of source documents.* Fields on a screen should be located on the same line and in the same order as fields on the source document. This factor is more important than absolute visual clarity.

The rule should not be interpreted literally, however; different caption sizes and the number of fields included on one line can cause minor distortions. Thus, the goal should be relative positioning, since the eye will not detect minor distortions in the exact image relationship.

If a source document contains nonentry fields, ink screening techniques can maintain the image relationship. If a source document contains a large number of these fields, the positioning of data entry fields on the screen may appear awkward. For consistency, however, the relative positioning rule must be maintained. The only exception would be a revised scheme that could eliminate the awkwardness while maintaining consistency within the application and the ability to locate specific fields easily.

Screens of this kind and their associated source documents cannot be developed separately. Constraints imposed by source document design considerations must be reflected in screen format design and vice versa. In fact, as was mentioned earlier, source document design is usually a greater restriction in the design process than screen design (Galitz, 1975). Design guidelines for source document design are discussed in chapter 13.

CAPTIONS

Structure and Size

- Captions should use abbreviations and contractions.
- Captions should not exceed eight characters.
- Abbreviations should not exceed three or four characters.
- Separate two or more abbreviations by hyphens.
- Display captions in normal intensity.

Formatting

- Single fields:
  - locate caption to left of entry field;
  - right justify caption to enter field;
  - separate from entry field by a unique symbol (such as a colon) and one space.

```
ORG:x_____
```

- Multiple occurrence fields:
  - row orientation—
    locate caption to left of entry fields;
    separate from entry field by a unique symbol (such as a colon) and one space;
    separate entry fields by a unique symbol with one space on each side of it.

```
CDS:  _____x:x_____ : _____ : _____ : _____
```

– columnar orientation—
    locate caption one line above column of entry fields;
    left-justify caption above first position of entry fields;
    precede entry fields by a unique symbol (such as a colon) separated
    from entry fields by one space.

```
ORD-NO
- - - - - - - - - - - - -
- - - - - - - - - - - - -
- - - - - - - - - - - - -
- - - - - - - - - - - - -
```

Structure and size. When a dedicated source document is used for keying, field captions are normally needed only for error detection or correction, or to find one's exact place on the screen when momentarily confused. Thus, captions have a supportive rather than a primary function in the data entry process, and abbreviations and contractions should be used.

The caption size limit is eight characters. This is a compromise between screen space utilization and clarity. It results in a good fit between standard (8½ by 11) documents and 80-character-wide screens (Galitz 1975), while maintaining an exact image relationship. Learning requirements do exist, but they are minimal. Since screen captions are derived from associated fields on the source document, the document provides a constant reference to aid in caption interpretation and learning.

The 8-character limitation should not be considered an absolute, since a longer caption may occasionally be needed to achieve clarity. Since caption pieces are small, hyphens should be used to tie them together visually. This will minimize misinterpretations and erroneous associations.

Formatting. Single data field captions should be located to the left of the entry field and separated by a unique symbol. The colon (:) is recommended for this purpose, because it provides a definitive and yet unobtrusive break between the two. The recommended approach for multiple occurring (repeating) fields is the columnar orientation. The caption should be placed above the data field and justified above the data field's first character entry position. This above-entry-field positioning will aid in distinguishing the single from multiple occurring fields. Components of larger captions should not be stacked above one another when the columnar approach is used. Maintain the caption on one line. If underscores are used as entry field delimiters for multiple occurring fields, the colons defining the beginning point of the field are not necessary. Colons are only necessary if entry field designators are not used, since they then become the only way a user has to determine how many occurrences of a field exist.

ENTRY FIELDS

Structure

- Optimally:
  - identify entire field by underscores;

```
ACCT:x_____
```

  - break up long fields through incorporation of slashes (/), dashes (-), other common delimiters, or spaces;
    if attribute character does not consume a character position:

```
      DT: __/__/__
  TEL-NO: (___) ___-____
```

    if attribute character consumes a character position:

```
      DT: __ __ __
  TEL-NO: ___ ___ ____
```

- Minimally, identify starting point of fields with unique symbols (separated by one space).

```
NM:x
STR:x
```

  - Optionally, identify ending point of long nonunderscored fields with a unique symbol (such as a semicolon). Separate symbol by one space.

```
STR:x
```

Highlighting

- Call attention to entry fields through a highlighting technique.

Structure. An entry field for this kind of screen should possess the following qualities:

- it should draw a user's attention to the fact that information must be keyed into it;
- it should not detract from the legibility of the characters keyed into the field.

As mentioned previously, Savage (1980) found that users overwhelmingly preferred something to indicate entry fields, and a follow-up study (Savage et al., 1982) found that the best alternative for defining an entry field appears to be the broken line underscore, which possesses an added advantage in that it visually resembles an entry field line on a paper form. It is also a desirable alternative in the next class of data entry screens where estimation of field length is more important. Thus, consistency between different kinds of screens is maintained.

To make entry fields more readable, it is desirable to break them up into logical pieces. If the attribute character does not consume a character position, slashes and dashes may easily be inserted into the entry field as illustrated above. If the attribute character does consume a character position, however, the best alternative is to break it logically through the use of spaces, which are actually unprotected attribute character positions. The entry field then becomes segments separated by auto skip cursor movements. This allows the keyer to still visualize the field as one entry field. To use slashes and dashes in this situation latter condition would be wasteful of space, as numerous attribute characters may be needed to break the field into segments.

If underscores are not possible, the caption symbol (such as the colon) used to signify the starting point of an entry field is acceptable. The entry field will usually start immediately after the symbol and one blank space. Absolute identification of field length is not essential if the system is operating with manual tabbing, because the terminal will identify the end by locking the keyboard.

Highlighting. If any field on this kind of data entry screen is highlighted, it should be the entry field not the caption, since entry fields are the strongest tie between source document and screen. A common highlighting technique is high intensity display of the field. The method chosen, however, should permit fields in error to be found quickly. Possible ways to call attention to error fields are to display them in reverse video or to turn off the highlighting when system edits are invoked.

FIELD ALIGNMENT

- Maintain image relationship with source document through placement of entry fields (not captions).

When a dedicated source document is used, the document/screen image relationship is maintained through placement of entry fields on the screen, as illustrated in figure 5.7. Captions need not be aligned. Note that the third field in the second line of the form (F-Medical Payments-Each Accident) is a non-entry field. It is shaded on the form and does not appear on the screen.

Figure 5.7 Maintaining a document/screen image relationship.

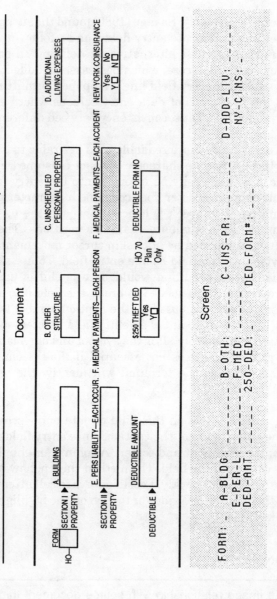

SPACING

Horizontal

- Optimally, leave a minimum of three spaces between one entry field and the caption of the following field. One space is acceptable if space constraints exist.

```
EFF-DT:  __  __  __xxxEXP-DT:  __  __  __xxx
```

Vertical

- Incorporate space lines where "visual" breaks or spaces occur on the source document.

When using a source document with horizontally arranged fields, it is preferable to leave three blank spaces between the last character of one field and the caption of the next. If space constraints exist, however, one blank space is acceptable.

Vertical spacing between rows of fields on a screen will follow the spacing conventions of the source document. If source document rows are single spaced, the screen rows will be single spaced also. If a gap between source document rows appears, there should be a gap between screen rows. This is another method of maintaining an image relationship between document and screen.

It is important to keep in mind that this spacing is relative. Some source documents may be designed for purposes of clarity, with what appears to be a space line between rows of document fields. From a screen design standpoint, these wider-spaced document rows should be considered as consecutive rows and the screen spacing accomplished accordingly. Leave a space line on a screen only when a wider than usual gap exists on the document.

COMPLETION AIDS AND PROMPTING

Completion Aids

- None necessary.

Prompting

- None necessary.

Completion aids are a form of guidance on the structure of data to be keyed within a field. Prompting messages are instructions to the user on what to do with, or how to work with, the screen being presented. Neither should be necessary on this kind of screen. With a dedicated source document, the structure is obvious from the design of the form. The data keyed is simply that coded on the document.

HEADINGS

Section Headings

- Locate section heading directly above its associated data fields.
- Indent related field captions or row headings a minimum of three spaces from the beginning of the section heading.
- Spell out fully.

```
CUSTOMER  INFORMATION

      NAME:  _____

xxxBTH-DT:  __  __  __

       OCC:  _____
```

Most source documents will contain section headings identifying related groups of document fields. These section headings may be incorporated on the screen following the rules given above. Note that with varying size captions, the three-space indention is to the longest caption.

This indention of captions and spelling out of the section heading is intended to make the heading visually distinguishable from the captions on the screen. They will be obvious to the screen user by their size and location. Other techniques may, of course, be used to achieve the same objective without resorting to positional cues. These techniques might be double-size characters or underlining. Whichever method is chosen should always permit easy discrimination of the section headings from other components of the screen.

Sub-Section or Row Headings

- Optional.
- Locate to left of first row of associated entry fields.
- Abbreviate or spell out fully.
- If directly adjacent to entry field, separate from entry field by a unique symbol (such as a colon) and one space.

```
        I N V - C D
    1 : x _ _ _ _ _ _ _ _
    2 : x _ _ _ _ _ _ _ _
    3 : x _ _ _ _ _ _ _ _
```

- If adjacent to field caption, indent related caption a minimum of three (3) spaces and incorporate "greater-than" (>>) symbols.

```
    P R O P E R T Y  > >          B L D G :   _ _ _ _ _ _ _ _
    L I A B I L I T Y x > > x x x   M E D :   _ _ _ _ _ _ _ _
```

Some source documents contain one or more row sub-section or headings to describe the subject of the entry fields in that row. These headings may be included on screens if space permits.

A meaningful convention to designate row headings is two "greater-than" symbols (>>). They direct attention to the right and indicate that everything that follows refer to this category. In the example above, the caption BLDG: and all fields that follow on that line refer to PROPERTY.

This convention can also be used to clean up a line of captions containing redundant words. The redundant word within each caption is removed and incorporated into the row heading as, for example, DATES >>.

Field Group Headings

- Center field group heading above the captions to which it applies.
- Relate to these captions by a broken dashed line ended by pointed brackets.
- Spell out fully.

Single Occurrence Fields

```
    < - - - - - - H O M E O W N E R S - - - - - >
    E F F - D T :  _ _  _ _  _ _     E X P - D T :  _ _  _ _  _ _
```

Multiple Occurrence Fields

```
    < - - - - - H O M E O W N E R S - - - - >
     F O R M         E F F - D T        E X P - D T
    _ _ _ _ _ _ _    _ _  _ _  _ _      _ _  _ _  _ _
    _ _ _ _ _ _ _    _ _  _ _  _ _      _ _  _ _  _ _
    _ _ _ _ _ _ _    _ _  _ _  _ _      _ _  _ _  _ _
```

Occasionally a group heading above a series of related captions may be needed. It may be centered above the captions to which it applies and related to them through a broken dashed line ended by pointed brackets ("greater-" and "less-than" symbols). This provides closure to the grouping. Field group headings will normally be spelled out fully.

TITLE

- Locate the title in a centered position at the top of the first screen in a transaction.
- Clearly and concisely describe the purpose of the transaction or screen.
- Spell out fully using an uppercase font.

A screen title need only appear on the first screen in a transaction. It should clearly and concisely describe the purpose of the transaction or screen and be spelled out fully in an uppercase font.

SCREEN IDENTIFIER

- For multiscreen transactions place a page number or screen identifier in the upper right-hand corner.

A page number or screen identifier should be incorporated on each screen to uniquely identify and allow users to know their location within a transaction. This number may simply be "page n of x" or it may incorporate a mnemonic code that is a contraction of the screen title, for example, "POL02" or "AUTO03," the last two digits indicating the number of the screen in the series. For easy identification the screen number may be surrounded by unique symbols such as asterisks (***)—for example *** POL02 *** or *** PAGE 1 OF 4 ***. This will reinforce its identification as the screen number.

Every screen must have a way of being uniquely identified through its titling and/or screen numbering convention.

ERROR/STATUS MESSAGES AND COMMAND AREA

- Uniquely identify error and status messages through:
  - a consistent location,
  - use of a contrasting display feature such as:
    Reverse video,
    Highlighting,

Preceding error message by a unique series of symbols (such as asterisks),

Lower case characters;

– Separating from the body of the screen.
* Uniquely identify command area through:

– a consistent location,
– separating from the body of the screen.

Recommended locations for error/status messages and command area have been described in chapter 4. They must attract the user's attention and be easily discernible from the body of the screen. This is accomplished most effectively by locating them outside the body of the screen and using contrasting display features, special symbols, and consistent locations. Again, each must be identified by its structure and location without actually having to be read.

SECTION 5-2. EXAMPLES

Example 1. A portion of a source document and its associated screen. Note the left and right justification and alignment of entry fields (not captions) to maintain the document/screen image relationship.

```
                        CHANGE / ENDORSEMENT                    *** CHG01 ***

POLICY IDENTIFICATION

     EFF-DT:  ------                               POL #:  ------
    INSD-NM:  ------                               ACCT #: ------
    AGCY-NM:  ------        BR-CD: ---            PROD-CD: ---

SECTION I ENDORSEMENTS

 48: - 1DES:  ---------        ADDL-LIM: ------            48-PR: ---
       2DES:  ---------        ADDL-LIM: ------
       3DES:  ---------        ADDL-LIM: ------

 49: - 2LIM:  ------  PR-GR: --  C/O: -  TER: ---  F&E: ------  P-C: ---
       3LIM:  ------  PR-GR: --  C/O: -  TER: ---  F&E: ------  P-C: ---
                                        3LIM: ------

 50: - 2LIM:  ------                                       50-PR: ---
 51: -  LIM:  ------                                       51-PR: ---
 69: -  LIM:  ------                                       69-PR: ---
216: - TYPE:  -                                           216-PR: ---
```

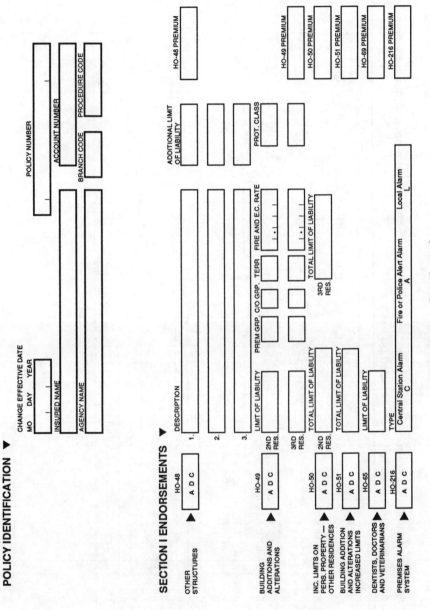

Example 1.—*Continued*

133

Example 2. Again, a portion of a source document and its associated screen. Note the several nonentry fields on the document which have not been included on the screen.

```
----------------------------------------------------------------------
                    PERSONAL AUTOMOBILE - SUPPLEMENT        *** PASUP ***
----------------------------------------------------------------------
APPLICANT INFORMATION
  AP-NM: _____                    POL#: ------
DRIVER INFORMATION
  DR-NM: _____ BTH-DT: ------ SEX: -- OCC: ------
  MR-ST: - LIC#: -------- ST: -- YR-LIC: -- GD-ST: - DR-TR: - IMP: -
VEHICLE INFORMATION
  VEH-YR: -- N/U: - MAKE: ------    ID#: -------- HP: - SYM: -
  VEH USE: - MILE: -- AV/MI: ----   MOD: - DRM: - CLS: -- TER: --
LIENHOLDER INFORMATION
  VEH#: -
  LN-NM: ------------------
  LN-NM2: ------------------
  ML-AD: ------ ST: -- ZIP: -----
  CITY: ------
PAYOR INFORMATION
  PY-NM: ------                   ACCT#: ----
  Y-NM2: ------                   TEL#: --- --- ----
  PY-AD: ------ ST: -- ZIP: -----
  CITY: ------
----------------------------------------------------------------------
```

Personal Automobile Application—Supplement

APPLICANT INFORMATION

APPLICANT NAME

POLICY NUMBER

DRIVER INFORMATION

DRIVER NAME (from license)

DATE OF BIRTH
MO   DAY   YEAR

SEX

OCCUPATION (if student miles from home)

MARITAL STATUS

DRIVERS LICENSE NUMBER

STATE   YEARS LICENSED

GOOD STUDENT

DRIVER TRAINING

IMPAIRED DRIVER

CAR   CAR   CAR

VEHICLE INFORMATION

YR/PUR   VEH. YR   NEW/USED?   MAKE MODEL AND BODY STYLE

New   Yes

VEHICLE IDENTIFICATION NUMBER

HP   SYMBOL   CYL   DRIVER

USE   MILES   ANN/MI

ALTERNATE GARAGE

MODIFIED
New   Yes

DAMAGE
New   Yes

CLASS   YEAR   GARAGED
New   Yes

LIENHOLDER INFORMATION

VEHICLE NUMBER

LIENHOLDER ACCOUNT #

LIENHOLDER NAME

MAILING ADDRESS

CITY

STATE   ZIP CODE

PAYOR INFORMATION (Complete only if policy payor is other than the insured.)

PAYOR NAME

PAYOR ACCOUNT NUMBER

PAYOR ADDRESS

PAYOR TELEPHONE NUMBER

CITY

STATE   ZIP CODE

Example 2.—Continued

135

Example 3. A columnar-organized document and screen with row headings. Again note the nonentry fields.

```
                                                      *** FA/FI ***

                    FARM / FIRE SCHEDULE


         PREM     CNS   DED    W-DED   AMT-INS   CNST

FIRE:    ------   --    ------         ------    --
EC::     ------         ------  -----            --
V&MM:    ------   --    ------
AOP:     ------   --    ------         ------
SPEC-EC: ------   --    ------
```

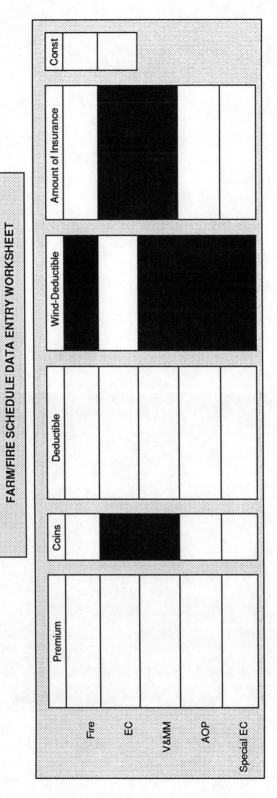

Example 3. *Continued*

137

SECTION **5-3**

Data Entry Screens Used Without a Dedicated Source Document

SCREEN ORGANIZATION

- The screen should provide optimum visual clarity and represent the organization of the world from which data is collected.

If data entry screens must be developed without dedicated source documents, their design should be based on the organization of the manuals, documents, papers, or notes from which the data is keyed. If the data is being provided by a person, such as a customer or sales agent, it must be organized in a manner meaningful to that person. Since these information organization variables cannot always be controlled, an exact correspondence between source material and screen isn't usually achievable. Thus, the screen format must be the controlling force in the development. A person usually identifies a field on the screen and then seeks data or information for keying from appropriate source materials or people. The rules for optimizing screen visual clarity should be applied here. Data entry will be enhanced by visual "anchor points" built into the screen that permit easy and efficient eye movements back and forth between the screen and source materials. Data entry will also be enhanced by minimizing required visual references to the screen. Every attempt should be made to reflect in the screen format the organization of the world from which entry data is taken.

If the sequence of data collected for entry is arbitrary or cannot be predicted, it may be preferable to develop a command language dialogue to identify each entry rather than have a user remember and reorder items to conform to the screen. The data then may be keyed in the order in which it is received, each field being identified by a unique keyed label.

CAPTIONS

Structure and Size

- Fully spell out in a meaningful language to the user.
- Display in normal intensity.
- Use an uppercase font:
    - a lowercase font may be used for long, very descriptive captions.

Formatting

- Single Fields:
    - locate caption to left of entry field;
    - separate caption from entry field by a unique symbol and one space. The colon (:) is the recommended symbol.

        ORGANIZATION: x_____

- Multiple Occurrence Fields:
    - row orientation—
        ○ locate caption to left of entry fields;
        ○ separate from entry field by a unique symbol (such as a colon) and one space;
        ○ separate entry fields by a unique symbol (such as a colon) with one space on each side of the symbol.

        CODES: _____ x : x _____ : _____ : _____ : _____

    - columnar orientation—
        ○ locate caption one line above column of entry fields;
        ○ left-justify caption above first position of entry fields;
        ○ precede entry fields by a unique symbol (such as a colon) separated by one space.

        ORDER NUMBER
        _____
        _____
        _____
        _____

Structure and size. Since a dedicated source document does not exist, screen captions are used to identify what information must be keyed into a field. Normal entry requires that the screen user read the caption, find the information in source materials or through conversation with someone else (or perhaps even create the entry from memory), and then key the information. Since data to be keyed must be identified from the screen, captions must clearly and concisely describe the information required.

Captions should be fully spelled out in the user's natural language. Captions that are ambiguous, imprecise, or unclear will impair performance until they are learned. In general, abbreviations and contractions should not be used. To achieve the alignment recommendations to be discussed shortly, an occasional abbreviation or contraction may be necessary. If so, choose those that are common in the everyday language of the application or those that are meaningful and easily learned.

Formatting. Formatting conventions will be identical to those for source document-oriented data entry screens. For single fields the caption will precede the entry field; for multiple occurring fields the caption will be above. The colon (:) will be the symbol to break caption from data.

ENTRY FIELDS

Structure

- Optimally:
    - identify entire field by underscores;

      ```
      ACCOUNT:x_____
      ```

    - break up long fields through incorporation of slashes (/), dashes (-), other common delimiters, or spaces—
      - if attribute character does not consume a character position:

        ```
                   DATE:  __/__/__
        TELEPHONE NUMBER:  (___)  ___-____
        ```

      - if attribute character consumes a character position:

        ```
                   DATE:  __ __ __
        TELEPHONE NUMBER:  ___ ___ ____
        ```

- Minimally, identify starting point of field with unique symbol (separated by one space).

  ```
    NAME:x
  STREET:x
  ```

– Optionally, identify ending point of long nonunderscored fields with a unique symbol (such as a semicolon). Separate symbol by one space.

```
                    STREET:x
```

Highlighting

* Call attention to entry fields through a highlighting technique.

Structure. In addition to possessing the qualities described for data entry screens with source documents (attracting attention; not detracting from entry legibility), entry fields for this class of screens should:

* provide some indication of the nature of the desired response,
* indicate the appropriate number of characters for the entry.

The Savage et al. (1982) study concluded that the broken underscore is a good technique for estimating field size. Pointed brackets (<>) were found to create the most errors in estimating field lengths, and column separators (a dot between each character position) to take the longest time to estimate field length.

To make entry fields more readable, again it is desirable to break them up into logical pieces. If the attribute character does not consume a character position, slashes and dashes may be easily inserted into the entry field as illustrated above. If the attribute character does consume a character position, the best alternative is to break it logically with spaces.

Highlighting. While the caption initially fulfills a more important role on this kind of screen than in the other kinds, to maintain consistency between all screen kinds, it is recommended that the entry field receive the highlighting. Again, high intensity may be used for this purpose, but the method chosen must be visually different from that used to communicate errors to the screen user.

FIELD ALIGNMENT

---

* Vertically align entry fields and captions into columns.

```
          POLICY NUMBER:      _____
          ACCOUNT NUMBER:     _____
          EFFECTIVE DATE:     __ __ __
          EXPIRATION DATE:    __ __ __
          POLICY STATUS:      _____
```

To aid users in finding their position quickly, fields should be columnized. Space constraint tradeoffs will sometimes result in two or even three columns of fields on one screen. It is important to remember that if the screen cursor moves from left to right and from top to bottom, related columnized fields will be placed *adjacent* to one another. A terminal whose cursor can be programmed to move down a column will result in a more efficient entry process, though, as eye movements between fields are greatly reduced and finding one's place is easier.

This is because the visual "anchor point" remains at about the same place on the screen as the eye moves back and forth between successive fields and source materials. If left-to-right field orientation is maintained, the anchor point jumps from side to side in a less efficient manner. So, columnize the organization of elements for top-to-bottom entry whenever possible.

FIELD JUSTIFICATION

1. First Approach

- Left-justify both captions and entry fields.
- Leave one space between the longest caption and the entry field column.

```
POLICY NUMBER:        _____
ACCOUNT NUMBER:       _____
EFFECTIVE DATE:       __ __ __
EXPIRATION DATE:x__ __ __
POLICY STATUS:        _____
```

2. Second Approach

- Left-justify entry fields and right-justify captions to entry fields.
- Leave one space between each.

```
        CORPORATION:x_____
              TITLE:x_____
 SOCIAL SECURITY NO:x___ __ ____
```

Field justification can be accomplished in either of two ways. Approach 1 results in both captions and entry fields left-justified into columns. Approach 2 right-justifies the captions up against the left-justified column of entry fields (see examples above). Each approach has advantages and disadvantages, as previously discussed in chapter 4. Whichever method is chosen should be consistently followed in a system's screen design.

Again, examples at the end of this and succeeding chapters reflect both styles to enable the reader to see and evaluate them.

KEYING ORDER

Cursor Moves from Left to Right

- For a large number of data fields, order sequentially from left to right.

```
FIRST PRIZE:  _____      SECOND PRIZE:  _____
THIRD PRIZE:  _____      FOURTH PRIZE:  _____
FIFTH PRIZE:  _____      SIXTH  PRIZE:  _____
```

- For a small number of data fields (about 15 or less) order sequentially from top to bottom.

```
        FIRST  PRIZE:   _____
        SECOND PRIZE:   _____
        THIRD  PRIZE:   _____
        FOURTH PRIZE:   _____
        FIFTH  PRIZE:   _____
        SIXTH  PRIZE:   _____
```

Cursor Can Move in any Direction

- Order sequentially from top to bottom.

```
          FIRST  PRIZE:   _____
         SECOND  PRIZE:   _____
          THIRD  PRIZE:   _____
         FOURTH  PRIZE:   _____
          FIFTH  PRIZE:   _____
          SIXTH  PRIZE:   _____
```

Ordering data fields for keying will be determined by the screen's cursor movement requirements as well as the amount of information to be keyed. For screens whose cursor moves left to right, ordering will, of course, have to be left to right. However, if there are few enough data fields to permit top-to-bottom movement, this should be done. Eye movements and the keying process will be more efficient in a top-to-bottom orientation.

For screens whose cursor can be programmed to move in any direction, top-to-bottom ordering is always recommended. If more than one column of elements exist on the screen, cursor movement will be from the bottom of one column to the top of the next.

SPACING

Horizontal

- Leave a minimum of five spaces between the longest entry field in one column and the leftmost caption in an adjacent column.

```
FIRST PRIZE: _____xxxxxSECOND PRIZE: _____
THIRD PRIZE: _____         FOURTH PRIZE: _____
FIFTH PRIZE: _____         SIXTH PRIZE:  _____
```

Vertical

- Leave at least one space line between columnized "groups" of related information.

```
DRIVER NAME:          _____
LICENSE NUMBER:       _____
RESTRICTIONS:         _____
EXPIRES:              __ __ __

VEHICLE TYPE:         _____
MODEL YEAR:           ____
HORSEPOWER:           ___
PLATE NUMBER:         _____
```

- For long columns of related elements, leave a space line after every fifth row. (If space permits, leave a space after every third row.) Never exceed seven rows without leaving a space line.

```
POLICY NUMBER:        _____
ACCOUNT NUMBER:       _____
EFFECTIVE DATE:       __ __ __
EXPIRATION DATE:      __ __ __
POLICY STATUS:        __ __ __

POLICY FORM:          __
PROPERTY:             _____
LIABILITY:            _____
DEDUCTIBLE:           ____
ENDORSEMENT:          _____

MODEL
_____
_____
_____
_____
_____

_____
_____
_____
_____
_____
```

To separate columns visually, leave a minimum of five spaces between the longest entry field in one column and the leftmost caption in the next column. To improve readability of field rows, leave a blank line after every fifth row; if space permits, leave a blank line after every third row.

Optimum spacing between columns of elements will be affected by the weighting of the elements within each column. The objective is for captions to be visually tied to their related entry fields and columns of elements to be visually broken up. Thus, spacing between columns should be enough to meet this objective.

COMPLETION AIDS AND PROMPTING MESSAGES

Completion Aids

- Incorporate completion aids on a screen as necessary, in a manner that visually distinguishes them, such as:

```
1)         DATE (MMDDYY):        __ __ __
           RATE (NN.N):          ____
           CODES (AB,CD,EF):     __
           AREA (Square Feet):   _____

2)         DATE: MM DD YY
           RATE: NN.N

3)         DATE:    __ __ __      (MMDDYY)
           RATE:    ____          (NN.N)
           CODES:   __            (AB,CD,EF)
           AREA:    _____        (Square Feet)
```

Prompting Messages

- Incorporate prompting messages on a screen, as necessary:
  - in a position just preceding the part, or parts, of a screen to which they apply;
  - in a manner that visually distinguishes them, such as a unique type style or enclosing the message in parentheses;
  - using a lowercase font style.

```
(The following are necessary for changes only.)
                KIND:    _____
              AMOUNT:    _____
      EFFECTIVE DATE:    __ __ __
```

Completion aids and prompting messages must be easily discernible from the body of the screen. This is accomplished most effectively by using contrasting display features, special symbols, and consistent locations. The message must stand out as an instruction or prompt by its size, shape, and/or location without it actually having to be read.

Before incorporating completion aids or prompting messages into a screen, make sure they are really needed since they can quickly become visual noise. In most cases a frequently used screen, or a frequently used system, might not require them.

Completion aids. Field completion aids can be used to provide some indication of the kind of data to be encoded within a field. Some methods are illustrated above. Approach 1, the completion aid within the caption, suffers from excess noise in the visual field once the field structures are learned. Because the aid is placed within the area normally consumed by the caption, the caption itself is also moved farther away from the entry field to which it relates. This can cause longer, and unnecessary, eye movements. Approach 2 puts the completion aid in the data field itself, and the key entry simply replaces it. The disadvantage here is that the aid is erased during data entry and is not available should the screen user ever question an entry's correctness. Approach 3 is advantageous in that it removes noise from the primary visual focus of attention (caption and entry field) for the experienced person but may be easily found by one who is inexperienced. Its disadvantage is that it still leaves noise on a screen, and care must be exercised to design the screen so that the completion aids are properly associated with the correct entry field. All things considered, approach 3 is the one that is recommended.

Required fields may be indicated on a screen by a special character such as the asterisk (*) illustrated in the RATE field. Again, use required field indicators with discretion, since the system edits will quickly let a user know if any are omitted.

Prompting. Prompting messages are instructions to the screen user on what to do with, or how to work with, the screen being presented. They are analogous to instructions on filling out a paper form. Prompting messages should be positioned just preceding that part of the screen to which they apply. They should be visually distinguishable, using a lowercase font style.

HEADINGS

Section Headings

- Locate section headings on line above related screen fields.
- Indent captions a minimum of five spaces from the start of the heading.
- Fully spell out in an uppercase font.
- Display in normal intensity.

```
COVERAGES
xxxxxDWELLING:        _____
         OUTBUILDINGS:  _____
         LIABILITY:     _____
PREMIUMS
         BASIC:         _____
         ENDORSEMENT:   _____
         TOTAL:         _____
```

The indention of captions makes the section headings visually distinguishable from the captions on the screen. They will be obvious to the screen user by their location. If the right-justified caption-to-entry-field approach is used, indention greater than five spaces may be necessary. Other techniques than positional cues may, of course, be used to set off section headings, such as double-size characters or underlining. The method chosen, however, should always permit easy discrimination of the section headings from other components of the screen.

Sub-Section, or Row, Headings

- Locate to the left of topmost row of associated data fields.
- Fully spell out in an uppercase font style.
- Display in normal intensity.
- Separate from the adjacent caption through use of a unique symbol, such as "greater-than."
- Separate symbol from heading by one space and from caption by three spaces.

```
ANIMALSx>>xxxxELEPHANTS: _____     KANGAROOS:    _____
              CAMELS:    _____     POLAR BEARS:  _____

BIRDS >>       KIWIS:    _____     COCKATOOS:    _____
               EAGLES:   _____     HAWKS:        _____
```

- If both section and sub-section, or row, headings are included on a screen, the sub-section, or row, heading should be indented a minimum of five character positions beneath the section heading.

```
ZOO POPULATION
xxxxxANIMALS >>     ELEPHANTS: _____     KANGAROOS:    _____
                   CAMELS:    _____     POLAR BEARS:  _____
```

A meaningful convention to designate subsection, or row, headings is the "greater-than" symbol (>). It directs attention to the right and serves to indicate that everything that follows refer to this category. The subsection is broken by a space line.

Like captions, these sub-section, or row, headings may also be right-justified instead of left-justified as illustrated below:

```
ANIMALS >>
  BIRDS >>
```

Field Group Headings

- Center field group headings above the captions to which they apply.
- Relate to these captions by a broken dashed line ended by pointed brackets.
- Spell out fully in an uppercase font.
- Display in normal intensity.

```
< - - - - - - - -AUTOMOBILE - - - - - - - >

DRIVER                                LICENSE NUMBER
_____               _____
_____               _____
_____               _____
```

Occasionally a group heading above a series of related captions may be needed. It may be centered above the captions to which it applies and related to them through a broken dashed line ended by pointed brackets ("greater-" and "less-than" symbols). This provides closure to the grouping. Field group headings will normally be fully spelled out.

TITLE

- Locate the title in a centered position at the top of the first screen in a transaction.
- Clearly and concisely describe the purpose of the transaction or screen.
- Spell out fully using an uppercase font.

A screen title need only appear on the first screen in a transaction. It should clearly and concisely describe the purpose of the transaction or screen and be spelled out fully in an uppercase font.

SCREEN IDENTIFIER

- For multiscreen transactions place a page number or screen identifier in the upper right-hand corner.

A page or screen identifier should be incorporated on each screen to uniquely identify and allow users to know their location within a transaction. This number may simply be "page n of x," or it may incorporate a mnemonic code that is a contraction of the screen title—for example, "POL02" or "AUTO03," the last two digits indicating the number of the screen in the series. For easy identification the screen number may be surrounded by unique symbols such as asterisks (***)—for example *** POL02 *** or *** PAGE 1 OF 4 ***. This will reinforce its identification as the screen number.

Every screen must have a way of being uniquely identified through its titling and/or screen numbering convention.

ERROR/STATUS MESSAGES AND COMMAND AREA

- Uniquely identify error and status messages through:
    - a consistent location,
    - use of a contrasting display feature such as:
      Reverse video,
      Highlighting,
      Preceding error message by a unique series of symbols (such as asterisks),
      Lowercase characters;
    - separating from the body of the screen.
- Uniquely identify command area through:

    - a consistent location,
    - separating from the body of the screen.

Recommended locations for error/status messages and command area have been described in chapter 4. They must attract the user's attention and be easily discernible from the body of the screen. This is accomplished most effectively by locating them outside the body of the screen and using contrasting display features, special symbols, and consistent locations. Again, each must be identified by its structure and location without actually having to be read.

SECTION 5-3. EXAMPLES

Example 1. This example uses the same data elements as illustrated in section 5-2, example 2 for "with source documents." Because a source document is now not presumed to exist, the fields have been columnized and expanded into two screens for visual clarity. Both captions and fields are left-justified.

```
    PERSONAL AUTOMOBILE - SUPPLEMENT              *** PASP01 ***

APPLICANT
 NAME:  _____
DRIVER
 NAME:  _____    POLICY #: _____
 OCCUPATION: _____
 SEX: _                            BIRTH DATE: __ __ __
                                   MARITAL STATUS: __ _
LICENSE
 LICENSE #: _____       STATE: __
 YRS LICENSED: __                  IMPAIRED: _
 TRAINING: _                       GOOD STUDENT: _
VEHICLE
 YEAR: __                          NEW/USED: _
 MAKE: _____               ID #: _____
 HORSEPOWER: ___                   SYMBOL: __
 USE: _                            MILES WORK: ___
 ANNUAL MILES: _____               MODIFIED: _
 DAMAGED: _                        CLASS: ____
 TERRITORY: _
```

151

```
                                                    *** PASP02 ***

LIENHOLDER
    VEHICLE #:  ----------------
    NAME 1:     -------------------
    NAME 2:     -------------------
    STREET:     -------------------
    CITY:       ----------- ST: -- ZIP: ---------

PAYOR: NAME 1:  -------------------
       NAME 2:  -------------------
       STREET:  -------------------
       CITY:    ----------- ST: -- ZIP: ---------

    ACCOUNT #:   ----- --- ----
    TELEPHONE #: --- ----
```

Example 1. *Continued*

Example 2. This screen illustrates right-justified captions, sub-section headings, and completion aids.

```
                              *** ANMCAT ***

              ANIMAL CATALOGUE

    NAME >>         COMMON: ------------------------------
                SCIENTIFIC: ------------------------------

DESCRIPTION >>      COLOR: --------------
                   HEIGHT: -----
                   LENGTH: -----
                   WEIGHT: -----

    HABITAT >>  ACTIVITY TIMES: -                (D,N)
                   TERRAIN: -----------
                      FOOD: -----------

    OFFSPRING >>     NUMBER: --
              SEASON OF YEAR: --          (SPR,SUM,FAL,WIN)
```

Example 3. This example illustrates a group of multiple occurrence fields in a columnar orientation with field group headings (ITEM and COST). Section headings (CUSTOMER and CREDIT CARD) follow the "above-fields" approach.

```
                          CATALOG ORDER

CUSTOMER
 NAME:        -------------------------------
 ADDRESS:     -------------------------------
 CITY:        ------------- STATE: -- ZIP: -----
 TELEPHONE:   --- --- ----

         <- - - - ITEM - - - - ->      <- - COST - - ->
 PG #  CATLG #  QTY  SIZE  DESCRIPTION  WGT  ITEM  MAIL  TOTAL
 ---   ------   ---  ---   -----------  ---  ---   ---   ---
 ---   ------   ---  ---   -----------  ---  ---   ---   ---
 ---   ------   ---  ---   -----------  ---  ---   ---   ---
 ---   ------   ---  ---   -----------  ---  ---   ---   ---
 ---   ------   ---  ---   -----------  ---  ---   ---   ---

                                        HANDLING: ---
                                        TOTAL:    ---

CREDIT CARD
 KIND:             --
 NUMBER:           -------------
 EXPIRATION DATE:  ------
```

Inquiry Screens 6

Inquiry screens are used to display the results of an inquiry request or the contents of computer files. Their design objective is human ease in locating data or information. Thus, they should be developed to optimize human scanning. Scanning is made easier if eye movements are minimized, required eye movement direction is obvious, and a consistent pattern is followed.

SCREEN ORGANIZATION

- Only display information necessary to perform actions, make decisions, or answer questions.
- Group information in a logical or orderly manner, with the most frequently requested information in the upper left corner.
- For multiscreen transactions, locate most frequently requested information on the earliest screens.
- Do not pack the screen. Use spaces and lines to perceptually balance the screen.
- Columnize, maintaining a top-to-bottom, left-to-right scanning orientation.

Information contained on an inquiry screen should only be what is relevant. Forcing a user to wade through volumes of data is time consuming, costly, and error prone. Unfortunately, relevance is most often situation specific. A relevant item one time a screen is displayed may be irrelevant another time it is recalled.

Inquiry screen organization should be logical, orderly, and meaningful. When information is structured in a manner that is consistent with a person's organizational view of a topic, more information is comprehended (Kintish, 1978).

Finding information on an inquiry screen can be speeded by a number of factors. First, if information is never used, do not display it. Limit a transaction or screen to what is necessary to perform actions, make decisions, or answer questions.

Second, for multiple-screen transactions locate the most frequently sought information on the earliest transaction screens, and the most frequently sought information on a screen in the upper left-hand corner.

Third, to aid in locating any particular item, provide easily scanned and identifiable groupings of information and, within each group, easily scanned and identifiable data fields. This is done through columnization with a top-to-bottom, left-to-right orientation. This means permitting the eye to move down a column from top to bottom, then moving to another column located to the right and again moving from top to bottom. This also means, if the situation warrants it, permitting the eye to move easily left to right across the top of columns to the proper column, before beginning the vertical scanning movement.

Top-to-bottom scanning will minimize eye movements through the screen and enable human perceptual powers to be utilized to their fullest. Inquiry screens are often visually scanned not through the captions but through the data fields themselves. A search for a customer name in a display of information often involves looking for a combination of characters that resembles the picture of a name that we have stored in our memory. The search task is to find a long string of alphabetic characters with one or two gaps (first name, middle initial, last name, perhaps). A date search might have the user seeking a numeric code broken by slashes. Other kinds of information also have recognizable patterns and shapes. Field captions usually play a minor role in the process, being necessary only to differentiate similar looking data fields. This leads to two key requirements in the design of inquiry screens: call attention to data fields, and make the structural differences between data fields as obvious as possible. Differences are most noticeable in a columnar field structure, since it is easier to compare data fields when one is above the other.

Data entry screens have been designed to achieve other objectives and seldom yield good inquiry screens. The left-to-right cursor movement results in a screen organization incompatible with the organization that is best for fast scanning.

Captions

Structure and Size

- Fully spell out in a meaningful language to the user.
- Display in normal intensity.

- Use an uppercase font:
  - a lowercase font may be used for long, very descriptive captions.

Formatting

- Single Fields:
  - locate caption to left of entry field;
  - separate caption from entry field by a unique symbol and one space—the colon (:) is the recommended symbol.

ORGANIZATION: MARKETING

- Multiple Occurrence Fields:
  - locate caption one line above column of data fields;
  - center caption above column of data fields.

CITY
PHILADELPHIA
PHOENIX
PITTSBURGH
PORTLAND

Structure and size. Captions on inquiry screens, while supporting the data itself, must still clearly and concisely describe the information displayed. They are important for inexperienced screen users and for identifying similar looking data or infrequently used data. As such, they should be fully spelled out in the natural language of the user. In general, abbreviations and contractions should not be used. To achieve the alignment recommendations to be discussed shortly, an occasional abbreviation or contraction may be necessary, but choose those that are common in the everyday language of the application or those that are meaningful and easily learned.

Captions for commonly used fields obvious to all screen users may, optionally, be left off inquiry screens. The most obvious example is name, address, city, state, and zip code. The shape and structure of the data itself is sufficient to identify it. This will give the screen a cleaner look and eliminate some potential noise. Never leave a caption off, however, unless all screen users can identify the data all the time.

For lengthy, very descriptive captions a lowercase font may be used.

Formatting. Caption formatting rules are most similar to those for data entry screens without source documents. For multiple occurrence fields the caption will be *centered* above its related data field, however.

DATA FIELDS

- Provide visual emphasis to the data fields.
- Display directly usable information:
  - fully spell out all codes;
  - include natural splits or predefined breaks in displaying data.

338302286	072179	162152
338-30-2286	07/21/79	16:21:52

  - display data strings of five or more numbers or alphanumeric characters with no natural breaks in groups of three or four characters with a blank between each group.

```
K349612094                          K349 612 094
```

- Left-justify text and alphanumeric formats.

```
        NAME:    JOHN SMITH
        STREET:  612 PINE ST.
```

- Right-justify lists of numeric data.

```
        BASIC:          965
        SURCHARGE:       82
        TOTAL:        1,047
```

- Identical data should be consistent despite its origin.

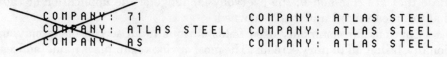

```
COMPANY: 71                 COMPANY: ATLAS STEEL
COMPANY: ATLAS STEEL        COMPANY: ATLAS STEEL
COMPANY: AS                 COMPANY: ATLAS STEEL
```

Visually emphasize data fields. Data fields should be visually emphasized to attract attention. This will enable the screen user to immediately find and begin scanning the display for the relevant information. High intensity is recommended to accomplish this.

Display directly usable information. Whereas data on a data entry screen is often keyed in the form of a code, data on the inquiry screen should be displayed fully spelled out. An entry code, for example, might be keyed "AS," but the inquiry screen should display "Atlas Steel." Again, this will reduce learning requirements for the screen viewer.

A data display should also reinforce the human tendency to break things into groups. People handle information more easily when it is in chunks.

Justification. In general, columnized text and alphanumeric data should be left-justified and numeric data should be right-justified. In aligning data fields, keep in mind how the fields will look in relation to one another when they contain information. The visual scan should flow relatively straight from top to bottom. This may require that some data fields be right-justified in the column that is created, not left-justified.

Consistency. Identical data taken into the system in different formats should be displayed in the same formats on inquiry screens.

DATA ORGANIZATION

• Organize data in accepted and recognizable orders.

```
SANDY SCHMIDT                          8:30  AM
1422 WHEELER RD                       10:56  AM
KIRKLAND, IL 60146                     2:06  PM
                                       4:33  PM
```

• In lists where there is no obvious frequency, pattern, or order, and in long lists (more than seven items), arrange information in alphabetic order.
• For long lists leave a space line between groups of related data, or about every five rows. Never exceed seven rows without inserting a space line.

```
              ADAMS
              BARNWELL
              CHARLES
              DENTON
              EDWARDS

              FRANKHAUSER
              GOLDEN
              HAMMER
              INGOLDBY
              JACKSON
```

Data must always be organized to be meaningful and consistent with human expectations.

FIELD ALIGNMENT

- Vertically align captions and data fields into columns.

```
POLICY NUMBER:     HGB-9011
ACCOUNT NUMBER:      796624
EFFECTIVE DATE:    02/01/88
EXPIRATION DATE:   02/01/91
POLICY STATUS:     ACTIVE
```

Columnization is necessary for efficient visual scanning and ease in find-ing the desired information. Since the scan will be downward, information organization will flow from top to bottom.

FIELD JUSTIFICATION

---

1. First Approach

- Left-justify both captions and data fields.
- Leave one space between the longest caption and the data field column.

```
NAME:        WILLIAM L. HASKIN
TITLE:       VICE PRESIDENT
DEPARTMENT:  ENGINEERING
```

2. Second Approach

- Left-justify data fields and right-justify captions to data fields.
- Leave one space between each.

```
      NAME: WILLIAM L. HASKIN
     TITLE: VICE PRESIDENT
DEPARTMENT: ENGINEERING
```

Again, field justification can be accomplished in either of two ways. Ap-proach 1 results in both captions and entry fields left-justified into columns. Approach 2 right-justifies the captions up against the left-justified column of entry fields (see examples above). Each approach has advantages and disad-vantages, as previously discussed in chapter 4. Whichever method is chosen should be consistently followed in a system's screen design.

Again, examples at the end of this and other chapters reflect both styles, to enable the reader to see and evaluate them.

HEADINGS

Section Headings

- Locate section heading on line above related screen fields.
- Indent captions a minimum of five spaces from the start of the heading.
- Fully spell out in an uppercase font.
- Display in normal intensity.

```
COVERAGES
xxxxxDWELLING:            200,000
       OUTBUILDINGS:       15,000
       LIABILITY:       1,000,000
PREMIUMS:
       BASIC:                 335
       ENDORSEMENT:            64
       TOTAL:                 399
```

This indention of captions is intended to make the section heading visually distinguishable from the captions on the screen. They will be obvious to the screen user by their location. If the right-justified caption-to-entry-field approach is used, indention greater than five spaces may be necessary. Other techniques besides positional cues may, of course, be used to achieve the same objective. Alternatives might be double-size characters or underlining. The method chosen, however, should always permit easy discrimination of the section headings from other components of the screen.

Sub-Section, or Row, Headings

- Locate to the left of top-most row of associated data fields.
- Fully spell out in an uppercase font style.
- Display in normal intensity.
- Separate from the adjacent caption through use of a unique symbol such as "greater than."
- Separate symbol from heading by one space and from caption by three spaces.

```
ANIMALSx>>xxxELEPHANTS:  4,163    KANGAROOS:    1,411
             CAMELS:       982    POLAR BEARS:     59

BIRDS >>     KIWIS:        141    COCKATOOS:      136
             EAGLES:         3    HAWKS:        3,612
```

- If both section and sub-section, or row, headings are included within a screen, the sub-section, or row, heading should be indented a minimum of five character positions beneath the section heading.

```
ZOO POPULATION
xxxxxANIMALS >>      ELEPHANTS:  4,163      KANGAROOS:    1,411
                     CAMELS:       982      POLAR BEARS:     59
```

Again, the "greater than" symbol (>) is a good way to designate sub-section, or row, headings. It directs attention to the right and serves to indicate that everything that follows refer to this category. The sub-section is broken by a space line.

Like captions, these sub-section, or row, headings may also be right-justified instead of left-justified, as illustrated below:

```
              ANIMALS  >>
                BIRDS  >>
```

Field Group Headings

- Center field group heading above the captions to which it applies.
- Relate to these captions by a broken dashed line ended by pointed brackets.
- Spell out fully in an uppercase font.
- Display in normal intensity.

```
< - - - - - - -AUTOMOBILE - - - - - - - >
    DRIVER                    LICENSE NUMBER
MARY GRABOWSKI                G433 5857 6445
JON  GRABOWSKI                G433 8990 9051
HAROLD GRABOWSKI              G433 8990 9590
```

Occasionally, a field group heading above a series of related captions may be needed. It may be centered above the captions to which it applies and related to them through a broken dashed line ended by pointed brackets ("greater-" and "less-than" symbols). This provides closure to the grouping. The heading should be spelled out fully.

SPACING

Horizontal Spacing—Single Fields

Without Section Headings

- Leave at least five spaces between the longest data field in one column and the left-most caption in an adjacent column.

```
MAKE:   OLDSMOBILE        LIST PRICE:    $18,424
MODEL:  NINETY-EIGHTxxxxxDOWN PAYMENT:    4,000
DOORS:  2                 BALANCE OWED:   14,424
```

With Section Headings

- Leave at least five spaces between the longest data field in one column and the section heading in an adjacent column.

```
                                    FINANCING
AUTOMOBILE
     MAKE:   OLDSMOBILE              LIST PRICE:    $18,424
     MODEL:  NINETY-EIGHTxxxxx       DOWN PAYMENT:    4,000
     DOORS:  2                       BALANCE OWED:   14,424
```

Lines Substituted for Spaces

- Where space constraints exist, vertical lines may be substituted for spaces.

```
                          |
     MAKE:   OLDSMOBILE    | LIST PRICE:    $18,424
     MODEL:  NINETY-EIGHTx |xDOWN PAYMENT:    4,000
     DOORS:  2             | BALANCE OWED:   14,424
                          |
```

To visually separate columns, leave a minimum of five spaces between the longest entry field in one column and the left-most caption in the adjacent column.

Optimum spacing between columns will ultimately be affected by the weighting of the elements within each column. Captions should be visually tied to their related entry fields, and columns of elements should be visually broken apart. Thus, spacing between columns should be enough to achieve this.

Where space constraints exist, an excellent way to provide visual separation is to incorporate a line between adjacent columns, as illustrated above. This is also clearly conveys to the screen viewer that the desired scanning motion is downward.

Horizontal Spacing–Multiple Occurrence Fields

Without Group Headings

- Leave at least three spaces between the columns of fields.

```
          MAKE         MODEL        YEAR
          CHRYSLERxxxNEW YORKER    1987
          FORD         TAURUS      1988
          PONTIAC      BONNEVILLExxx1988
```

With Group Headings

- Leave at least three spaces between columns of related fields.
- Leave at least five spaces between groupings.

```
< - - - - - OWNED - - - - - >      < - - - - - LEASED - - - - - >
    MAKE          MODEL     YEAR        MAKE          MODEL     YEAR
CHRYSLERxxxNEW YORKER    1987xxxxxTOYOTA      COROLLA      1988
FORD         TAURUS      1988    CADILLAC     FLEETWOOD    1986
PONTIAC      BONNEVILLExxx1988    MERCURY      COUGAR       1987
```

Multiple occurrence fields must also provide adequate visual separation of columns of fields. Again, these are minimum guidelines and greater separation may be necessary.

Vertical Spacing

- Leave at least one space line between columnized "groups" of related information.

```
           NAME:  WILLIAM BRADFORD
            AGE:  34
         HEIGHT:    6 Ft., 2 In
         WEIGHT: 194

     OCCUPATION: DIVER
YEARS EXPERIENCE:  11
         DEGREE: M.S.
          MAJOR: ACCOUNTING
```

- For long columns of related elements, leave a space line after every fifth row. (If space permits, leave a space after every third row.) Never exceed seven rows without inserting a space line.

```
AMERICA'S LARGEST CITIES
          FIRST:  NEW YORK
         SECOND:  LOS ANGELES
          THIRD:  CHICAGO
         FOURTH:  PHILADELPHIA
          FIFTH:  SAN FRANCISCO

          SIXTH:  DETROIT
        SEVENTH:  BOSTON
          EIGTH:  HOUSTON
          NINTH:  WASHINGTON
          TENTH:  DALLAS
```

To permit the eye to move easily across the screen data fields, to reduce screen density, and to satisfy the human need for groupings, space lines must be left on screens. This is accomplished in the ways shown above.

TITLE

- Locate the title in a centered position at the top of the first screen in a transaction.
- Clearly and concisely describe the purpose of the transaction or screen.
- Spell out fully using an uppercase font.

Since an inquiry screen in a series can often be directly reached from a control screen, a screen title should appear on all screens in a transaction. It should meaningfully describe the inquiry screen's contents and be spelled out fully in an uppercase font.

SCREEN IDENTIFIER

- For multiscreen transactions place a screen identifier or page number in the upper right-hand corner.

A page number or screen identifier should appear on each screen to uniquely identify screens and to allow users to know their location within a transaction. This number may simply be "page n of x," or it may incorporate a mnemonic code that is a contraction of the screen title, for example, "POL02" or "AUTO03," the last two digits indicating the number of the screen in the series. For easy identification, the screen number may be surrounded by unique symbols such as asterisks (***), for example *** POL02 *** or *** PAGE 1 of 4 ***. This will reinforce its identification as the screen number.

Every screen must have a way of being uniquely identified through its titling and/or screen numbering convention.

ERROR/STATUS MESSAGES AND COMMAND AREA

- Uniquely identify error and status messages through:
  - a consistent location;
  - use of a contrasting display feature such as
    reverse video,
    highlighting;

preceding error messages by a unique series of symbols (such as asterisks);

lowercase characters;

– separating from the body of the screen.

• Uniquely identify command area through:
  – a consistent location
  – separating from the body of the screen.

Recommended locations for error/status messages and command area have been described in Chapter 5. They must attract the user's attention and be easily discernible from the body of the screen. This is accomplished most effectively by locating them outside the body of the screen and using contrasting display features, special symbols, and consistent locations. Again, each must be identified by its structure and location without actually having to be read.

CHAPTER 6 EXAMPLES

Example 1. The "personal automobile" data elements illustrated in section 5-2, example 2, and section 5-3, example 1, are now columnized for easy visual scanning on an inquiry screen. Section headings are included and captions follow the right-justified approach. Visual separation of the left and right sides of the screen is aided by a vertical broken line. Data elements within sections are organized into logical groupings. The name and address fields on screen 2 are only briefly captioned as NAME.

```
                                             *** PAGE 1 OF 2 ***

        PERSONAL AUTOMOBILE - SUPPLEMENTAL INFORMATION

POLICY      POLICY #: 556 904          VEHICLE
                                                    YEAR: 1987
                                                NEW/USED: NEW
DRIVER                                              MAKE: MERCEDES
            NAME: MARTHA JENKINS                    ID #: S988 670925G
             SEX: FEMALE                      HORSEPOWER: 160
      BIRTH DATE: 09/21/63                        SYMBOL: K
  MARITAL STATUS: SINGLE
      OCCUPATION: MODEL
                                              MILES/WORK: WORK
                                                     USE: WORK
       LICENSE #: J6689 5543              MILES/WORK: 13
           STATE: ALASKA                 ANNUAL MILES: 15,000
  YEARS LICENSED: 7                          MODIFIED: NO
                                              DAMAGED: NO

        IMPAIRED: NO
        TRAINING: YES                            CLASS: 6
    GOOD STUDENT: YES                        TERRITORY: 38
```

```
                                            *** PAGE 2 OF 2 ***


LIENHOLDER
   VEHICLE #: 1
      NAME: NORTHERN LIGHTS BANK
            800 DIAMOND BLVD.
            ANCHORAGE, AK 99515

  PAYOR  NAME: EMILY JENKINS
              644 SWIFT CURRENT WAY
              ANCHORAGE, AK 99503

      ACCOUNT #:: NONE
    TELEPHONE #:: (907) 555-4601
```

Example 1. Continued

168

Example 2. A one-column inquiry screen with left-justified captions using the sub-section heading concept.

```
-----------------------------------------------------------------
          INVOICE                                    *** INV ***
-----------------------------------------------------------------

CUSTOMER >>   NAME:         REGINALD JONES
              ADDRESS:      44 DOLPHIN WAY
                            CLAXTON, GA 30417

              TELEPHONE:    (314) 555-5672

ITEM >>       CATALOG #:    762J
              QUANTITY:     1
              SIZE:         EXTRA LARGE
              DESCRIPTION:  GOLF GLOVE
              COLOR:        WHITE

CHARGES >>    ITEM:      $  9.95
              MAIL:         .79
              HANDLING:    1.50
              TOTAL:     $ 12.24

CREDIT CARD >>  KIND:       AMEX
                NUMBER:     3700 690 5432
                EXP. DATE:  5/89
-----------------------------------------------------------------
```

Multipurpose Screens   7

Information is entered into a system through a data entry screen, and the contents of the system are viewed through an inquiry screen. Sometimes, however, it may seem desirable to use a single screen for more than one purpose—perhaps to initially enter data into the system (data entry) and then call it back to see what is there (inquiry), or to view the contents of the system's data base (inquiry) and then make changes or corrections (data entry). Is a combination or multipurpose screen a viable alternative?

From a human perspective a multipurpose screen does make sense if a person needs to deal with different classes of screens at different times. Learning will be aided because only one organization of elements will be confronted. The problem is that the organization of the screen often cannot be optimized for both situations. The left-to-right movement of the cursor for data entry is not compatible with the desired top-to-bottom scanning of the screen during inquiry. What, then, is the sensible approach concerning multipurpose screens?

IMPLEMENTATION

- If different people will be using screens for different reasons, create separate screens to achieve their intended purposes.
- If the same people will be using screens for different reasons, consider creating multipurpose screens. Structure these multipurpose screens in the direction of their most frequent usage.

Since a screen usually cannot be created that satisfies both data entry and inquiry needs, develop separate screens for users who will be using them in only one way. If there is a group within an organization whose job is to enter data into the system, fashion data entry screens for this group. If there is another group whose purpose is to review computer records (such as customer service), develop screens following the inquiry screen guidelines presented above. The usability objectives of each group will be best served by this approach.

If the same groups will be using screens for different reasons, however, consider creating multipurpose screens. Structure them in the direction of their most frequent usage based on an analysis of what the most frequent usage is. If, for example, a screen will be used to change or correct a computer record, and few items of information are changed at a time, the optimum arrangement is the inquiry screen approach. Scanning will be optimized to aid in finding elements to be changed. When the field is located, the cursor is moved to it before the change can be made. While the left-to-right movement of the cursor may be across unrelated fields, this illogical movement is less important than making it easy to find what must be changed.

If screens will be heavily used in a variety of ways, and creation of a multipurpose screen may severely affect usability in one or more of those ways, the best alternative is to create separate screens, each optimized for its intended purpose. This will result in more far-reaching benefits than those achieved by the reduced learning requirements of the multipurpose screen.

Question and Answer Screens

A question and answer screen is characterized by short alternating communications between a user and a system. Normally the system will provide a thought or prompt and the user will respond; or the user will make a short request and the system will respond. The dialogue proceeds on this basis, each participant sharing in a continual step-by-step interaction. This may be contrasted with the kinds of screens previously described where the communication is on a full screen basis—the screen using the entire available display area and the user being able to work with it before sending a response to the system.

A question and answer screen does not necessarily perform unique functions. They may be used for data entry or to display the results of inquiries. They are, however, not very efficient in performing these functions extensively because of the excessive amount of communication needed and the slowness of the process.

Question and answer dialogues are especially valuable when a system user has little or no training and a fast computer response time is expected. They can supplement full screen display techniques in the log-on process or when providing guidance and assistance.

DEVELOPMENT RULES

- Limit computer communication to one idea or question.
- Phrase questions as concisely as possible.

- Require short user responses.
- Display previous user answers for related questions.

In a question-and-answer dialogue, questions to the user should be displayed separately. Never require him to answer several questions at once. Computer questions and user responses should be as short and concise as possible. If questions are related, or if a user response is based on answers to previous questions, make sure the previous messages are visible, not having "scrolled" out of view. The proper context for answering the current question must be maintained.

FIELD FORMATTING

- Maintain field widths within a range of 25 to 40 characters.
- Locate in a left-centered position on the screen.

For reading ease field widths should not exceed 40 characters. For visual balancing purposes the fields should be located in a left-centered position on the screen. (On an 80-character-wide display, a 40-character-wide field should begin in about column 15.)

FIELD CHARACTERISTICS

- Provide a means to visually distinguish computer messages from keyed entries. For example:
  - always display computer message at high intensity, key entry at normal intensity,
  - display computer message in lower case, key entry in upper case;

```
Applicants name:

CAROL FORESTER
```

  - indent key entry several spaces to right of start of computer message;

```
APPLICANTS NAME:

     CAROL FORESTER
```

  - precede key entry by a unique symbol;

```
APPLICANTS NAME:

==>   CAROL FORESTER
```

– if questions are generally short, position key entry to right of question and align beyond longest expected caption.

```
APPLICANTS NAME:        CAROL FORESTER
```

Key entries and computer messages should be easily distinguishable from one another. This can be accomplished by using various display components, contrasting features, or variable spacing techniques summarized above.

TITLE

- Optional.
- Locate in a centered position at the top of the screen.
- Separate from first screen field by at least one blank line.

The necessity of a title should be based on the kind of question and answer screen created, following the guidelines described in the chapters on data entry screens and inquiry screens.

CHAPTER 8 EXAMPLES

Example 1. Computer messages are distinguished from key entries by letter case. Computer messages are in lower case, key entries in upper case.

```
Driver's name:
KARIN ROEPEL
Sex:
F
Birth date:
11 18 61
Marital status:
M
Occupation:
OFFICE MANAGER
Driver's license number:
T6994 334 556A
State:
OK
```

Example 2. Computer messages are distinguished from key entries by spatial positioning. Key entries are indented five character positions.

```
DRIVER'S NAME:
     KIMI ANDERSON
SEX:
     F
BIRTH DATE:
     09 21 63
MARITAL STATUS:
     S
OCCUPATION:
     MODEL
DRIVER'S LICENSE NUMBER
     G543 569 4453
STATE:
     IL
```

Example 3. Computer messages are distinguished from key entries by a unique symbol preceding them.

```
DRIVER'S NAME:
==>   BARRY MITCHELL
SEX:
==>   MALE
BIRTH DATE:
==>   JULY 17, 1959
MARITAL STATUS:
==>   SINGLE
OCCUPATION:
==>   FARMER
DRIVER'S LICENSE NUMBER:
==>   M432 6775 988
STATE:
==>   ILLINOIS
```

Example 4. Aligned key entries following computer messages.

```
DRIVER'S NAME:          LISA RENCH
SEX:                    F
BIRTH DATE:             08 05 61
MARITAL STATUS:         M
OCCUPATION:             STUDENT
DRIVER'S LICENSE NO:    R668 9870 254
STATE:                  NC
```

Menu Screens 9

A system will often contain large amounts of data and perform a variety of functions. Regardless of its purpose, the system must provide some means to tell users about the information it possesses or the things it can do. This is accomplished by displaying a screen listing the choices or alternatives the user has at appropriate points while using the system, or creating a string of screens that lead a user from a series of general descriptors on the first screen through increasingly specific categories on following screens until the lowest level screen is reached. This lowest level screen provides the desired choices. The common name for these kinds of screens is *menu screens*.

Menu screens are effective because they utilize the more powerful human capability of recognition rather than the weaker recall. Working with menus reminds users of available options and information that they may not be aware of or have forgotten.

Menu screens are not without problems, however. New system users might find learning larger systems difficult because information must be integrated across a series of displays (Engel and Granda, 1975; Dray et al. 1981; Billingsley, 1982; and Miller, 1981). As each menu is viewed in isolation, relationships between menus are difficult to grasp. Words and phrases with multiple meanings may be interpreted incorrectly because of the inability to see relationships (Bower et al. 1969). Ambiguities may be resolved on the basis of assumptions about menu structure that are incorrect (Cuff, 1980; Durding et al. 1977). The frequent result is that users make mistakes and get lost in the hierarchical structure.

Experienced system users, while finding menus helpful at first, may find them tedious as they learn the system. Continually having to step through a series of screens to achieve the desired objective can be time consuming and frustrating.

Therefore, the design of menu screens must consider the conflicting needs of both inexperienced and experienced users.

This discussion of menu screens begins with a categorization of the kinds of menus typically found on screens. Topics to follow include menu organization, ordering, selection, identification, and navigation techniques. Finally, some specific rules concerning caption wording, alignment, justification, spacing, and other considerations are presented.

KINDS OF MENUS

Shneiderman (1987) has identified three basic kinds of menus to be found on screens: single, linear sequence, and multipath. (See figure 9.1.) Both single and multipath menu categories contain several subclasses.

Figure 9.1 Kinds of menus.

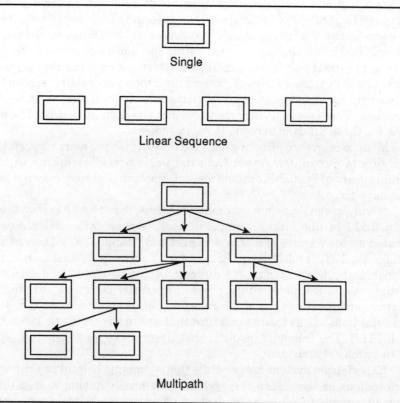

Single

Linear Sequence

Multipath

Single Menus.

A single menu is generally confined to one screen. It may encompass the whole screen or just a portion of it. In some instances it may extend beyond a single screen. Single menu subclasses are as follows.

Binary choice.   A binary menu simply asks the user to select from a pair of choices, yes/no, true/false, and so forth. Binary menus are commonly found in computer games.

Multiple item.   A multiple item menu presents the user with more than two choices. Several or more options may be displayed, and the user must select the proper alternative.

Extended.   In an extended menu a lengthy list of options is presented that extends beyond one screen. The last choice presented on the first screen leads to the second screen. The user, not finding the desired choice on the first screen, goes to the second screen and continues searching. To achieve efficiency, extended menus often have the more common choices on the first screen and less frequent choices on the second.

Pop-up.   Through use of windowing techniques, a pop-up or pull-down menu may appear on demand in a portion of the screen. Possible actions or choices that can be made at that moment are displayed. Because they cover other information on the screen, they tend to be small.

Permanent.   A permanent menu shows commands that can be applied to a displayed object or in the current situation. They are usually permanently displayed in a reserved area on the screen. Function key choices or labels in the bottom line of a screen reflect this approach.

Multiple selection.   A multiple selection menu permits more than one choice from the list of alternatives displayed.

Embedded.   An embedded menu permits a selection from choices within the data itself. A paragraph of text may have highlighted words that, when selected, provide additional information about the word or topic selected. Whereas the other kinds of single menus are explicit, an embedded menu is implicit, a by-product of another function.

Linear Sequence Menus

Linear sequence menus are a series of choices requiring two or more screens to complete. For example, setting the parameters for document printing may involve a number of decisions that must be made. These kinds of menus guide a complex decision-making process by presenting one choice at a time.

Multipath Menus

When the number of choices grows too large for easy comprehension, a semblance of order is established by categorizing alternatives and providing "paths" of choices to achieve the desired results. How the user is permitted to move through these paths, which together resemble a tree, gives each subclass its name. (See figure 9.2.)

Tree structure. A simple tree structure multipath menu permits the user to make a series of choices that takes him down through succeedingly lower level menus until his destination is reached. Movement back up a path is not permitted, nor is movement between paths.

Acyclic network. An acyclic network menu is a tree structure that permits downward movement between tree paths.

Cyclic network. A cyclic network menu is a tree structure that permits downward and upward movement between tree paths.

Multipath menu systems can make large numbers of choices easily available. On the other hand, they are very easy to get lost in.

ORGANIZATION

- Include:
  - all relevant alternatives,
  - only relevant alternatives.
- Provide hierarchical groupings of elements that:
  - contain logically similar items,
  - cover all possibilities,
  - do not overlap.
  - provide immediate access to critical or frequently chosen alternatives.
- Minimize number of menu levels within limits of clarity:
  - without logical categorization, limit choices per screen to 4-8,
  - with logical categorization, multi-column menus are permissible.
- Provide a general or main menu.

Relevant alternatives. A menu screen, or screens, should provide all relevant alternatives, and only relevant alternatives, at the point at which it is displayed. Including nonrelevant choices on a menu screen increases learning

Figure 9.2 Multipath menus.

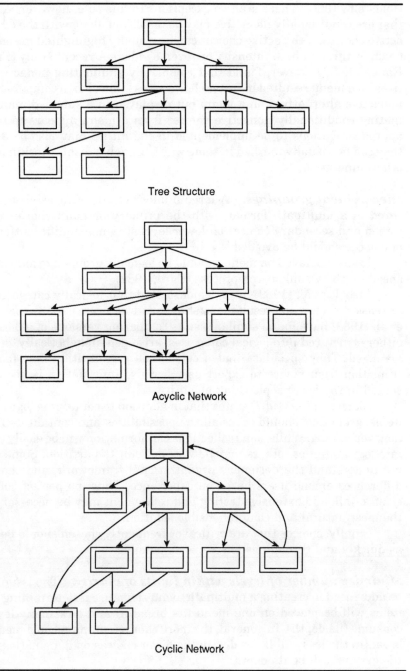

Tree Structure

Acyclic Network

Cyclic Network

requirements and has been found to interfere with performance (Baker and Goldstein, 1966). There are two exceptions to this rule, however. Alternatives that are conditionally nonactive may be displayed along with the conditionally active choices, if the active choices can be visually highlighted in some manner (such as through high intensity or reverse video). A recent study (Francik and Kane, 1987), however, found that completely eliminating nonactive alternatives on a menu resulted in faster choice access time, when compared to leaving nonactive alternatives on a menu but displayed in a subdued manner. Eliminating conditionally nonactive choices from a menu appears to be the best approach. Options to be implemented in the future may also be displayed if they can be visually marked in some way (through a display technique or some other annotation).

Hierarchical groupings. A large number of alternatives should be structured in a multipath format, with the primary or main choices on the top screen and secondary choices on lower level screens. Undifferentiated strings of choices should be avoided.

Items displayed on menus should be logically grouped to aid learning and speed up the visual search process (Card, 1982).

Liebelt et al. (1982) have demonstrated that logically categorized menus are easier to learn and result in faster and more accurate performance. McDonald et al. (1983) have found similar results comparing versions of a 64-item menu either structured into logical categories, arranged alphabetically, or randomly arranged. They speculate that a categorical organization may facilitate the transition from novice to expert user because information is visually represented in the way people think about it.

Shneiderman (1987) states that in addition to containing logically similar items, groupings should cover all the possibilities and contain items that are nonoverlapping. While some collections of information will be easily partitioned into logical groups, others may be very difficult to partition. Some users may not understand the designer's organizational framework, and there may be differences among users based on experience. Thus, no perfect solution may exist for all, and extensive testing and refinement may be necessary to create the most natural and comprehensible solution.

Finally, choices that are critical or frequently chosen should be accessible as quickly and through as few steps as possible.

Minimize number of levels within limits of clarity. The issue that must be addressed in creating a multipath menu structure is determining how many items will be placed on one menu (its breadth) and how many levels it will consume (its depth). In general, the more choices contained on a menu (greater breadth) the less will be its depth; the fewer choices on a menu (less breadth), the greater will be its depth.

A menu system with greater breadth and less depth has the following advantages:

- fewer steps, and shorter time, to reach one's objective. (Seppala and Salvendy, 1985),
- fewer opportunities to wander down wrong paths,
- easier learning by allowing the user to see relationships of menu items.

A broad menu's disadvantages are:

- a more crowded screen that reduces the clarity of the choice wording,
- increased likelihood of confusing similar choices because they are seen together,
- difficulties in displaying choices in the same area of the screen, which is preferred to displaying choices in different areas of the screen (Baker and Goldstein, 1966).

The advantages of greater depth are:

- less crowding on the screen,
- fewer choices to be scanned,
- easier hiding of inappropriate choices,
- easier display of all information in the same area of the screen,
- less likelihood of confusing similar choices since there is less likelihood that they will be seen together.

Greater depth disadvantages are:

- more steps, and longer time, to reach one's objective (Seppala and Salvendy, 1985),
- more difficulties in learning since relationships between elements cannot always be seen,
- more difficulties in predicting what lies below resulting in increased likelihood of going down wrong paths or getting lost,
- higher error rates (Tullis, 1985; Snowberry et al., 1983; Kiger, 1984; Seppala and Salvendy, 1985).

A good number of studies have looked at the breadth–depth issue in recent years. Some have concluded that breadth is preferable to depth in terms of either greater speed or fewer errors (Landauer and Nachbar, 1985; Tullis, 1985; Wallace, 1987), that a low number of levels (2 to 3) and an intermediate number of choices (4 to 8) results in faster, more accurate performance as opposed to fewer or greater numbers of levels and choices (Miller, 1981; Kiger, 1984), and that 4 to 8 choices per menu screen is best (Lee and MacGregor, 1985). Another study found that one level was easiest to learn (Dray et al., 1981), and a couple of studies have concluded that a menu could contain up to 64 items if it were organized into logical groups (Snowberry et al., 1983; Paap and Roske-Hofstrand, 1986). The least desirable alternative in almost all cases was deep level menu screens that simply presented the user with a binary choice (select one of two alternatives) on each screen.

The conclusion that one might derive from these studies is this. Fewer levels of menus aid the decision-making process, but trying to put too many choices on a single screen also has a negative impact. The final solution is a compromise: minimize the number of levels within limits of clarity. What is clarity? The studies seem to indicate that if the choices to be displayed cannot be segmented into logical categories, then confine the number of alternatives displayed to 4 to 8 per screen. If logical categorization is possible, and meaningful, logical category names can be established, then a larger number of choices can be presented, perhaps as many as 64. The maximum number of alternatives will, however, be dependent upon the size of the words needed to describe the alternatives to the user. "Wordy" captions will greatly restrict the number of alternatives capable of being displayed.

Provide a general menu.   The top level menu in a hierarchical menu scheme should be a general or main menu consisting of basic system options. This will provide a consistent starting point for all system activities and a "home-base" to which the user may always return.

CONTROL

- Permit only one selection per menu.
- When hierarchic levels of menus are used, permit one simple key action to:
    - return to the next higher level menu,
    - return to the general or main menu.
- Provide menu maps.

One selection per menu.   Requiring more than one choice per displayed menu can be confusing to the novice user.

Simple key actions.   Navigation through menu levels should be accomplished through simple key actions. It should always be very easy to return to the next higher level menu and the main or general menu.

Provide menu maps.   It is often difficult to maintain a sense of position or orientation as one wanders deeper into a multipath menu system. The result is that "getting lost" in the menu maze is quite easy to do. The value of a menu map in reducing disorientation has been demonstrated in three studies (Billingsley, 1982; Parton et al., 1985; Kaster and Widdell, 1986). In all cases, providing a graphic representation of the menu in map form, either in hard copy or on-line, resulted in fewer errors or wrong choices, faster navigation, and/or greater user satisfaction when compared to no guides or simply providing indexes or narrative descriptions of the menu structure. Kaster and Widdell also found that being able to view on the screen just the "path" one was following improved performance and learning.

So, menu maps or graphic representations of the menu structure are desirable. These maps should be included in the system documentation and also should be available through a HELP function. In addition, it is advantageous to either display on a menu screen the path of choices that has led to the current position, or make this path easily available through a pull-down window.

ITEM CAPTIONS

- Provide familiar, fully spelled-out descriptions of alternatives and choices available.
- Use either an upper- or lowercase font.
- Use concise phrasing.
- Provide distinctive wording.
- Word captions as commands to the computer.
- Bring main topic or keyword to the beginning.
- Be consistent between menus.

Menu captions, like captions on other screens, should comprise familiar, fully spelled-out words. While abbreviations may occasionally be necessary, they should be kept to a minimum. Captions should also be concise, containing as few words as possible, and distinctive, constructed of words that make a caption's intent as clear as possible. One way to improve caption distinctness is to avoid repeating the same word, or words, in a list of captions. Repeated words often signal the need for menu categorization.

Captions for menu options should be worded as commands to the computer, not questions to the user such as: COPY? (Y/N). Wording options as questions implies that the dialogue initiative is with the computer. An option or caption worded as a command (C = COPY) implies the initiative is with the user. Wording options as commands also permits the development of mnemonic codes for menu choices, which facilitates learning commands and bypassing menus as system familiarity is achieved.

Also, arrange the caption so that the descriptive and unique words appear at its beginning. This allows ease of visual scanning while the user is learning the menu. Finally, caption phrasing and wording should be consistent across all menus to further aid learning.

ITEM CAPTION ALIGNMENT, JUSTIFICATION, AND POSITIONING

Menus As Complete Screens

- Align alternatives or choices into columns.
- Left-justify captions.

```
CREATE
COPY
DELETE
EDIT
PRINT
EXIT
```

- Position in the center of the screen.

Menus Included On Other Screens

- Distinguish from other screen components through:
  - consistent positioning,
  - using a distinctive display technique to contrast with the remainder of the screen,
  - setting off with lines.
- Align alternatives or choices into columns, if possible.
- If a single row (horizontal) orientation must be maintained, organize for left-to-right readings.

```
CREATE    COPY    DELETE    EDIT    PRINT    EXIT
```

- If two or more rows are available:
  - organize for top-to-bottom, left-to-right reading,
  - left-justify captions.

```
CREATE    DELETE    PRINT
COPY      EDIT      EXIT
```

Menus as complete screens. For scanning ease, choices should be left-justified and aligned into columns. Parkinson et al. (1985) and Backs et al. (1987) have found columnar menus searched significantly faster than horizontally oriented menus. Position the aligned items in the center of the screen.

Menus included on other screens. When menus are included on other screens, such as with pop-up or permanent menus, space constraints often exist and the menu must somehow be easily differentiated from other screen components. This can be accomplished by always presenting the menu in the same location and using distinctive display techniques to contrast the menu with the remainder of the screen. Display techniques must, or course, be compatible with those used for other purposes on the remainder of the screen. A good way to set a menu off from the remainder of the screen is to enclose it in a box or, if it is at the screen's top or bottom, separate it with a horizontal line. Techniques chosen should be consistent throughout the system.

Choices should always be aligned in columns if possible. If a single row (horizontal) orientation is necessary, organize for left-to-right reading based on one of the ordering principles described earlier. If two or more rows are available for displaying choices, organize for top-to-bottom, left-to-right reading to facilitate visual scanning.

ORDERING

- Order lists of alternatives by their natural order, or
- For lists with a small number of options (seven or less), order by:
  - sequence of occurrence,
  - frequency of occurrence,
  - importance.
- Use alphabetic order for:
  - long lists (eight or more options),
  - short lists with no obvious pattern or frequency.
- Be consistent in ordering between menus.

Ordering Items and Choices

Within categories included on a menu, or in menus in which categories are not possible, items or choices must be ordered in a meaningful way.

Natural ordering. If items have a natural sequence, such as chapters in a book, months in the year, or physical properties such as increasing or decreasing sizes or weights, the ordering scheme should follow this natural sequence. These ordering schemes will have already been well learned by the screen viewer.

Small number of options. For groupings with a small number of options (about seven or less), sequence of use, frequency of use, or importance of the item is the best ordering scheme.

Alphabetic order.   For a large number of options, alphabetic ordering of alternatives is desirable. Alphabetic ordering is also recommended for small lists where no frequency or sequence pattern is obvious.

It has been found that alphabetically ordered menus can be searched much faster than randomly ordered menus (Card, 1982; McDonald et al., 1983; Perlman, 1984). Card, for example, found that an 18-item alphabetic menu was visually searched four times faster than a randomly organized menu. Search time was a function of saccadic eye movements through the display. Search patterns were random, but fewer eye movements were required with the alphabetic arrangement. After twenty trials, however, only one eye movement was required for all conditions and search time was the same. Learning does take place, but it will be greatly aided by the ordering scheme.

Consistency between menus.   Whereas ordering schemes may be different between menus, items found on more than one menu (such as EXIT or HELP) should be consistently positioned on all menus.

ITEM IDENTIFICATION

- Menu items may be identified by:
    - an ordinal code,
    - a mnemonic code,
    - or be unidentified.

Ordinal Identification

- Use numbers starting with one, not zero.

```
1    CREATE
2    COPY
3    EDIT
4    ERASE
5    PRINT
```

Mnemonic Identification

- Use a mnemonic or abbreviation that meaningfully describes the alternative. Simple truncation is the preferred method.

```
CR    CREATE
CO    COPY
ED    EDIT
ER    ERASE
PR    PRINT
```

No Identification

- The caption serves to identify the item.

```
CREATE
COPY
EDIT
ERASE
PRINT
```

Identification of Menu Choices

Identification of choices on a menu may take one of several forms. The common methods are the following.

Ordinal identification. With ordinal identification the identifier has no meaningful relationship with the item it describes. The advantage of an ordinal code is that it provides a simple and unique way to identify a choice, and few keystrokes are needed to communicate the selection.

The disadvantage of the ordinal code is that it makes remembering choices on other menu screens much more difficult. Alternative "3" on eight different menus will usually mean eight different things. Ordinal codes also cause problems when items are added to menus. If the original menu has items arranged in some logical order (such as sequence of use), adding a new alternative in its logical location in the listing of choices will cause a renumbering of alternatives appearing below it. This problem often results in menu listings on expanding systems not being ordered in some meaningful way because the designer chooses not to renumber and simply adds to the list at the bottom.

Ordinal codes commonly found on screens have been made up of letters of the alphabet or numbers. The advantages of sequential lettering are that 26 choices can be communicated with one keystroke and fewer errors occur because the letters are more spread out. Disadvantages include longer times to find choices (especially for those not familiar with a typewriter keyboard) and the potential for fostering erroneous associations. That is, letters of the alphabet associated with captions comprising letters can create associations that were not intended and that interfere with menu learning.

Using numbers as ordinal codes has the following advantages. Numbers are grouped more logically from both a spacing and ordering perspective, aiding visual scanning and making it easier to find the relevant key. Thus, selection speed is improved. Numbers also permit function keys to be substituted for typewriter key activation, and they exactly identify how many choices are available. Disadvantages of numbers are the necessity for making two keystrokes when more than nine choices exist and that numbering may imply an ordering or preference (number 1 is most important) that does not exist.

In a study comparing these two ordinal coding schemes, Perlman (1984) found that numbered ordinal codes were searched about twice as fast as lettered codes.

In consideration of the arguments above, the recommended ordinal code is numeric digits beginning with one (1). Never start with zero (0). While computers may start counting with zero, people never do.

Mnemonic identification. A mnemonically identified alternative has a meaningful relationship with the item it identifies. Mnemonics are extremely advantageous in that they aid the menu users' learning of the system choices, thereby facilitating the transition to a command language and avoiding the need to always step through a series of menu screens. Thus, the transition from novice to expert user is aided. Mnemonics also permit easy reordering of menu listings as items are added. They may be inserted in their proper places without renaming identifiers.

A disadvantage of a mnemonic scheme is that uniqueness must be maintained throughout the entire menu structure. This can create large identifiers that require more keystrokes to communicate a command to the system.

Three studies (Perlman, 1984; Shinar et al., 1985; Shinar and Stern, et al., 1987) have demonstrated that mnemonically coded menus can be searched significantly faster than menus with ordinal numeric codes. Mnemonic codes are preferable to ordinal codes, whenever they are possible.

No identification. Of course, items may not be identified at all, which implies that a user has to select an alternative by pointing at it with the screen cursor (using the keyboard or a control like the "mouse"), or by touching it with his finger. A problem with this method is that a transition to a command language is impossible.

ITEM IDENTIFICATION CODE POSITIONING

- Position code to the left of its associated caption and separate from caption by two blank spaces.
- Left-align all alphabetic codes.

```
CRxxCREATE
CO   COPY
ED   EDIT
ER   ERASE
PR   PRINT
"    "
"    "
EX   EXIT
```

- Right-align all numeric codes.

```
1 x x C R E A T E
2     C O P Y
3     E D I T
4     E R A S E
5     P R I N T
"         "
"         "
1 0   E X I T
```

- For horizontally arranged captions with space constraints, visually relating caption to code may be necessary:
    - use an equal (=) sign as the delimiter.

```
1 = C R E A T E    2 = C O P Y    3 = E D I T    4 = E R A S E    5 = P R I N T
```

Codes should be positioned to the left of the choice captions. Normally, a large space border around the menu choices is sufficient to visually relate the code to its respective caption. On screens where space to display a menu is restricted, such as with pop-up or permanent menus, visually tying the code to the caption may be necessary. A good symbol to accomplish this is the equal sign (=).

ITEM SELECTION TECHNIQUES

- Alternatives may be selected by:
    - one entry field per screen (single selection field),
    - one entry field for each choice (multiple selection fields),
    - pointing at the choice,
    - function keys.

Single Selection Fields

- Locate selection field directly underneath the column of choice codes (or first column if a multi-column menu screen).
- Separate from caption by a blank line.
- Identify with a unique and descriptive caption such as SELECTION or CHOICE.

```
9     P R I N T              P R    P R I N T
1 0   E X I T                E X    E X I T

S E L E C T I O N :  _ _      S E L E C T I O N :  _ _
```

Multiple Selection Fields

- Identify selection field by an underscore.
- Position selection field to left of choice.
- Leave two blank spaces between selection field and caption.

```
_ x x C R E A T E
_     C O P Y
_     E D I T
_     E R A S E
_     P R I N T
```

- If item codes are included, leave two blank spaces between selection field and code.

```
_ x x 1 x x C R E A T E
_     2     C O P Y
_     3     E D I T
_     4     E R A S E
_     5     P R I N T
```

Pointing

- Highlight the selected choice through a distinctive display technique.

Function Keys

- Use the function keys available on the keyboard to select a choice.

Selecting Items on a Menu Screen

Items on a menu screen may be selected in a variety of ways. One entry field may be provided on a screen, the single selection field method; an entry field may be associated with each choice, the multiple selection field method; the item may be pointed at by moving the cursor to the choice desired; or the keyboard's function keys may be used. Each method has advantages and disadvantages.

Single selection field. One entry field may be incorporated on a menu screen into which the code for the selective alternative is keyed. Single selection fields should be located in a consistent position at the bottom of the screen and must be identified with a unique and descriptive caption. The recommended location is at the bottom of the column of menu choices. The inexperienced user's eyes are permitted to scan down the column of alternatives until the desired alternative is found. The eyes then continue downward until the selection field is found. Eye movement from keyboard back to selection field to verify that the entry is correct is also minimized by this location. The experienced user who does not rely on scanning the menu listing to find a choice, but relies on memory instead, will also find this location acceptable, as it is consistent and minimizes the visual distance between the keyboard and the field itself. If command or choice stacking or "typeahead" is permitted (which is desirable as it permits the expert user to override the display of menus in a string), this selection field must be large enough to permit keying as many choices as needed.

On multi-column menu screens position the entry field at the bottom of the first column of choices. This will provide the most location consistency in systems containing menus of varying numbers of choice columns.

Multiple selection fields. With multiple selection fields the screen user moves the cursor to an entry field associated with an item and keys a value to indicate the item has been selected. For screens containing a small number of items, this method can be used quite efficiently. As the number of items on a menu increases, however, it becomes less efficient as the cursor must be moved greater distances. Where the single selection field method can become more efficient is difficult to say. As a rule of thumb, confine this technique to menus where one item must be selected from no more than five or six.

The multiple selection field method may also be effectively employed where more than one item must be selected from a large number of items. That is, the user may wish to select 3 or 4 items at one time from a list of 10 or 12 choices. Menus containing a larger number of choices may use this method, since distances between choices will, on the average, remain short. (If about 4 items are selected from 12 alternatives, approximately 1 in every 3 entry fields will have a value keyed into it.) Again, a rule of thumb would be to restrict the method to situations where on the average 1 item is selected for every several alternatives displayed.

Other advantages of the multiple selection field approach are that codes to identify alternatives are not necessary and that fewer opportunities exist for making typing errors. A disadvantage is that command stacking, or "typeahead" is not permitted.

Pointing. The pointing approach to choice selection resembles the multiple selection field approach, except that a value need not be keyed. Instead, the cursor is moved to the designated item through use of the cursor movement (arrow) keys, or an alternative control mechanism such as a "mouse"; or the user's finger is used to make the selection (if the screen is touch sensitive).

Depressing a key such as TRANSMIT or ENTER signals the choice to the computer.

If cursor movement is used, the item selected should be highlighted in some way through a distinctive display technique. Reverse video is often used for this purpose. Highlighting the choice gives direct visual feedback that the proper choice has been selected, reducing the possibility of errors in choice selection. If a touch sensitive screen is available and a finger is used to communicate a choice, the target area should be as large as possible. Single character positions on a screen make poor targets for most fingers. Also keep in mind that using a finger to signify a choice can be taxing on arm muscles, so this approach should only be used in casual or infrequent use situations.

Other advantages and disadvantages to pointing are similar to those of the multiple selection field approach. One study (Shinar et al., 1985) compared cursor pointing to single field entry of a one-character mnemonic code, and found that keying a mnemonic code was faster than pointing for more than five choices. This would seem to confirm that pointing is slower when codes are small and when more than five or six choices exist.

Function keys.   Menu alternatives may also be selected through use of Function keys. Item identification on the screen can incorporate the key number, and a choice is made by pressing the applicable key. The advantage of this approach is that it requires only one key stroke to implement a choice. Disadvantages are that usually fewer alternatives are available (some terminals may have few, if any, function keys), and that command stacking for the experienced user is not possible.

COMBINING IDENTIFICATION AND SELECTION TECHNIQUES

Item identification and selection techniques can be combined. An interesting example is described by Goodwin (1983). In the system described, called MENUS, several alternatives are implemented concurrently, including numbered ordinal identification codes, function keys, and mnemonic-like commands. An example of a menu from this system is illustrated in figure 9-3. Each menu contains a numbered listing corresponding to the number of the function key associated with this option. A system user may press the appropriate function key or key the one-digit number into the selection field. Since this does not allow the expert user to go directly to the wanted screen, a command code has also been provided through the creation of meaningful path names derived from one- and two-character alphabetic codes added to the command as the several levels of menus are navigated. To go from one menu to the next simply requires keying the meaningful code displayed on that menu. As code structures are learned, they may be strung together (stacked) to go directly to the menu or screen needed. Thus, all system users may use the approach with which they are most comfortable at any time.

Figure 9-3 An example of a standard MENUS system menu.

```
-------------------------------------------------------

              OFFICE SUPPORT TOOLS (O)
                 (parent:   MAIN)


    PF KEY      COMMAND        DESCRIPTION
      1          OM           Mail System
      2          OP           Personal Appointments (Calendar)
      3          OR           Reminder Files



      9          RMM          Return to MAIN Menu
     10          RPM          Return to Previous Menu (F)
     11          LVE          Leave MENUS
     12          LOG          Logoff of CMS



-------------------------------------------------------
```

ENTER YOUR SELECTION:

From Goodwin, N.C., "Designing a Multipurpose Menu Driven User Interface to Computer Based Tools," in *Proceedings of the Human Factors Society-27th Annual Meeting (1983)*, p. 820. Santa Monica, Calif.: Human Factors Society, Inc. Reproduced by permission of the publisher.

ITEM IDENTIFICATION TECHNIQUES

Multiple Selection Fields

- The recommended value to be keyed is Y, because:
  - it possesses a high association value (Yes, I would like to choose this alternative);
  - the letter Y is located at a convenient place on the standard typewriter keyboard (middle of center row).

Single Selection Fields

- Selection occurring on the same screen as the displayed alternatives:
  - permit keying a
    choice number,
    mnemonic abbreviation.

- Selection occurring on a screen different from the displayed alternatives
  – permit keying a
    mnemonic abbreviation,
    fully spelled-out item caption.

Multiple selection fields. With multiple selection fields any value may be keyed to indicate selection of the item or choice. It is recommended, however, that the value keyed be Y because of its high association value and convenient location on the standard typewriter keyboard.

Single selection fields. Single selection fields should permit keying of the ordinal or mnemonic code. If keying of choice is permitted on a screen other than the menu screen where the items are listed, fully spelled-out item captions should be permitted as well as mnemonic codes.

MENU NAVIGATION TECHNIQUES

- Permit typeahead—the keying of following menu screen codes on the displayed menu screen.
- Permit direct access—the keying of the desired menu screen name on the displayed screen.
- Permit menu macros—regularly used menu paths to be stored and keyed as commands.
- Permit one simple action to return to:

    – the next higher-level menu,
    – the general or main menu.

A criticism of many menu systems concerns is long and tedious path that may have to be traversed to reach one's objective. This is extremely bothersome if menus are several levels deep and/or response times are somewhat slower than desirable. These problems can be alleviated if users are permitted to go directly to their destination, avoiding intermediate stops along the way. Shneiderman (1987) has outlined three ways to improve menu navigation: typeahead, direct access, and menu macros.

Typeahead. Typeahead is command or choice "stacking." As paths through the menu system are learned, the needed choice codes can be keyed on higher level menus, and the destination screen will be directly displayed. If choice codes are mnemonics, the strings can achieve a mnenonic value themselves. The transition from novice menu user to expert command user can be gradual and graceful. As the user becomes experienced, he learns and remembers deeper paths. Infrequently used paths can still be supported by menus, as can the occasional memory lapse.

Typeahead requires a single entry field, which must be large enough to accommodate the deepest path that can be covered.

Direct access. If a name is assigned to each menu, it can be keyed on any menu and then its menu will be directly displayed. Again, learning is gradual and graceful, with full menu paths always available when needed.

This approach is most useful if there are only a few destinations that have to be remembered. Unique names must also be created for all menus.

Menu macros. Regularly used paths can be recorded as menu macros; that is, a command name can be established to cause the desired path to be traversed whenever the command is executed. In addition to simplifying access, this permits individual customization of the system.

Upward movement. One simple key action should be all that is necessary to return to the next higher level menu and the main or general menu.

CATEGORY HEADINGS

- Incorporate menu category headings whenever possible.
- Categories of menu items should:
  - contain logically similar items,
  - cover all possibilities,
  - not overlap.
- Distinguish the category heading from the choices by:
  - displaying it in an uppercase font.
  - positioning it in the line above its related choice captions and starting the category heading five spaces to the left of the aligned listing of choice captions, choice codes, or multiple selection entry fields.

```
CUSTOMER
      1   ACCOUNT
      2   INFORMATION
      3   STATUS
```

  - positioning the category heading to the left of the caption, code, or multiple selection entry field, separated by a "greater than" sign (>) and three spaces.

```
CUSTOMERx>xxx1   ACCOUNT
             2   INFORMATION
             3   STATUS
```

Category headings should be included whenever possible. They will reflect the hierarchical groupings recently discussed. Therefore, they should contain logically similar items, cover all possibilities, and not overlap. They should be easily distinguishable from the alternatives but should not detract attention from choices to be scanned. The recommended approach is the second one illustrated above: positioning the category heading to the left of the first item in the group and separating it with a "greater than" (>) sign. The first approach, indention of the category heading above the column of choices, is most practical and efficient on multi-column menus or on menus where horizontal spacing constraints exist.

SPACING

Vertical Spacing

- Leave a blank line between categories of information.

```
CUSTOMER                         CUSTOMER  >      1  ACCOUNT
    1  ACCOUNT                                    2  INFORMATION
    2  INFORMATION                                3  STATUS
    3  STATUS
                                 TRANSACTION  >   4  HISTORY
TRANSACTION                                       5  NUMBER
    4  HISTORY                                     6  TYPE
    5  NUMBER
    6  TYPE
```

- For long lists of alternatives, leave a blank line after every fifth item. Do not exceed seven items without inserting a space line.

```
                        BILL
                        CANCEL
                        CORRECT
                        DISPLAY
                        ENDORSE

                        FILE
                        ISSUE
                        PRINT
                        QUOTE
                        RENEW
```

Horizontal Spacing

- For multi-column arrangements on full screens, leave a minimum of five spaces between the longest item caption in one column and the first character position of the adjacent column category heading, code, or multiple selection field.
- Center the double column on the screen.

```
        BILL           FILE
        CANCEL         ISSUE
        CORRECTxxxxxPRINT
        DISPLAY        QUOTE
        ENDORSE        RENEW

    1   BILL        6  FILE
    2   CANCEL      7  ISSUE
    3   CORRECT     8  PRINT
    4   DISPLAY     9  QUOTE
    5   ENDORSExxxxx10 RENEW
```

- Where horizontal space constraints exist, consider separating columns by a dashed line.

```
        BILL      |  FILE
        CANCEL    |  ISSUE
        CORRECT   |  PRINT
        DISPLAY   |  QUOTE
        ENDORSE   |  RENEW

    1   BILL      |  6   FILE
    2   CANCEL    |  7   ISSUE
    3   CORRECT   |  8   PRINT
    4   DISPLAY   |  9   QUOTE
    5   ENDORSE   |  10  RENEW
```

- Where horizontal orientation of choices is necessary, leave a minimum of two spaces between adjacent captions, three spaces if available.

```
   CREATExxCOPY   DELETE   EDIT   PRINT   EXIT

 1=CREATExx2=COPY   3=DELETE   4=EDIT   5=PRINT   6=EXIT

 1=CREATExxx2=COPY   3=DELETE   4=EDIT   5=PRINT   6=EXIT
```

Vertical spacing. The vertical spacing guidelines outlined above are necessary to achieve visual groupings and separation. Parkinson et al. (1985) found that spacing between groups of information reduced menu search time. It is not desirable to leave space lines between elements within a group because they hamper visual perception of the group as a separate entity. If space is available on the screen, consider leaving an extra space line between groups instead. If a logical grouping contains six or seven items, a space line may be left after the last one instead of after five items, as recommended above. Do not, however, go beyond seven items within the logical grouping without including a space line.

Horizontal spacing. Horizontal spacing guidelines are intended to achieve visual separation and to convey the necessity of columnar scanning. Thus, these separation requirements should be considered minimums, and more space should be left between columns if available. Lengthy captions will usually require greater between-column spacing than that described above (unless a vertical line is drawn).

TITLE

- The title should reflect the nature of the choice to be made or the menu's purpose.
- Lower level menu titles should reflect the choice made above.
- Spell out fully.
- Locate in a centered position at the top of the screen.

Single menus should contain a title that reflects the menu's purpose or the nature of the choice to be made. In linear sequence menus, the title should reflect the stages in that sequence. Within multipath menus the title of a lower level menu should reflect the choice made in the menu above it. Titles should be spelled out fully, but wording should be concise.

SCREEN IDENTIFIER

- For multiscreen menus place a page number or screen identifier in the upper right-hand corner.

To uniquely identify a menu and allow users or screen identifiers to know their location within a series of menus, a menu number should be incorporated on each menu. This number may simply be "menu n of x," or it may incorporate a mnemonic code—for example, "MENU01," the last two digits indicating the number of the menu in the series. For easy identification the menu number may be surrounded by unique symbols such as asterisks (***)—for example, *** MENU01 *** or *** MENU 1 OF 4 ***

ERROR/STATUS MESSAGES AND INSTRUCTIONAL INFORMATION

- Uniquely identify messages and instructional information through:
  - a consistent location,
  - use of a contrasting display feature such as
    reverse video,
    highlighting,
    preceding message by a unique series of symbols (such as asterisks),
    lowercase characters;
  - separating messages from body of screen.

Messages must attract the user's attention and be easily discriminated from the body of the menu screen. This is accomplished most effectively by using contrasting display features or special symbols and a consistent location. Again, the message must be perceived as an instructional message or prompt by its size, shape, and/or location without it actually having to be read.

CHAPTER 9 EXAMPLES

Example 1. A menu containing mnemonic codes, category headings and a single selection field.

```
- - - - - - - - - - - - - - - - - - - - - - - - - - - - - - - - - - - - - - - - -

                                                      *** CNTRY ***

           COUNTRIES OF THE WORLD


     AFRICA >    CH   CHAD
                 KE   KENYA
                 LI   LIBERIA
                 MO   MOZAMBIQUE
                 UG   UGANDA

     ASIA >      BR   BRUNEI
                 HO   HONG KONG
                 IN   INDONESIA
                 SI   SINGAPORE
                 TH   THAILAND

     SELECTION:  __



- - - - - - - - - - - - - - - - - - - - - - - - - - - - - - - - - - - - - - - - -
```

Example 2. A menu containing ordinal codes, category headings and a single selection field.

```
----------------------------------------------------------
                                            *** ATHL ***



        FAMOUS AMERICAN ATHLETES

            BASEBALL PLAYERS
                1    Joe DiMaggio
                2    Willy Mays
                3    Stan Musial
                4    Ted Williams

            FOOTBALL PLAYERS
                5    Sammy Baugh
                6    Elroy Hirsch
                7    Walter Payton
                8    Bob Waterfield

        SELECTION: _


        --------------------------------------------------
```

Example 3. A menu containing multiple selection fields.

```
----------------------------------------------------------
                                            *** FURN ***


        FURNITURE STYLES

            __    Chippendale
            __    Colonial
            __    Duncan Phyfe
            __    Early American
            __    Empire

            __    French Provincial
            __    Hepplewhite
            __    Jacobean
            __    Louis XIV
            __    Victorian


        --------------------------------------------------
```

Color in Screen Design   **10**

The addition of color can add a new dimension to screen usability. Color draws attention because it attracts the user's eye. If used properly, it can emphasize the logical organization of a screen, facilitate the discrimination of screen components, accentuate differences, and make displays more interesting. If used improperly, color can be distracting and visually fatiguing, impairing the system's usability.

The discussion to follow begins by defining color. Next is a review of how color may be used in screen design and some critical cautions in its use. Then, the human visual system and the implications for color are discussed. Finally, guidelines are presented for choosing and using colors for both alphanumeric and graphic screens.

COLOR—WHAT IS IT?

Wavelengths of light themselves are not colored. What is perceived as actual color results from the stimulation by a received light wave of the proper receptor in the eye. The "name" that a color is given is a learned phenomenon, based on previous experiences and associations of specific visual sensations with color names. Therefore, a color can only be described in terms of a person's report of his or her perceptions.

The visual spectrum of wavelengths to which the eye is sensitive ranges from about 400 to 700 millimicrons. Objects in the visual environment often emit or reflect light waves in a limited area of this visual spectrum, absorbing light waves in other areas of the spectrum. The dominant wavelength being "seen" is the one that we come to associate with a specific color name. The visible color spectrum and the names commonly associated with the various light wavelengths are shown in figure 10.1.

Figure 10.1 The visible spectrum.

Color	Approximate Wavelengths in Millimicrons
Red	700
Orange	600
Yellow	570
Yellow-green	535
Green	500
Blue-green	493
Blue	470
Violet	400

COLOR USES

- Use color as a formatting aid to:
  - relate or tie fields into groupings,
  - differentiate groupings of fields,
  - relate fields that are spatially separated,
  - emphasize or call attention to important fields.
- Use color as a visual code to identify:
  - screen components,
  - sources of data,
  - status of data.

Color Uses

Color may be used as a formatting aid in structuring a screen, or it may be used as a visual code to categorize information or data.

As a formatting aid. As a formatting aid, color can provide better structure and meaning to a screen. It is especially useful when large amounts of data must be included on a screen and spacing to differentiate components is difficult to employ.

For example, differentiation of logical groupings of fields can be enhanced by displaying them in different colors. Spatially separated but related fields can also be tied together through a color scheme.

Color can also replace highlighting as a means of calling attention to a field or fields. Color is much more flexible than other techniques because of the number of colors that are available. Color as an attention-getting mechanism must, however, be chosen in light of the psychological and physiological considerations, to be described shortly.

As a visual code.   A color code shows what category the data being displayed falls into. It has meaning to the screen's user. A properly selected color coding scheme permits a user to identify a relevant category quickly without having to first read its contents. This permits focusing concentration on this category while the remaining data is excluded from attention.

One common color coding scheme to differentiate screen components is to display captions and data fields in different colors. Another is to identify data from different sources—data added to a transaction from different locations, or text added to a message from different departments, may be colored differently. Color coding to convey status might involve displaying, in a different color, data that passed or failed system edits. Color can also be used as a prompt, guiding a person through a complex transaction.

Color as a visual code must be relevant and known. Relevance is achieved when the code enables a user to attend only to the data that is needed. A relevant code, however, will be useless unless it is also understood by the persons who must use it. Not knowing a code's meaning will only distract and degrade performance.

POSSIBLE PROBLEMS WITH COLOR

- Color's high attention-getting quality may be distracting if it causes a person to:
  - notice differences in color, regardless of whether the differences have any real meaning,
  - visually group items of the same color together, regardless of whether these grouped items are related.
- Indiscriminate or poor use of color on one screen may interfere with color's attention-getting capacity on another screen.
- The sensitivity of the eye to different colors and color combinations varies, some being visually fatiguing.
- Some people have color viewing deficiencies.

The simple addition of color to a screen will not guarantee improved performance. When used improperly, color may even impair performance by distracting the viewer and interfering with the handling of information. Possible problems in dealing with color may be caused by the perceptual system itself and/or the physiological characteristics of the human eye.

High attention-getting capacity.   Color has an extremely high attention-getting capacity, which causes the screen viewer to associate or "tie together" screen elements of the same color, whether or not such an association should be made. The user thus might search for relationships and differences that do not exist or that are not valid. The result is often bewilderment, confusion, and slower reading. The effect achieved is often described as a "Christmas tree."

Interference with use of other screens. Indiscriminate or poor use of color on some screens will diminish the effectiveness of color on other screens. The rationale for color will be difficult to understand and its attention-getting capacity severely restricted.

Varying sensitivity of the eye to different colors. All colors, in the eye of the viewer, are not equal. The eye is more sensitive to those in the middle of the visual spectrum, which appear brighter than those at the extremes. Thus, text comprising colors at the extremes is generally more difficult to read. Also, some combinations of colors strain the eye's accommodation mechanism. The perceived appearance of a color is affected by a variety of factors, including color size, ambient illumination level, and other colors in the viewing area. Failure to consider the eye, and how it handles color, can lead to mistakes in color identification, misinterpretations, slower reading, and, perhaps, visual fatigue.

Color viewing deficiencies. Another disadvantage of color is that about 8 percent of males and 0.4 of females have some form of color perception deficiency—"color-blindness." The most common form of color blindness is red-green, which affects about 2.5 percent of the population. The visual color spectrum in this form of color blindness ranges from blue to white to yellow. For an individual with a color perception deficiency, all the "normal" colors may not be discernible.

The use of color in screen design must always keep these possible problems clearly in focus. The designer must work to minimize their disruptive and destructive effects. Always keep in mind that poor use of color is worse than not using it at all.

COLOR AND SCREEN DESIGN—WHAT THE RESEARCH SHOWS

The effectiveness of color in improving the usability of a display has yielded mixed research results. On a positive note, color has been shown to improve performance (Kopala, 1981; Sidorsky, 1982), to improve visual search (Christ, 1975; Carter, 1982), to be useful for organizing information (Engel, 1980), and to create positive user reactions (Tullis, 1981). On the other hand, it has also been shown that color does not improve performance (Tullis, 1981), may impair performance (Christ and Teichner, 1973; Christ, 1975), and is less important than display spacing (Haubner and Benz, 1983). It has also been demonstrated that poor character–background color combinations lead to poorer performance (McTyre and Frommer, 1985).

Research has found, moreover, that as the number of colors on a display increases, the time to respond to a single color increases, and the probability of color confusions increases (Luria, et al., 1986). Many studies have found that the maximum number of colors that a person can handle is in the range of 4 to 10, with emphasis on the lower numbers (for example, Brooks, 1965; Halsey and Chapanis, 1951; Luria et al., 1986).

The conclusion to be derived from these studies is that for simple displays, color may have no dramatic impact. Indeed, a monochromatic display may serve the purpose just as well. As display complexity increases, however, so does the value of color. When it is used, though, the value of the color will be dependent on the task being performed, the colors selected, how many are used, how they are used, and the viewing environment.

COLOR AND HUMAN VISION

To understand how color should be used on a screen, it is helpful to know something of the physiology of the human eye. The reader requiring a detailed discussion of this subject is referred to Murch (1983, 1984A).

The lens.   The lens of the eye, controlled by muscles, focuses wavelengths of light on the retina. The lens itself is not color corrected. The wavelengths of light creating different colors are focused at different distances behind the lens, the longer wavelengths (red) being focused further back than the shorter wavelengths (blue). The result is that colors of a different wavelength than the color actually being focused by the lens appear out of focus. To create a sharp image of the out-of-focus colors requires a refocusing of the eye. Excessive refocusing (such as between red and blue) can lead to eye fatigue.

The effect of this focusing for most people is that reds appear more distant and blues appear closer. It can give a three-dimensional appearance to what is being viewed. A critical problem is that the wavelength of light creating blue can never be brought into focus on the retina, but is always focused in front of it. A sharp blue image is impossible to obtain.

Very pure colors require more refocusing than less pure colors. Therefore, a color with a large "white" component will require less refocusing.

The lens does not transmit all light wavelengths equally. It absorbs more wavelengths in the blue region of the spectrum than those in the other regions. Additionally, as the lens ages, it tends to yellow, filtering out the shorter blue wavelengths. Thus, as people get older, their sensitivity to blue decreases.

The retina.   The retina is the light sensitive surface of the eye. It comprises two kinds of receptors, rods and cones, that translate the incoming light into nervous impulses. Rods are sensitive to lower light levels and function primarily at night. Cones are stimulated by higher light levels and react to color. The sensitivity of cones to colors varies, different cones possessing maximum sensitivity to different light wavelengths. About two-thirds (64 percent) of the cones are maximally sensitive to longer light wavelengths, showing a peak response at about 575 millimicrons. These cones have traditionally been referred to as "red" sensitive cones. In actuality, however, the peak sensitivity is in the yellow portion of the visual spectrum (see figure 10.1). About one-third (32 percent) of the cones achieve maximum sensitivity at about 535 millimicrons and are commonly referred to as "green" sensitive cones. The remainder (2 percent) primarily react to short light wavelengths, achieving maximum sensitivity at about 445 millimicrons. These are known as "blue" sensitive cones. Any lightwave impinging on the retina evokes a response, to a greater or less degree, from most or all these cones. A perceived "color" results from the proportion of "stimulation" of the various kinds.

Rods and cones vary in distribution across the retina. The center is tightly packed with cones and has no rods. Toward the periphery of the retina, rods increase and cones decrease. Thus, color sensitivity does not exist at the retina's outer edges, although yellows and blues can be detected further into the periphery than reds and greens. The very center of the retina is devoid of "blue" cones, creating a "blue-blindness" for small objects fixated upon.

The receptors in the eye also adjust, or adapt, their level of sensitivity to the overall light level and the color being viewed. Adaptation to increases in brightness improves color sensitivity. Color adaptation "softens" colors.

The brightness sensitivity of the eye to different colors also varies. It is governed by output from the "red" and "green" cones. The greater the output, the higher the brightness, which results in the eye being most sensitive to colors in the middle of the visual spectrum and less sensitive to colors at the extremes. A blue or red must be of a much greater intensity than a green or yellow to even be perceived.

The ability of the eye to detect a form is accomplished by focusing the viewed image on the body of receptors to establish "edges." Distinct edges yield distinct images. Edges formed by color differences alone cannot be accurately focused and thus create fuzzy and nondistinct images. A clear, sharp image requires a difference in brightness between adjacent objects, as well as differences in color.

The components of the eye—the lens and retina—govern the choices, and combinations, of colors to be displayed on a screen. The proper colors will enhance performance; improper colors will have the opposite effect, as well as greatly increase the probability of visual fatigue.

COLORS IN CONTEXT

Colors are subject to contextual effects. The size of a colored image, the color of images adjacent to it, and the ambient illumination all exert an influence on what is actually perceived. At the normal viewing distance for a screen, maximal color sensitivity is not reached until the size of a colored area exceeds about a three-inch square. Smaller size images become desaturated (having a greater white component) and change slightly in color. Also, small differences in actual color may not be discernible. Blues and yellows are particularly susceptible to difficulties in detecting slight changes. Finally, small adjacent colored images may appear to the eye to merge or mix. Red and green, for example, might appear as yellow.

Adjacent images can influence the perceived color. A color on a dark background, for example, will look lighter and brighter than the same color on a light background. A color can be *induced* into a neutral foreground area (gray) by the presence of a colored background. A red background can change a gray into a green. Induced colors are the complementary of the inducing color. Complementary afterimages can also be induced by looking at a saturated color for a period of time.

Colors change as light levels change. Higher levels of ambient light tend to desaturate colors. Saturated colors will also appear larger than desaturated colors.

CHOOSING CATEGORIES OF INFORMATION FOR COLOR

- Choosing categories of information for color requires a clear understanding of how the information will be used.
- Some examples:
  - if different parts of the screen are attended to separately, color code the different parts to focus selective attention on each in turn;
  - if decisions are made based on the status of certain types of information on the screen, color code the types of status the information may possess;
  - if screen searching is performed to locate information of a particular kind or quality, color code these kinds or qualities for contrast;
  - if the sequence of information use is constrained or ordered, use color to identify the sequence;
  - if the information displayed on a screen is packed or crowded, use color to provide visual groupings.

Color chosen to classify data on a screen must aid the transfer of information from the display to the user. This requires a clear understanding of how the information is selected and used. The examples above describe some common ways of classifying information for color coding purposes.

It is important to remember, however, that data on one screen may be used in more than one way. What is useful in one context may not be in another and may only cause interference. Therefore, when developing a color strategy, consider how spatial formatting, highlighting, and messages may also be useful.

CHOOSING COLORS TO DISPLAY

General Considerations

- Design for monochrome first.
- Use colors conservatively.
- For best absolute discrimination, select no more than four to five colors widely spaced on the color spectrum:
  - good colors: red, yellow, green, blue, white.
- For best comparative discrimination, select no more than six to seven colors widely spaced on the color spectrum:
  - other acceptable colors: orange, yellow-green, blue-green, violet.
- Use bright colors to emphasize and nonbright colors to de-emphasize:
  - the brightness of colors from most to least is white, yellow, green, blue, red.
- To emphasize separation use contrasting colors:
  - red and green, blue and yellow.
- To convey similarity use similar colors:
  - orange and yellow, blue and violet.
- To indicate that actions are necessary, use warm colors:
  - red, orange, yellow.
- For text use desaturated or spectrum center colors:
  - yellow, green.
- For backgrounds use darker, spectrally extreme colors:
  - blue, black, red, magenta.
- For peripheral viewing use blue or yellow.
- Conform to human expectancies:
  - in the job,
  - in the world at large.
- Order colors by their spectral position.
- Be consistent in color use.

Colors chosen for display on a screen must consider these factors: the human visual system, the possible problems that may arise, the contextual effects that may occur, the environment in which the terminal is used, and the task of the user. The primary objective of color is aiding the transfer of information from the display to the viewer.

Design for monochrome first. A screen should be as capable of being effectively used as if it were in a monochrome environment. Spatial formatting, messages, and display techniques described earlier such as highlighting and upper- and lowercase characters should all be utilized to give it a structure that makes it easily used if the viewer is color blind, if it ever becomes necessary to use the screen on a monochrome terminal, or if the color fails.

Use colors conservatively.   Only enough colors to achieve the design objective should be used. More colors increase response times, increase the chance of errors due to color confusions, and increase the chance of the "Christmas tree" effect. If two colors serve the need, use two colors. If three colors are needed, of course use three.

For best absolute discrimination, use four to five colors.   The population of measurable colors is about 7.5 million (Geldard, 1953). From this vast number, the eye cannot effectively distinguish many more than a handful. If color discrimination is important, only a small number of colors may be used.

   If absolute color discrimination is necessary (a color must be correctly identified while no other color is in the field of vision), select no more than four to five colors widely spaced along the color spectrum. Selecting widely spaced colors will maximize the probability of their being correctly identified. Good choices are red, yellow, green, blue and white.

   Good two color opponent pairs are red/green and yellow/blue. All of these colors except blue are easy to resolve visually. Be extremely cautious in the use of blue on alphanumeric screens.

For best comparative discrimination, use six to seven colors.   If comparative discrimination is necessary (a color must be correctly identified while other colors are in the field of vision), select no more than six to seven colors widely spaced along the visual spectrum. In addition to red, yellow, green, blue, and white, other acceptable colors would be orange, yellow-green, blue-green, and violet. Again, be cautious in the use of blue on alphanumeric screens.

Use bright colors for emphasis.   The eye is drawn to brighter colors, so use them for the more important screen components. The data itself is the most important component on almost all screens, so it is a good candidate for the brightest color. The brightness of colors, from most to least, is white, yellow, green, blue, and red.

   Keep in mind, however, that under levels of high ambient illumination, colors frequently seem washed out or unsaturated. If some means of light attenuation is not possible, or if characters chosen are not bright enough to counter the illumination, color should be used with caution.

Use contrasting colors to emphasize separation.   To emphasize the separation of screen components, use contrasting colors. Good pairs would be red/green, and blue/yellow.

Use similar colors to convey similarity.   Similar colors indicate a similar meaning. Related elements can be brought together by displaying them in a similar color. Blue and green, for example, are more closely related than red and green.

Use warm colors to indicate actions. The warm colors (longer wavelengths) should be used to signify actions or responses. The cool colors should be used to provide status or background information. Warm colors advance, forcing attention, while cool colors recede or draw away.

Use desaturated or spectrum colors for text. Desaturated or spectrum center colors (yellow and green) will appear brighter to the eye.

Use darker, spectrally extreme colors for backgrounds. To provide adequate contrast with the text or data, spectrally extreme colors such as red, blue, black or magenta make good display backgrounds. Blue is especially good because of the eye's increased sensitivity to it in the periphery. Some other background considerations include the following:

- a neutral background helps set off a full color;
- related screens can be visually grouped by a common background color;
- a background in the complement color of the main image will minimize visual afterimages;
- if dark characters are displayed, use more subtle pastel-like colors for backgrounds.

Use blue or yellow for peripheral viewing. The eye is most sensitive to blue and yellow in its peripheral viewing area.

Conform to human expectancies. Use color meanings that already exist in the user's job or the world at large. They are ingrained in his behavior and difficult to unlearn. A common expectancy is that dealing with status. For example, three common associations are:

$$Red = Stop\ or\ danger$$

$$Amber = Caution$$

$$Green = Go\ or\ normal$$

Order colors by their spectral position. If an ordering of colors is needed, such as high to low, levels of depth, etc., arrange colors by their spectral position. There is evidence that people see the spectral order as a natural one (Fromme, 1983). The spectral ordering is red, orange, yellow, green, blue, indigo, violet and white.

Be consistent in color use. Consistency should exist within a screen, an application, and a set of applications. Changing color meanings will lead to difficulties in interpretation, confusion, and errors. In general, broadly defined meanings (such as red indicating a problem) permit more scope for variations without inconsistency.

Alphanumeric Screens

- Use effective foreground/background combinations (see Table 10.1).
- Use effective character combinations (see Table 10.2).
- Use no more than four colors at one time.

For alphanumeric screen components, colors selected should have adequate visibility, contrast, and physiological harmony.

Use Effective Foreground/Background Combinations

Lalomia and Happ (1987) established effective foreground/background color combinations for the IBM 5153 Color Display. From a color set of 16 different foregrounds and eight different backgrounds, 120 color combinations were evaluated for 1) response time to identify characters, and 2) subjective preferences of users. The results from each measure were ranked and combined to derive an overall measure of color combination effectiveness. The best and poorest color combinations are summarized in Table 10.1. In this table "Best" means the specified combination was in the top 20 percent for overall effectiveness; "Poor" means it was in the bottom 20 percent. Those combinations comprising the "middle" 60 percent are indicated by a dash (–).

The results yield some interesting conclusions:

- The majority of good combinations possess a bright or high intensity color as the foreground color;
- The majority of poor combinations are those with low contrast;
- The best overall color is black;
- The poorest overall color is brown;
- Maximum flexibility and variety in choosing a foreground color exists with black or blue backgrounds (these backgrounds account for almost one/half of the good combinations);
- Brown and green are the poorest background choices.

Use effective character combinations. Smith (1986) has recommended the two- and three-color combinations summarized at the left of Table 10.2 as being effective for dark background screens. She cautions against using the combinations described on the table's right side. She also suggests that light background screens should contain pastel colors with dark characters.

Table 10.1 Effective foreground/background combinations (from Lalomia and Happ, 1987).

FOREGROUND	BACKGROUND							
	BLACK	BLUE	GREEN	CYAN	RED	MAGENTA	BROWN	WHITE
BLACK	x	-	-	Good	-	Good	-	Good
BLUE	-	x	-	-	Poor	-	-	Good
H.I. BLUE	-	-	Poor	Poor	-	-	Poor	Poor
CYAN	Good	-	Poor	x	-	-	Poor	-
H.I. CYAN	Good	Good	-	Good	Good	Good	-	-
GREEN	Good	Good	x	Poor	Good	-	-	Poor
H.I. GREEN	-	Good	-	-	Good	Good	-	-
YELLOW	Good	Good	-	Good	-	-	-	-
RED	-	-	Poor	-	x	Poor	-	-
H.I. RED	-	-	Poor	-	-	x	-	-
MAGENTA	-	-	Poor	-	Poor	Poor	Poor	-
H.I. MAGENTA	Good	-	Good	-	-	-	-	-
BROWN	-	Poor	Poor	-	-	Poor	x	-
GRAY	-	-	-	-	Poor	-	-	-
WHITE	Good	Good	Good	Poor	-	-	Poor	x
H.I. WHITE	Good	-	Good	Good	-	-	-	-

(H.I. = High Intensity)

Table 10.2 Effective two- and three-color combinations for dark background screens from Smith (1986).

TWO COLOR COMBINATIONS

GOOD	POOR
White / Green	Red / Blue
Gold / Cyan	Red / Green
Gold / Green	Red / Purple
Green / Magenta	Red / Yellow
Green / Lavender	Red / Magenta
Cyan / Red	White / Cyan
	White / Yellow
	Blue / Green
	Blue / Purple
	Green / Cyan
	Cyan / Lavender

THREE COLOR COMBINATIONS

GOOD	POOR
White / Gold / Green	Red / Yellow / Green
White / Gold / Blue	Red / Blue / Green
White / Gold / Magenta	Red / Magenta / Blue
White / Red / Cyan	White / Cyan / Yellow
Red / Cyan/ Gold	Green / Cyan / Blue
Cyan / Yellow / Lavender	
Gold / Magenta / Blue	
Gold / Magenta / Green	
Gold / Lavender / Green	

Use no more than four colors at one time. While not experimentally verified, experience indicates that more than four colors are displayed at one time on an alphanumeric screen gives rise to a feeling of "too much." So, while more than four colors may be displayed over a period of time or on a series of screens, do not display more than four colors at one time on a single screen.

GRAPHIC SCREENS

- Use no more than six colors at one time.
- Provide images of an adequate size for the task.
- Surround images:
    - in a neutral color,
    - in a color complementary to main image.
- To give impression of size and weight, use saturated or warm colors.
- For concentration levels, to indicate:
    - high, use saturated colors,
    - low, use desaturated colors.
- For status, to indicate:
    - proper, normal, or OK, use green, white, or blue,
    - caution, use yellow or gold,
    - emergency or abnormal, use red.
- For measurements, to show:
    - grids, use gray.
    - data points, use yellow,
    - variance or error bars, use blue,
    - out of specified range data, use red,
    - labels, use lavender, limegreen, and/or cyan.
- For fine detail, use black, white, and gray.

Use no more than six colors at one time. Experience indicates that displaying more than six colors at one time on graphic screens is "too much."

Provide adequate size images for the task. Smaller images are subject to color distortions. The larger the image, the less likely a distortion will occur.

Provide a proper image surround. A neutral background will help set off a full color. A background in the complementary color of the main image will minimize visual afterimages.

Use saturated or warm colors to give impression of size and weight. Saturated colors appear larger than nonsaturated colors. Warm colors appear larger than cool colors (Tedford et al., 1977).

Concentration levels, status, and measurements.   The colors shown in the guidelines above should be used to achieve the various objectives (Smith, 1986).

Use black, white, and gray for fine detail.   The perception of fine detail will be degraded by color. Black and white work much better.

AVOID DISPLAYING

- Highly saturated, spectrally extreme colors at the same time:
    - red and blue, yellow and purple.
- Colors of equal brightness.
- Colors lacking contrast:
    - for example, yellow and white, black and brown, reds, blues, and browns against a light background.
- Colors in small areas.
- Colors for fine details.
- Text, thin lines, or small shapes in pure blue.
- The periphery of large-scale displays in red and green.
- Color to improve legibility of densely packed text.
- Adjacent colors only differing in the amount of blue they possess.
- Low brightness colors for older viewers.
- Too many colors at one time.

The proper use of color in screen design also suggests some things to avoid.

Highly saturated, spectrally extreme colors at the same time.   Because the eye cannot focus on all colors at the same time, spectrally extreme combinations such as red/blue and yellow/purple can be visually fatiguing.

Colors of equal brightness.   Colors of equal brightness cannot be easily distinguished. A brightness difference must exist between adjacent colors.

Colors lacking contrast.   Colors lacking contrast also cannot be easily distinguished. Examples of colors with poor contrast are yellow/white, black/brown, and red, blue, and brown against a light background.

Colors in small areas.   Distortions may result when color is used in small areas.

Colors for fine details.   Black, gray, and white will provide much better resolution.

Text, thin lines, or small shapes in pure blue. Because the eye cannot resolve blue, text, thin lines, or small shapes in blue will always look fuzzy.

The periphery of large-scale displays in red and green. The eye is not sensitive to red and green in its periphery. Be careful to avoid small images or shapes in this area.

Color to improve legibility of densely packed text. Space lines after about every five rows will work much better than color to improve legibility of densely packed text.

Adjacent colors only differing in the amount of blue they possess. Because of the eye's difficulty in dealing with blue, differences in color based on varying amounts of blue in the color's mixture will not be noticed.

Low brightness colors for older workers. The aging process reduces the amount of light passing through the eye lens. All colors will look less bright, and colors that are dim to begin with may not be legible.

Too many colors at one time. Do not overuse color. Too many colors at one time may make a screen confusing or unpleasant to look at. Use only enough colors to fulfill the needs of the application.

Graphics 11

The visual, spatial, or physical representation of information—as opposed to numeric, alphanumeric, or textual presentation—is known as graphics. Graphic design is the art of conveying visual concepts from a source through a medium to a viewer. In screen design the computer is the source, a visual display terminal is the medium, and the system user is the viewer.

Graphic presentation of information utilizes a person's information processing capabilities much more effectively than other presentation methods. Properly used, it minimizes the necessity for perceptual and mental recoding and reduces short-term memory loads. It also permits faster information transfer between computer and user by permitting more visual comparisons of amounts, trends, or relationships; more compact representation of information; and simplification of the perception of structure. Graphics can also reduce errors, as well as the necessity for training and practice, and has also been shown to enhance problem solving (Polya, 1957) and improve retention (Wertheimer, 1959).

Nevertheless, graphics may not be the best alternative in all situations. Some studies have found textual presentation of information (Shneiderman, 1977, 1982A; Stern, 1984) or tabular display of information (Tufte, 1983) superior to graphics. So, it is the content of the graphic that is critical to its usefulness. The wrong information or a cluttered presentation may actually lead to greater confusion, not less.

There are three types of graphics in screen design: statistical; component relationships, such as flow charts or decision trees; and iconic, the graphical representation of objects or actions.

STATISTICAL GRAPHICS

A well designed statistical graphic display consists of complex ideas communicated with clarity, precision, and efficiency. It gives its viewer the greatest number of ideas, in the shortest time, in the smallest space, and with the least clutter as possible. It will also induce the viewer to think of substance, not techniques or methodology. It will provide coherence to large amounts of information by tying them together in a meaningful way, and it will encourage data comparisons of its different pieces by the eye. A well designed graphic display also avoids data distortions by telling the truth about the data.

Much of this material on statistical graphics is based upon Tufte (1983) and Smith and Mosier (1986).

Utilization

- Reserve for material that is rich, complex, or difficult.

Graphics should be reserved for large data sets with real variability. The power of graphics should not be wasted on simple linear changes or situations where one or two numbers would summarize the result better. Tufte (1983) says that tables usually out-perform graphics on small data sets of 20 or fewer numbers, or when data sets are noncomparative or highly labeled.

Data Presentation

- Emphasize the data.
- Minimize the nondata.
- Minimize redundant data.
- Show data variation, not design variation.
- Provide proper context for data interpretation.
- Restrict the number of information-carrying dimensions depicted to the number of data dimensions being illustrated.
- Employ data in multiple ways, whenever possible.
- Maximize data density.
- Employ simple data coding schemes.
- Avoid unnecessary embellishment:
    - grids,
    - vibration,
    - ornamentation.

The most important part of a graphics display, as with an alphanumeric display, is the data itself.

Emphasize the data, minimize the nondata. A user's attention should be drawn to the measured quantities. The largest share of the graphic's "ink" should present data. Nondata such as elaborate grid lines, gratuitous decoration, and extensive, detailed, and wordy labels draw attention to themselves and hide the data. So, nondata should be minimized or, if possible, eliminated completely.

Minimize redundant data. Redundant data—information that depicts the same number over and over—should also be minimized or eliminated. The height illustrated in figure 11.1, one inch, can be unambiguously established in at least five ways, says Tufte. They are:

1) Height of left line,
2) Height of shading,
3) Height of right line,
4) Position of top horizontal line,
5) Number itself.

Any four of the five ways can be erased and the height still established. These are four more ways than are needed.

Redundancy, on occasion, will be useful, however. It may aid in providing context and order, facilitating comparisons, and creating an aesthetic balance. Use redundancy only if necessary.

Show data variation, not design variation. Each part of a graphic generates visual expectations about its other parts. The expectancies created in one part of a graphic should be fulfilled in other parts so that the viewer does not confuse changes in design with changes in data. Scales should move in regular intervals; proportions should be consistent for all design elements. If the viewer does confuse changes in design with changes in data, ambiguity and deception result.

Figure 11.1. One inch. (From Tufte, 1983)

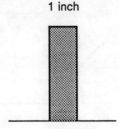

1 inch

Provide the proper context for data interpretation. Graphics often lie by omission. Data for making comparisons or establishing trends must always be included to provide a proper point of reference. "Thin" data must be viewed with suspicion. The graphic in figure 11.2, for example, might have a number of possible interpretations, as illustrated in figure 11.3. All important, possible questions must be foreseen and answered by the graphic.

Figure 11.2. A change between 1982 and 1983 without proper context for interpretation.

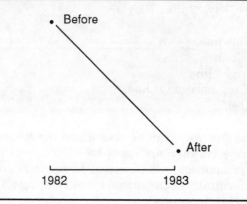

Figure 11.3. Changes between 1982 and 1983 with proper contexts for interpretation.

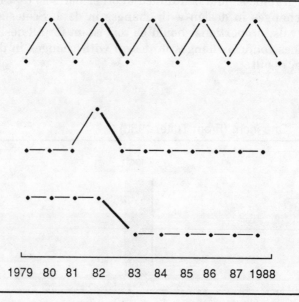

Restrict the number of information-carrying dimensions depicted to the number of data dimensions being illustrated. Displaying one-dimensional data in a multi-dimensional format is perceptually ambiguous. With multi-dimensional data, changes in the physical area on the surface of the graphic do not produce an appropriate proportional change in the perceived area. Examples of multi-dimensional formats to display one-dimensional data would be different sized human bodies to connote populations or different sized automobiles to connote numbers of cars. Often the impression on the viewer is that the change is actually much greater than it really is. This problem can be avoided if the number of information-carrying dimensions on the graphic are restricted to the number of data dimensions being illustrated.

Employ data in multiple ways, whenever possible. Parts of a graph can be designed to serve more than one graphical purpose. A piece of data may at the same time convey information and perform a design function usually left to nondata. A grid to aid readability of a bar chart, instead of being inscribed on the graphic background, may be constructed within the bar itself, as illustrated in figure 11.4.

One part of a graph might show several pieces of data. The size of what is being measured can be conveyed through element size, and the intensity of the measured element can be conveyed through color or level of shading. Population maps, for example, can indicate community size through dot size and population density through intensity of dot shading.

The data itself may also serve as the graph. Figure 11.5, from Ayres (1919) (as described in Tufte, 1983), uses data (a U.S. Army Division numerical designation) to create a graphic that tells: 1) the number of divisions serving

Figure 11.4. Piece of data performing a non-data function (From Tufte, 1983).

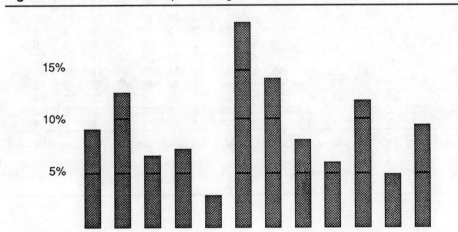

Figure 11.5. U.S. Army Divisions in France in World War I (Ayres, 1919 in Tufte, 1983).

Jun	Jul	Aug	Sep	Oct	Nov	Dec	Jan	Feb	Mar	Apr	May	Jun	Jul	Aug	Sep	Oct
																8
																38
																31
															34	34
															86	86
															84	84
															87	87
														40	40	40
														39	39	39
														88	88	88
														81	81	81
														7	7	7
														85	85	85
													36	36	36	36
													91	91	91	91
													79	79	79	79
													76	76	76	76
												29	29	29	29	29
												37	37	37	37	37
												90	90	90	90	90
												92	92	92	92	92
												89	89	89	89	89
												83	83	83	83	83
												78	78	78	78	78
											80	80	80	80	80	80
											30	30	30	30	30	30
											33	33	33	33	33	33
											6	6	6	6	6	6
											27	27	27	27	27	27
											4	4	4	4	4	4
											28	28	28	28	28	28
											35	35	35	35	35	35
											82	82	82	82	82	82
										77	77	77	77	77	77	77
									3	3	3	3	3	3	3	3
									5	5	5	5	5	5	5	5
								32	32	32	32	32	32	32	32	32
							41	41	41	41	41	41	41	41	41	41
						42	42	42	42	42	42	42	42	42	42	42
		26	26	26	26	26	26	26	26	26	26	26	26	26	26	26
	2	2	2	2	2	2	2	2	2	2	2	2	2	2	2	2
1	1	1	1	1	1	1	1	1	1	1	1	1	1	1	1	1

Jun Jul Aug Sep Oct Nov Dec | Jan Feb Mar Apr May Jun Jul Aug Sep Oct

1917   1918

in France each month for the period shown, 2) what divisions were in France each month, and 3) how long each division stayed in France each month.

Graphics can be designed to have multiple viewing depths. The top level is what is seen from a distance—the overall structure. A population density map of the United States viewed from this level shows patterns of habitation with heavy concentration in some areas and sparse concentration in others. The second level is what is seen up close and in detail. City names may be associated with areas of high population concentration, and population corridors connecting major urban complexes may be identified. The third level is what is seen implicitly, underlying the graphic. Here, the map reveals the effect of landform—mountains, valleys, lakes, and rivers—on population distribution.

Finally, graphics may be designed to have different viewing angles or lines of sight. The Ayres graphic (Figure 11.5) can be viewed from three visual angles. The upward-moving horizon conveys the ever increasing number of American divisions in France in World War I; the vertical identifies which divisions were in France in each month; and the horizontal identifies the length of each division's stay.

The danger in employing data in multiple ways is that it can thus generate graphical puzzles. A sign of a puzzle is that the graphic, instead of being interpreted visually, must be interpreted verbally. Symptoms of a puzzle are frequent references to a legend to interpret what is presented and extensive memorization of design rules before one can comprehend what is presented. By contrast, a well designed multiple function graphic permits a quickly learned, implicit translation of the visual to verbal.

Maximize data density.   In graphics more information is better than less information—the greater the amount of information displayed on a screen, the larger number of visual comparisons can be made, improving comprehension. This is so because the eye can detect large amounts of information in a small space. As mentioned earlier, simple things belong in a table or in the text.

Data density of a screen can be maximized in two ways: enlarging the data matrix, or shrinking the graphic. Enlarging the data matrix involves displaying as much information as possible. If the graphic becomes overcrowded, techniques such as averaging, clustering, smoothing, or providing summaries can reduce the numbers to be displayed. Shrinking the graphic means reducing it in size, but screen resolution may impose limitations on how much shrinking can be performed.

Employ simple data coding schemes.   If visual differentiation in the types of data being displayed is necessary, use simple coding methods in the areas being depicted. Elaborate schemes or patterns can be eye straining (as will be illustrated shortly) and can actually impede the flow of information. Some possible acceptable coding alternatives include:

- Varying densities or shades of gray,
- Labeling with words instead,
- Varying colors.

In using color, the considerations discussed in chapter 10 should be kept in mind.

Avoid unnecessary embellishments.   The pieces of a graphic display must tell the viewer something new. An unnecessary embellishment is information or "chartjunk" that does not add anything new to the meaning of the graphic. It is decoration, or noise, that hinders assimilation of the message the graphic is trying to communicate. Nondata and redundant data are forms of chartjunk. Three other common kinds are vibration, heavy grids, and ornamentation.

Grids.   A grid on a graphic display carries no information, contributes noise, and focuses attention away from the data. An excessively heavy grid can even mask the data.

Grids should be suppressed or eliminated so they do not compete with data. When a grid serves as an aid in reading or extrapolating, it should, of course, be included. Its tendency to overwhelm can be reduced by constructing it with delicate lines or muted colors.

Vibration.   The eye is never absolutely still; it produces continuous, slight tremors that aid visual acuity. The result, when small patterns of lines, boxes, or dots are viewed, is the distracting sensation of vibration or shimmer, a kind of optical art. Examples of this effect can be seen in the patterns in figures 11.6 and 11.7. While eye catching, vibrations also strain the eye. The data coding schemes described above can serve as alternatives to vibration producing symbols.

Ornamentation.   When the quantitative information on a graphic is overwhelmed by decoration, the result is a designer's self-tribute—more effective as a piece of art hung on the wall than as an effective conveyer of information. Ornamentation can take many forms: extensive use of color when it is not necessary, creating multi-dimensional graphics when single-dimensional will do; pointless use of different of vibrating patterns; or forcing data into a graphic when a table would work much better. Ornamentation is really a symptom of "See what I can do with my computer" rather than an effort to provide the system user with the proper data in the most comprehensible way possible. The best graphic display is the simplest graphic display.

Figure 11.6. Examples of patterns creating vibrations. (From Tufte, 1983).

Figure 11.7. Examples of patterns creating vibrations. From professional journals.

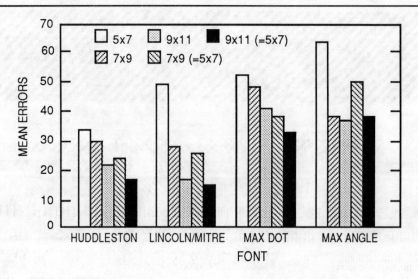

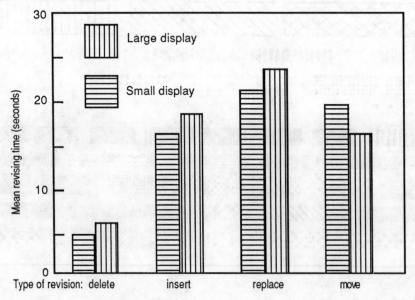

Figure 11.7. *Continued*

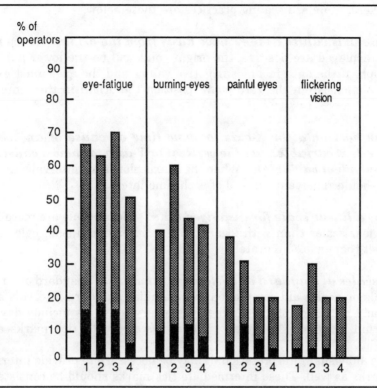

Scaling

- Values on an axis should increase as they move away from the origin.
- Use the horizontal axis (X) to show time or cause of an event (the independent variable).
- Use the vertical axis (Y) to show a caused effect (the dependent variable).
- Employ a linear scale for displayed data.
- Mark scales at standard or customary intervals.
- Start numeric scales at zero (0).
- Display only a single scale on each axis.
- For large data matrices, consider displaying duplicate axes.
- Provide aids for scale interpolation.
- Provide scaling consistency across two or more related displays.
- Clearly label each axis in a left-to-right reading orientation.

Scaling is the positioning of data in relation to the measurement points or markers. Standard scaling practices are those below.

Increase axis values as they move away from the origin. If the numeric values displayed are positive, the origin point will be the lower left point of the graph. If the data includes negative values and the axes must extend in both directions from the zero point, position the origin in the center of the graph.

Use the horizontal or X-axis to show time or cause of an event (the independent variable); use the vertical or Y-axis to show a caused effect (the dependent variable). When the X-axis plots time intervals, the labeled points should represent the end of each time interval.

Employ a linear scale for displayed data. Most people are more familiar with linear scales than with logarithmic or other non-linear scales and will interpret them more accurately.

Mark scales at standard or customary intervals. Standard or customary intervals on scales aid comprehension. Familiar standard intervals are 1, 2, 5, 10, and multiples of 10; familiar customary intervals include days of the week; and months of the year. Construct scales with tick marks at these intervals.
To aid visual interpretation, it may be necessary to provide intermediate tick marks as well. These intermediate tick marks should be consistent with the scale interval shown.

Start numeric scales at zero. Using zero as the starting point on scales aids comparisons. If a zero point is omitted, this omission should be clearly indicated on the display.

Display only a single scale on each axis. Avoid multiple scales associated with a single axis. For all but the most experienced users, multiple scales can be confusing and can lead to interpretation errors. Meanings can also be greatly distorted.
If multiple-scale graphs must be used, permit the user to select any data curve individually and have the computer highlight its corresponding scale.

Display duplicate axes for large data matrices. The readability of large data matrices is improved if the X-axis scale appears at the top as well as the bottom of the graph, and the Y-axis scale at the right as well as the left side.

Provide aids for scale interpretation. Where reading accuracy is extremely critical, provide computer aids for interpretation, such as:

- Displaying a fine grid upon request,
- Vertical and horizontal rules that the user can move to the intersection point.
- Letting the user "point" at a data item and the computer then provide the exact values.

When grid lines are displayed, ensure that they are not confused with data by making them thinner. Also ensure that grid lines do not obscure data elements by positioning them behind depicted data (and thus invisible).

Provide scaling consistency. If comparisons must be made between multiple graphs or charts, use the same scale for each. Data sets that are scaled differently will lead to interpretation errors.

Clearly label each axis. Each scale axis should be clearly labeled in conventional left-to-right reading orientation. A complete description with measurement units should be provided.

Proportion

- Provide accurate proportion of displayed surfaces to data they represent.
- Provide proper proportion by:
    - conforming to data shape,
    - the width being greater than the height.

Provide accurate proportion of displayed surfaces to data they represent. The displayed surfaces on graphics should be directly proportional to the numerical quantities they represent. Failure to do this can create false impressions of magnitudes of differences in sizes or changes. Violations of this principle can be measured by the "lie factor," which is calculated as follows:

$$\text{Lie Factor} = \frac{\text{Size of effect shown in graphic}}{\text{Size of effect in data}}$$

Lie factors equal to 1 accurately represent the underlying numbers. Lie factors more than 1.05 or less than .95 indicate distortion. Most lie factors involve overstating an effect in the graphic, with factors of 2 to 5 being very common. Graphics with lie factors of 50 or more are occasionally seen.

This kind of graphical distortion can be eliminated through clear, detailed, and thorough labeling, to be addressed shortly.

Provide proper proportion. When the relative proportions of a graphic are in balance, it looks better. Graphics should tend toward the horizontal, assuming a greater length than height. There are a number of reasons for this recommendation. First, the eye has greater practice in detecting deviations from a horizon. Second, it is easier to read words arranged left to right rather than stacked one above the other, and a wider horizontal plane aids left-to-right word positioning. Third, many graphics plot cause and effect relationships, with effect on the vertical axis and cause on the horizontal. An elongated horizontal axis helps describe the causal variable in more detail. Fourth, mathematical aesthetic properties exist more for wide than high shapes (see chapter 4). Fifth, visual preferences appear to exist for these same shapes. However, if the data being displayed suggests a graphic shape square or higher than wide, conform to the shape suggested by the data.

Labeling

- Employ clear, detailed, and thorough labeling.
- Maintain a left-to-right reading orientation.
- Integrate labeling with drawing.

The labeling principles for graphic screens should follow the principles outlined for alphanumeric screens.

Employ clear, detailed, and thorough labeling. Words should be fully spelled out. Both upper- and lowercase should be used: with lowercase for textual information. Use the simplest and shortest forms of words possible.

Maintain a left-to-right reading orientation. Display all labels horizontally. Avoid words that are organized vertically or words that run in different directions. Whereas nonhorizontal words on hard copy graphics can be read by turning the paper, this is impossible on a screen.

Integrate words and numbers with drawing. Explanations on graphics help the viewer and should be incorporated as much as possible. Words are data, and they can occupy space freed up by eliminating nondata or redundant data. Integrating words and captions with the graphic eliminates the need for a legend and the eye movements back and forth required to read it. Also, incorporate messages to explain the data, and label interesting or important data points. Pictures and words used together aid comprehension.

Using the same type style for graphics and text aids the visual integration of the two. Do not use ruled lines to separate them.

Curves and Line Graphs

- Display data curves or lines that must be compared in a single graph.
- Display no more than four to five curves or lines in a single graph.
- Identify each curve or line with an adjacent label whenever possible.
- If a legend must be included, order the legend to match the spatial ordering of the curves or lines.
- For tightly packed curves or lines, provide data differentiation through a line coding technique such as different colors or line types.
- Highlight curves or lines representing important or critical data.
- When comparing actual to projected data:
    - use solid curves or lines for actual data,
    - use broken curves or lines for projected data.
- Display a reference index if displayed data must be compared to a standard or critical value.
- Display differences between two data sets as a curve or line itself.

Curves and line graphs can be used to show relations between sets of data defined by two continuous variables. They are especially useful for showing data changes over time, being superior to other graphic methods for speed and accuracy in interpreting data trends. With a "curve" the data relations are summarized by a smoothed line. With a "line" the data plots are connected by straight line segments. This kind of graph implies a continuous function. If the data point elements are discrete, it is better to use a bar graph.

Display data to be compared in one graph.   If several curves must be compared, display them in one combined graph to facilitate the comparisons.

Display no more than four to five curves or lines in one graph.   As more curves or lines are added to a graph, visual discrimination among them becomes more difficult. The maximum number of lines should be limited. If one particular line or curve must be compared with several others, consider multiple graphs where the line of interest is compared separately with each other line.

Identify each curve or line with an adjacent label.   A label associated with each curve or line is preferable to a separate legend. If direct labeling is impossible due to the "tightness" of the lines, a legend may be the only alternative. If a legend is used, visually differentiate the lines (colors, line types, etc.) and include the coding scheme in the legend.

Order legends to match the spatial ordering of the curves or lines.   If the legends are to be used with a series of graphs, however, maintain one consistent order for the legends on all the graphs.

For tightly packed curves or lines, use a coding technique for line differentiation. Common coding techniques include different colors and line types. Do not exceed the maximum number of alternatives for the coding technique selected, as shown in Figure 11.8. If color coding is used, choose colors on the basis of the considerations described in chapter 10. Line width and dot size coding should be avoided because of their similarity to grids and scatterplot data points. If a series of related graphs are line coded, be consistent in the selection of techniques for corresponding data.

Highlight important or critical data. If one curve or line in a multiple line graph is of particular significance, highlight that curve (high intensity, different color, etc.) to call attention to it. The coding scheme selected should be different from that selected for spatial differentiation.

Actual vs. projected data. Use solid curves or lines for actual data; use broken curves or lines for projected data.

Display reference indexes if necessary. When a curve or line must be compared to some standard or critical value, display a reference curve or line reflecting that value.

Directly display differences. If the difference between two sets of data must be determined, display the difference itself as a separate curve or line. This is preferable to requiring the user to visually compare the two values and calculate the difference between them.

If the difference between the related curves is of interest, consider a band chart where both lines or curves are displayed and the area between them coded through texture, shading, or color.

Surface Charts

- Order the data categories so that:
  - the least variable is at the bottom,
  - the most variable is at the top.
- Use different texture or shading coding schemes to differentiate the areas below each curve or line.
- Incorporate labels within the bands of data, if possible.

If the data being depicted by a curve or line represents all the parts of a whole, consider developing a surface chart. In this kind of graph the curves or lines are stacked above one another to indicate aggregated amounts, and the area between each curve or line is differentially coded, usually by textures or shadings. A surface chart is similar to a segmented bar chart.

*Order data categories to show least variable at bottom and most vari-
able at top.* Irregularities in the bottom curve or line will affect those above
it. This can make it difficult for a user to determine whether the irregularity
in the upper curves reflects "real" data differences or is the result of this style
of graph. Displaying least variable data at the bottom will minimize this effect.
If the data itself implies that some logical organization must be followed, and
the resulting organization creates confusing distortions in the curves, this
method should not be used.

Use different texture or shading coding schemes. Ensure that the coding
scheme chosen for each area is visually distinguishable from all others.

Incorporate labels within the bands of data. Labels with left-to-right
reading orientation should be included within the textured or shaded bands,
if possible. Legends should only be incorporated where space constraints exist
within the bands.

Scatterplots

- Limit use to two-dimensional displays of data.
- Visually distinguish points of particular significance through a highlighting
  technique.

Scatterplots can be used to show relationships among individual data
points in a two-dimensional array. Three-dimensional scatterplots, while possible, do not yield clear, unambiguous displays. Points of particular significance
on scatterplots can be made distinctive through highlighting techniques such
as high intensity, different colors, or different shapes. Correlations and trends
on scatterplots can be indicated by the superimposition of curves (thus combining with the scatterplot another kind of graphic display).

Bar Graphs

- Orient bars consistently, either horizontally or vertically.
- Make the spacing between bars less than the bar width.
- If different bars must be easily distinguished, provide differentiation through
  a coding technique.
- Highlight bars representing important or critical data.
- Provide a consistent ordering to related groups of bars.
- Display a reference index if displayed data must be compared to a standard
  or critical value.
- Identify each bar with an adjacent label.

- When a great many pieces of data must be compared, consider using histograms or step charts.

Bar graphs can be used to show differences between separate entities or to show differences in a variable at discrete intervals. Bar graphs may extend from a common origin or baseline, or they may extend between separately plotted high and low points.

Orient bars consistently. Bars may be oriented either horizontally or vertically. A consistent orientation should be maintained for bars displaying similar information. In general, frequency counts are displayed in vertical bars, and time durations in horizontal bars.

Space bars for ease of visual comparison. Comparison of bars should be accomplishable without eye movement. Generally, the spacing between bars should be less than the bar width. If many bars are to be displayed, the alternating pattern of bright and dark bands that results can be visually disturbing to some viewers. In this case it is better to completely eliminate the spacing between bars (The graph is then called a Histogram).

Visually distinguish different groups of bars. If different groups of bars must be easily distinguished, provide differentiation through a coding technique such as color, texture, or shading.

Highlight important or critical data. If one bar represents data of unusual significance, call attention to that bar through a different coding technique.

Consistently order related groups of bars. Related groups of bars should be ordered in a consistent manner.

Display reference indexes if necessary. When bars must be compared to some standard or critical value, display a reference line to aid that comparison.

Identify each bar with an adjacent label. A label associated with each bar, in left-to-right reading orientation, is preferable to a separate legend. If groups of bars are repeated, it is only necessary to label one group rather than all bars in all groups.

Consider histograms or step charts when a great many pieces of data must be compared. Histograms or step charts are bar graphs without spaces between the bars.

Segmented or Stacked Bars

- Order the data categories in the same sequence.
- Order the data categories so that:
  - the least variable is at the bottom,
  - the most variable is at the top.
- Use different texture or shading coding schemes to differentiate the areas within each bar.
- Clearly associate labels with bars and segments.

If both the total measures and the portions represented by segments are of interest, consider segmented or stacked bars. This kind of graph is similar to a surface chart.

Order the data categories in the same sequence. To provide consistency, order the data categories in the same sequence.

Order data categories to show least variable at bottom and most variable at top. Irregularities in the bottom segment will affect those above it. This can make it difficult for a user to determine whether the irregularity in the upper segments reflects "real" data differences or is the result of this style of graph. Displaying least variable data at the bottom will minimize this effect. If the data itself implies that some logical organization must be followed, this logical organization should be followed.

Use different texture or shading coding schemes. Ensure that the coding scheme chosen for each segment is visually distinguishable from all others.

Associate labels with bars and segments. Labels, with a left-to-right reading orientation, are preferable to legends. Legends should only be used if space does not allow labels.

Pie Charts

- Pie charts should be used with caution.
- If pie charts are used:
  - use five segments or less;
  - directly label each segment in the normal orientation for reading;
  - include numbers with the segment labels to indicate percentages or absolute values;
  - highlight segments requiring particular emphasis through a contrasting display technique or by "exploding" it.

Pie charts can be used to show an apportionment of a total into its component parts. Bar graphs, however, usually permit more accurate estimates of proportions.

Use pie charts with caution.   Experts caution against the use of pie charts because:

- they provide no means of absolute measurement,
- they cannot represent totals greater than 100 percent,
- they can only represent a fixed point in time,
- human estimation of relationships is more accurate with linear than with angular representations.

If pie charts are used, the guidelines below should be followed.

Use five segments or less.   To minimize confusion, provide adequate differentiation of pieces and permit accurate labeling.

Directly label each segment in the normal reading orientation.   To provide maximum association of label with data and for reading clarity, use a left-to-right reading orientation.

Include numbers with the segment labels to indicate percentages or absolute values.   Only by including numbers with segment labels can numeric values be accurately established.

Highlight segments requiring emphasis.   Use a contrasting display technique or "explode" segments requiring emphasis by displacing them slightly from the remainder of the pie.

FLOWCHARTS

- Displayed steps should be designed to:
  - follow some logical order, or
  - minimize path length.
- Orient following common reading conventions such as left to right or top to bottom.
- Follow common flowchart coding conventions to distinguish elements.
- Use arrows in conventional ways to indicate directional relationships.
- Highlight elements requiring particular attention through a contrasting display technique.
- Require only one decision at each step.
- Display options to be considered in a logical order.
- Be consistent in all option ordering and wording.

If the data to be displayed flows in a complex, yet sequential, process, consider using a flowchart to schematically represent it. Flowcharts can also be used to aid problem solving in which a solution can be reached by answering a series of questions. They are not useful when tradeoffs must be made.

Order steps logically or to minimize path length. One logical ordering scheme is to follow a sequence of operations or processes from start to finish. Other potential ordering schemes include placing the most important decisions first or the decisions that can be made with the most certainty. If no logical order is apparent, order the flowchart to minimize the length of the path through it. If some decision paths are more likely to occur than others, minimize the length of the most likely path.

Orient for conventional reading. Follow a left-to-right and top-to-bottom orientation.

Follow common coding conventions to distinguish elements. Follow existing shape coding conventions for the kinds of "boxes" being displayed. Adhere to standards and user expectations.

Use arrows in conventional ways. Use arrows to indicate directional relations and sequential links.

Highlight elements requiring particular attention. Contrasting display techniques, such as high intensity or color, should be used to call attention to relevant paths or elements. Color is particularly effective in this regard.

Require only one decision at each step. Multiple decisions reduce flowchart size. But requiring multiple decisions such as "Is A true and B false?" can be confusing. Require that only single decisions be made.

Display options to be considered in a logical order. Use orders that are natural, sequenced numerically, or meaningful.

Consistently order and word all choices. Consistency always aids learning.

ICONS

The symbolic representation of objects, such as office tools or storage locations, and optional actions on a screen began with XEROX's STAR, continued with Apple's LISA and MACINTOSH, and has been building ever since. The reasoning behind icon development has been the same reasoning behind graphics generally—more effective use of human information processing capabilities and reduction in short term memory loads—as described at the beginning of this chapter. This reasoning has been bolstered by a small body of research that has found, for example, that symbols are recognized faster and more accurately than text (Ells and Dewar, 1979), that they are effective in conveying simple instructions (Dickey and Schneider, 1971), and that they can be easily learned (Walker et al., 1965).

This body of "positive" symbol research is now being confronted by some studies finding that symbolic representation of information may not necessarily be better, and in some cases may be worse than textual or alphanumeric displays. Examples of this research include Stern (1984), who found that graphic instructions on an automated bank teller machine were inferior to textual instructions; Remington and Williams (1986), who found that numeric symbols elicited faster responses than graphic symbols in a visual search task; Cairney and Sless (1982) and Zwaga and Boersema (1983), who found that some current or proposed symbols were not very effective, and Brems and Whitten (1987), who found that users preferred a "command name" interface over an iconic interface. The conclusion based upon the research, and what experience has shown, is that some concepts are very hard to convey symbolically, that the content of a graphic representation is a critical determinant of its effectiveness, that the success of a "symbolic" system depends upon the skill of a designer in choosing effective icons, and user preferences should be considered.

The usability of icons is dependent on the following factors:

Familiarity.   How familiar is the object being depicted? Familiarity will reduce learning time (Carroll and White, 1973; Wingfield, 1968). How familiar are the commonly seen icons in figure 11.8? Lack of familiarity requires learning the icon's meaning. Many unfamiliar icons require a great deal of learning.

Experience makes words and numbers often more familiar to a person than symbols. Confusion matrices have been developed through extensive research for alphanumeric data (0 versus O, 1 versus I). Graphic symbols may be more visually similar.

Directness of link.   How "sign-like" is the icon; how well does it convey its intended meaning? For concrete objects and actions direct links are more easily established. Adjectives, adverbs, conjunctions, and prepositions can cause problems, however. Also, how does one easily convey concepts like bigger, smaller, wider, or narrower?

Context.   The context of a symbol may change its meaning. Does the "rabbit" symbol illustrated in figure 11.8, if seen on a road sign in a national park, mean "go faster"?

Complexity.   The more abstract or complex the symbol, the more difficult it is to extract or interpret what is its meaning. In the 1984 Stern study the more concrete graphic messages were easier to comprehend than the more abstract.

Figure 11.8.   Some common icons. What do they stand for? (From Micro Switch, 1984) See page **243** for the answers.

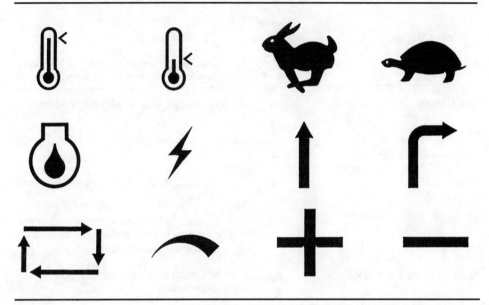

Expectancies.   The symbol may be comprehended, but a false conclusion may be reached about the desired action because of an incorrect expectancy. Bailey (1984) reported that a study of international road signs found that 8 percent of all drivers never saw the "slash" through the symbol on a road sign, which indicates "do not" do the pictured action. Their expectancy was that they could do it.

Efficiency.   A graphics screen may be less efficient, consuming more screen display space than a word or requiring more physical actions by the user. A telephone directory of 50 names and numbers listed on an alphanumeric screen may consume the same screen space required for 15 file cards. Raising an arm or moving a "mouse" may be slower than simply typing.

Discriminability.   Symbols chosen must be visually distinguishable from other symbols. A person's powers of differentiation for shapes and other forms of codes have been experimentally determined over the years. The maximum number of codes for effective human differentiation, including geometric shapes, are summarized in figure 11.9. A person's ability to discriminate alphabetic or alphanumeric information is much more potent.

Figure 11.9. Maximum number of codes for effective human differentiation.

Encoding Method	Recommended Maximum	Comments
Size	3	Considerable space required; location time longer than for colors and shapes.
Line Length	3–4	Will clutter display with many signals.
Line width	2–3	
Solid and broken lines	3–4	
Brightness	2–3	Creates problems on screens with poor contrast.
Flashing	2–3	Confusing for general encoding but the best way to attract attention; interacts poorly with other codes.
Number of dots or marks	5	Minimum number best for quick assimilation.
Geometric shapes	10	High mnemonic value.
Color	6–8	No extra space required; short location time.
Orientation (location on display surface)	4–8	

Data derived from Martin 1973, and Barmack and Sinaiko 1966.

The impact on the user of a poorly designed iconic screen is similar to that of a poorly designed alphanumeric screen: excessive learning, confusion, information overload, and possible rejection. New techniques may still result in old problems. Research, and experience, leads to the following design guidelines.

Icons

- Use for familiar objects and actions.
- Clearly and simply reflect objects represented.
- Conform to standards, where they exist.
- Keep number of symbols to under 20, preferably under 12.
- Test for behavioral expectations.
- Incorporate alphanumeric labels for confusing symbols.

Use for familiar objects and actions.   Shneiderman (1987) suggests that simple metaphors, analogies, or models with a minimal set of concepts is the best place to start in developing icons. He also suggests that mixing metaphors from two or more sources should be avoided, and that an inviting emotional tone should be established. A sewage disposal system would be an inappropriate metaphor for an electronic mail system wastebasket.

Clearly and simply reflect objects represented.   Avoid ornamentation. Use simple, clean lines.

Conform to standards, if they exist.   Many symbols have already been established by the International Standards Organization (ISO) and other organizations. Consult all relevant reference books before inventing new symbols or modifying existing ones.

Keep the number of symbols to under 20, preferably under 12.   Restricting the size of the symbol set will aid symbol differentiation.

Test for behavioral expectations.   Choosing the right objects and actions, and the symbols to represent them, will not be easy. So, as in alphanumeric screen design, adequate testing, and possible refinement of developed symbols, should be built into the design process.

Incorporate alphanumeric labels for confusing symbols.   The ability to comprehend confusing symbols can be greatly improved by adding alphanumeric labels to the symbols. Add labels or captions whenever necessary.

In conclusion, graphic screens, like alphanumeric screens, always improve as they are designed, edited, tested, and refined. This process should be built into the design cycle to achieve a most usable, and visually pleasing, final product.

The icons depicted in figure 11.8 have the following meanings (reading from left to right):

Hot	Turn
Cold	Automatic
Fast	Variable Regulation
Slow	(Increase/decrease)
Engine Oil	Plus/Positive
Ammeter/Generator	Minus/Negative
Straight	

Source Documents 12

A well-designed source document will

- Produce manual subsystem processing times.
- Permit the user to perform rapid
  - coding,
  - use of coded data,
  - data entry.
- Reduce errors
  - made in coding,
  - made in data interpretation,
  - stored in the system data base.

Ideally, the development of data entry screens is accomplished in conjunction with that of the source documents from which data is keyed. The system development effort which permits joint screen and document development usually yields the most effective human-machine data entry interface.

The screen designer should also, ideally, be the person who develops the source documents, since occasional design tradeoffs affecting both documents and screens must be performed. A designer who fully understands both components is in the best position to make the necessary judgments.

In this chapter a series of design guidelines is presented to enable a screen designer to develop a source document of sufficient detail for presentation to an organization's Form Design department. The focus is on document organization and style, and the desired product is a hand-printed draft from which a Form Design department can create the final printed version.

GENERAL DESIGN CRITERIA

- A well-designed source document meets the following criteria:
    - It reflects the needs and idiosyncracies of its human users;
    - It allows hand, typed, or hand/typed completion;
    - It permits development of associated screen formats in its image;
    - It is economical regarding composition, paper, and printing within utilization ease limits;
    - It is consistent within itself, within related forms, within an application, and within an organization.

A well designed source document, like a well designed screen format, must meet certain broad criteria, as outlined above. In the pages that follow, guidelines for achieving these criteria are described. One important caution, however: document economy is a desirable design goal but only within human ease of use limits. Too often documents and forms are developed with composition economy as the dominant design factor. Since various analyses show that form handling costs are about 100 times their composition and printing costs, this is a false economy. The most important design objective must be utilization ease.

SOURCE DOCUMENT DESIGN CONSIDERATIONS

The guidelines begin with a brief discussion of the philosophy that data should be collected at its source. Following a reiteration of the importance of design consistency is a general review of the alternative document design concepts available. Then an extensive series of document design guidelines are presented.

Source Data Collection

- Collect data at its source.
- Use the data collection vehicle as the source document for data entry.
- Never require transcription of data from one document to another.

Data transcription is an error-prone process. Any time a data transcription occurs the chance of errors being introduced into a data base is increased.

Galitz (1973) surveyed a sample of insurance agents regarding their attitude toward a source document (an application form) that, while imposing completion constraints, became the vehicle from which data entry keying was performed. A large majority (85 percent) said they would complete the document. More than one-half (53 percent) said they would complete the document even if it took half again as long to complete as the existing form. These agents realized the personal advantages to be gained by improving the quality of data reaching the system data base.

Design Consistency

---

* Incorporate and use documents developed following a single design philosophy.

The larger the number of different documents that must be processed, the slower will be the overall data entry rate. Each dissimilar document to be keyed necessitates a certain amount of operator learning. The more similar the documents, the faster the learning. Significant differences between documents can impair data entry rates on all documents, as rules, formats, and handling requirements negatively impact one another.

This effect is minimized if a wide variety of source documents are developed according to the same standards. Processing in batches also has a positive effect on overall data entry rate, but this is usually not under control of the designer and is not usually a design consideration.

Alternative Source Document Design Concepts

---

* Caption preceding fill-in area.
* Caption within fill-in area.
* Caption above fill-in area (floating box).

The most common source document design concepts, illustrated in figure 12.1, find the caption preceding, within, or above the fill-in area. Most currently available forms utilize one of these techniques. For source document design purposes, the first alternative, caption preceding fill-in area, can be readily eliminated as a viable method. Among its deficiencies are inefficient use of screens in matching a source document and poor visibility of fill-in fields.

The acceptable alternatives are the latter two: captions within and above fill-in areas. Table 12.1 provides a general comparison of these design alternatives by a number of factors. The recommended approach to source document design is the caption-above or floating box approach. Among its advantages are that it minimizes the visibility of irrelevant information, provides the best visibility of fill-in data (white boxes are generally imposed on a light-colored background), and fosters ease in keeping one's place in a document through built-in perceived visual rulers. This method also provides the best "perceptual

Figure 12.1 A, B, and C   Alternative Source Document Design Concepts

A   Caption Preceding Fill-In Area:

Description and No. of messengers _____

Average amount each: Money $ _____ Securities $ _____ Checks $ _____

Merchandise $ _____

Type of conveyances used _____

Average daily receipts plus bank: Money $ _____ Securities $ _____

Checks $ _____ How often are bank deposits made? _____

Payroll Money $ _____ Checks $ _____ How often? _____

No. of employees on duty in premises _____ Guards _____ No. guards _____

Holdup alarm _____ Hours of business _____

Are checks cashed? _____ How much extra cash is brought in? $ _____

Are all checks listed? _____

Public sale of: Travelers Checks $ _____ Money Orders $ _____ Others $ _____

Exposures within the Banking Premises: Amount of Money $ _____ Securities $ _____ contained within

a leased safe deposit box or boxes or Securities $ _____ held by a bank for safekeeping in any Banking Premises

or similar recognized places of safe deposit, at _____

_____

(STREET AND NUMBER)   (CITY OR TOWN)   (COUNTY)   (NAME OF BANK)   (STATE)

B Caption Within Fill-In Area:

INSURED INFORMATION

Insured			Business of Insured

Insured is:
- [ ] Individual
- [ ] Corporation
- [ ] Joint Venture
- [ ] Partnership
- [ ] Other:

Address		State	Zip Code

County		Name and Telephone Number of Person to Contact for Loss Control Survey

Mortgagee	Item No.(s)	Previous Carrier(s) & Policy Number(s)

Address		State	Zip Code

C Caption Above Fill-In Area (Floating Box):

3. RESIDENCE AND INSURED INFORMATION ▼

INSURED NAME (last, first, middle initial)

STREET ADDRESS (MAILING)

CITY   STATE   ZIP CODE

INSURED PREMISES OTHER THAN MAILING ADDRESS
[ ] Y Yes
▲ If yes, be sure to complete Premise Address

RESIDENCE TELEPHONE NUMBER
(Area)

INSURED BIRTH DATE
MO   DAY   YEAR

MARITAL STATUS
[ ] M Married   [ ] S Single   If Married ▲

SPOUSE EMPLOYED
[ ] Y Yes   [ ] N No

INSURED OCCUPATION   SPOUSE OCCUPATION

PREMISES ADDRESS (If other than mailing)

CITY   STATE   ZIP CODE

COUNTY IN WHICH INSURED PREMISES LOCATED

PROPERTY LEGAL DESCRIPTION ATTACHED
(If Required)
[ ] Y Yes

249

Table 12.1 The most common document design concepts.

Caption Within Fill-In Area	Floating Box Design
Coding Factors	
• Sufficient writing space • Permits hand or typed entry • Permits clearly stated captions • Clear Association—captions to fill-in data	• Sufficient writing space • Permits hand or typed data • Permits clearly stated captions • Clear Association—captions to fill-in data • Easy to achieve consistent size writing space • Best visibility of fill-in area • Easy to incorporate coding aids • Easy to minimize visibility of irrelevant information
Processing Factors	
• Fill-in data readable	• Fill-in data readable • Best visibility of fill-in area
Data Entry Factors	
• Fill-in data readable • Screen fields easily associated with form captions	• Fill-in data readable • Screen fields easily associated with form captions • Form/screen relationship easily maintained • Best visibility of fill-in data • Easy to minimize irrelevant information • Perceptual ease in keeping place on form
Composition and Economy Factors	
• Sometimes more efficient use of form space	• Usually more efficient use of screens • Easiest to conform to screen design guidelines

match" between document and screen. The floating boxes are easily identifiable as separate entities and can be most easily associated with fields on a screen.

Sless (1987), in evaluating the floating box form, found that it helps both those coding the form and those processing the information contained on the form. The areas where answers go are obvious, how much work is involved in filling out the form can be ascertained by a glance, and checking for verification that all fields are completed is made easier. Information can also be retrieved easier with this style form.

Sless also uncovered a particular problem with the Caption Within Fill-In Area forms. In many cases people filling out this style form began to write the required data after the captions instead of at the beginning of the boxes. As a result, the space available for writing wasn't used.

The primary disadvantages of this approach are its newness and its frequent association with computers. Some resistance to forms like this has been caused by these factors. Form users, however, have shown a willingness to use self-coding source documents when they perceive the benefits (Galitz, 1973). These kinds of documents have been successfully used in some information systems for 15 to 20 years.

In the guidelines that follow, both the caption-above and floating box concepts will be addressed. The document designers should "test the water" in their own organizations to ascertain what document design standards do exist and what potential feelings toward the floating box approach might be. Where no severe roadblocks are encountered (or where confrontation of existing roadblocks may be desired), the floating box method is suggested.

SOURCE DOCUMENT PHYSICAL CHARACTERISTICS

Most of a source document's physical characteristics are specified by an organization's Form Design department. The following concepts are presented to familiarize the source document designer with the variables that must be considered, and to provide background for discussions with that department. The designer will find that greater care exercised in the specification of all document requirements will usually yield the desired product much more quickly.

Source Document Physical Characteristics

Size

- 8½″ × 11″.
- 8½″ × 7″.
- 8½″ × 5½″.

Margins

- At least ⅓″ on all sides.

Type Style

- Clear, simple styles such as Univers or Helvetica.

Type Size

- A minimum of 5 points for captions and check box codes. Section headings and form title should be larger, possibly 10 to 14 points.

Line Rules

- Utilize line rules of varying widths to identify major document components. For example,
  - section divisions—heavy lines,
  - subsection divisions—medium lines,
  - fill-in fields—light lines.

Turns

- Utilize the book-turn method for documents printed on both sides.

Colors

- Paper:
  - white or yellow.
- Titles, headings, captions, and codes:
  - black ink.
- Rules:
  - basic color or black ink.
- Background (floating box approach):
  - basic colors screened at about 30 percent.

Source document design can be accomplished simply by choosing a standard form size (such as 8½″ × 11″) and laying out fields and information within a ⅓-inch margin on all sides. Depending on printing requirements, exact margin requirements may vary slightly from this recommendation, but this approximation will permit Form Design to easily make any necessary adjustments.

Type style and size and line rules will ultimately be selected by the Form Design department in light of organization standards and legibility requirements. The document designer should feel free to make recommendations, however.

Turns refer to the method by which documents printed on both sides are turned over. "Book turn" means printing the front and back side of source documents head to head (with the top of each side back to back on the page). The paper is then turned, as the page of a book is turned. This is contrasted to the "tumble turn," where the top of the backside of a document is opposite and bottom of the front side. Turning requires grasping the bottom of the page and flipping it to the top as the page is turned. The most important point is not whether a document requires book- or tumble-turning, but that one consistent method is chosen. Confusion and frustration can result if a mix of documents requires turning by the different methods.

Color is a vital ingredient of forms developed with the floating box method. Best legibility is usually obtained if all alphanumerics (title, headings, captions, and codes) are printed in black ink and the document background is a basic color screened at about 30 percent. Some colors, if used for alphanumerics, may provide adequate contrast with the background, but these should be carefully selected.

DOCUMENT ORGANIZATION

- Provide clear design and clean reproduction by using perceptual groupings.
- Arrange information according to an acceptable combination of:
    - sequence of use,
    - frequency of use,
    - function,
    - importance.
- Use orderly and logical data sequence (top to bottom, left to right).
- Permit development of a screen format that is an exact image of the form.
- Minimize irrelevant information.

People's reactions to a form, like a screen, will be influenced by their first perceptions. The form may be perceived as cluttered, busy, and confusing, or conversely, meaningful and with evident purpose. The former is most often the result of trying to jam too much within its boundaries. The latter can only occur through plentiful use of "white space" and segmentation into logical pieces.

It is very important that source document design occur within constraints imposed by the physical limitations of the screens to which they are related. The design of the source document must permit development of a screen, or screens, in its exact image. The design of the source document must be the controlling factor, as this data collection vehicle must make sense to the person who is filling it out. Experience has shown that the standard 8½-inch form width is usually the primary constraining factor in developing a source document and related screen. That is, one usually runs out of space on the form before one runs out of space on a typical 80-column-wide screen (while using the methods described in this book).

Information arrangement on source documents should be based on sequence and frequency of use, function, and importance—principles described earlier.

To reiterate:

Sequence of use grouping involves arranging information items in the order in which they are commonly received or transmitted, or in natural groups. A person's address, for example, is normally given by street, city, state, and zip code. Another example of natural grouping is the league standings of football teams, which appear in order of best to worst records.

Frequency of use is a design technique based on the principle that information items used most frequently should be grouped at the beginning of the form. The second-most frequently used items are grouped next, and so forth.

Function involves grouping information items according to their purpose. All items pertaining to insurance coverage, for example, may be placed in one location. Such grouping also allows convenient group identification for both preparer and user.

Importance grouping is based on the information's importance to the task being performed. Important items are placed in the most prominent positions.

Source document design normally reflects a combination of these techniques. Information may be organized functionally, but within each function individual items may be arranged by sequence or importance. Numerous permutations are possible.

SOURCE DOCUMENT CONTENT

Captions

- Provide intelligent and clearly stated captions.
- Spell out fully using words meaningful to the form coder.
- Clearly associate captions with fill-in areas.

Floating Box

- Center caption above fill-in area.

Caption

- If fill-in area is excessively long, position caption above upper-left corner.

Caption

- For columnar-oriented multiple fields, center caption above topmost fill-in area.

Caption

Caption Within Fill-In Area

- Position caption in upper left-hand corner.

Caption

- For columnar-oriented multiple fill-in areas center caption above topmost fill-in area separated by a line.

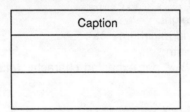

Caption

- Do not mix methods on one document or family of documents.

Captions must clearly communicate to the form coder what data or information must be placed in a fill-in field. Which fill-in field should receive the data or information must also be obvious. These simple rules are often violated in the design of forms. How often have you found yourself encoding the wrong information, or putting it in the wrong place? The rules described above, for the alternative design methods, are intended to eliminate the chances of these errors occurring.

Fill-In Areas

- Maximize visibility of fill-in areas.
- Provide sufficient writing space.
- Develop for completion by handwriting, typewriter, or both, as necessary.

FLOATING BOX

Hand Only Composition

- Vertical spacing:
  Multiples of 1/6″;
- Fill-in area height:
  Optimally—1/3″;
  Minimally—1/5″;
- Fill-in area width:
  Optimally—1/4″ per expected character;
  Minimally—1/6″ per expected character.

Typewriter Only Completion

- Vertical spacing:
  Multiples of 1/6″;
- Fill-in area height:
  Optimum and minimum—1/5″;
- Fill-in area width:
  Minimally—1/10″ per expected character (plus an additional 1/10″ per field).

Hand or Typewriter Completion

- Vertical spacing:
  Multiples of 1/6″;
- Fill-in area height:
  Optimum and minimum—1/5″;
- Fill-in area width:
  Optimally—1/5″ per expected character;
  Minimally—1/6″ per expected character.

CAPTION WITHIN FILL-IN AREA

Hand Only Completion

- Vertical spacing:
  Multiples of 1/6″;
- Fill-in area height:
  Optimally—1/2″;
  Minimally—1/3″;

– Fill-in area width:
Optimally—at least ¼″ per expected character;
Minimally—at least ⅛″ per expected character.

Typewriter Only Completion

– Vertical spacing:
Multiples of ⅙″;
– Fill-in area height:
Optimum and minimum—⅓″;
– Fill-in area width:
Minimally—¹⁄₁₀″ per expected character (plus an additional ¹⁄₁₀″ per field).

Hand or Typewriter Completion

– vertical spacing:
multiples of ⅙″;
– fill-in area height:
optimum and minimum—⅓″;
– fill-in area width:
optimally—at least ⅕″ per expected character;
minimally—at least ⅛″ per expected character.

Some source documents are always completed by hand, others by hand or typewriter. Some are always completed by typewriter. The method of completion is the driving factor in establishing field sizes and spacing. The guidelines summarized above provide optimums and minimums for the various alternatives. The optimums are always recommended, the minimums only if absolutely necessary. The requirements described can be illustrated as follows:

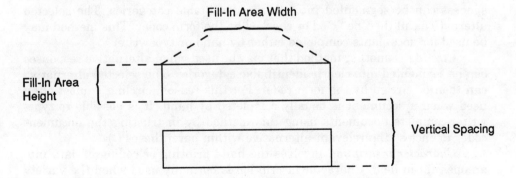

Many forms lack sufficient writing space for encoding information. Information legibility can be severely impaired if the size of fill-in areas is reduced to squeeze too many elements onto one piece of paper. In a study by a large insurance company (Galitz, 1973), adequate spacing for form completion or encoding was ranked by insurance agents as the most important factor in simplifying forms.

Coding Techniques—Alternatives

Ballot Box Checking

- Should be used when the required responses can be segmented into clearly identifiable categories.
- May be used for hand or typewriter completed documents.
- Do not exceed six or seven alternatives for a field.

Circling

- Should be used when the required responses can be segmented into clearly identifiable categories.
- Use only for hand completed documents.
- Do not exceed six or seven alternatives per field.

Character Inscription

- Should be used when the variety of information to be coded is too great to be categorized.
- May be used for hand or typewriter completed documents.

Coding is the process by which data is manually written or typed into a fill-in field. It is most commonly accomplished through ballot box checking, alternative circling, and character inscription.

Ballot box checking is a method commonly used when alternative responses can be segmented into clearly identifiable categories. The selected alternative can then be "x"ed or checked by the form coder. This method may be used for documents completed either by hand or typewriter.

Circling is another method that may be used when alternative responses can be segmented into clearly identifiable categories. The selected alternative can then be circled by the form coder. For this reason, circling is most often used when a document is usually completed by hand. It is possible to type-writer-complete documents using this method by instructing the document coder to enclose the relevant alternative within parentheses ( ).

Character inscription involves the hand printing or coding of data into an open fill-in field. Character inscription is normally used when the variety of information to be coded is too great to be categorized. Names and addresses are good examples of data requiring this kind of coding technique.

The advantages of the ballot box checking and circling approaches are that they rely upon the coder's more effective powers of recognition rather than recall, and legibility is guaranteed because the codes are printed. (Hand-inscribed characters may occasionally suffer in legibility.) The chief disadvantage of these methods is the amount of space that may be consumed to develop one field. Therefore, six or seven is about the maximum number of alternatives that should be included within this type of field. A larger number of alternatives usually requires reverting to the character inscription method. One reasonable compromise which may be implemented for fields with more than six or seven alternatives, and some alternatives infrequently occur, is to use ballot box checking or circling for the frequent alternatives and character inscription for the infrequent ones.

Coding Techniques—Design

Ballot Box Checking

- Place the alternative caption above the box.
- Center the check box below the alternative caption.
- Position the code to the right of the check box.
- Leave space equal to at least one-half of the combined length of an alternative ballot box, caption, and code between each alternative in the field.

LOCATION			APPROVED	
Los Angeles	New York	Chicago	Yes	No
☐ LA	☐ NY	☐ CH	☐ Y	☐ N

LOCATION			APPROVED	
Los Angeles	New York	Chicago	Yes	No
☐ LA	☐ NY	☐ CH	☐ Y	☐ N

Circling

- Place the alternative caption above the code.
- Center the code below the alternative caption.
- Leave space equal to the least one-half of the length of an alternative caption between each alternative in a field.

LOCATION			APPROVED	
Los Angeles	New York	Chicago	Yes	No
LA	NY	CH	Y	N

LOCATION			APPROVED	
Los Angeles	New York	Chicago	Yes	No
LA	NY	CH	Y	N

Character Inscription

- The code is inscribed in a free-form manner.

CITY

While either the ballot box or circling technique may be used, the circling technique is recommended because it results in a less cluttered looking fill-in field. When a two-part document can be developed (part one, or the top page, is coded and part two, or the back page, becomes the document from which key entry is performed), data irrelevant to the user of each document part may be left off that document part. For example, using the ballot box technique illustrated above, part one would look like:

CITY

and part two:

LOCATION			APPROVED	
Los Angeles ☐	New York ☐	Chicago ☐	Yes ☐	No ☐

LOCATION			APPROVED	
☐ LA	☐ NY	☐ CH	☐ Y	☐ N

Coding Aids

FIELD SIZE INDICATORS

- For fill-in fields requiring a fixed number of characters in field:
  - fields may be partitioned using ¹⁄₁₂″ high thin (000 rule) tick marks.

PRODUCER CODE

PRODUCER CODE

  - fields may be segmented into logical pieces using ¹⁄₁₂″ high thicker (two point) tick marks.

- For fill-in fields in which a variable number of characters may be coded in field:

Floating Box

    – inscribe the maximum number of characters permitted in upper left-most corner of fill-in field;
    – Increase field width by one character space.

LOAN NUMBER

12

Caption Within Fill-In Field

    – locate the maximum number of characters permitted immediately to the right of caption.

LOAN NUMBER (12)

To expedite completion, various coding aids may be built into a document. Included are field size indicators, assumed value indicators, dollar signs, decimal points, and required field completion indicators.

Field size indicators are optional in document design. They may take the form of either tick marks to identify the individual character positions in a field, or a numeric value to simply indicate the maximum number of characters that may be encoded within its boundaries. Tick marks, when used, should only be incorporated within fields requiring a fixed number of characters. Incorporating tick marks within variable length fields constrains the coder for the worst case condition, which is seldom achieved. Two studies (Wright and Barnard, 1975; and Barnard et al. 1978) found that field spacing constraints, including tick marks, actually impair performance in terms of speed of information entry and legibility of the final product. These investigators concluded that spatial constraints are deleterious to the perception of individual letters. Possible causes are that they contribute noise to the visual field or that they may modify the way characters are written so that they become less legible.

Since the reading process is holistic (using a word's general features such as its overall shape and letter sequence probabilities), spatial arrangements that distort perceptual features may disrupt the reading process.

In light of these findings, use tick marks only for fixed length fields that generally contain less meaningful data (rates, factors, etc.) with less established perceptual features. The tick marks will also remind the document coder that all character positions must be filled. For variable length fields generally containing more meaningful data, restrict field size indicators, if used at all, to a simple value that indicates maximum field size. The probability of exceeding field size is low, and if it happens it will be immediately detected at data entry, where remedial action can be taken. Excessive restrictions to the coding process itself do not seem worth the effort involved for the small gains to be made.

Coding Aids (Continued)

ASSUMED VALUE INDICATORS

Floating Box

- Place value to right and outside of fill-in field.

DEDUCTIBLE   LIMIT

```
┌──────────────┐              ┌──────────────────────┐
│              │              │                      │
│              │ 00           │                      │ 000
└──────────────┘              └──────────────────────┘
```

Caption Within Fill-In Field

- Place value within fill-in field.
- Increase field size to compensate for assumed value indicator inclusion.

DEDUCTIBLE   LIMIT

```
┌──────────────┐              ┌──────────────────────┐
│              │              │                      │
│           00 │              │                  000 │
└──────────────┘              └──────────────────────┘
```

DOLLAR SIGNS

Floating Box

- Place dollar sign to left and outside of fill-in field.

AMOUNT

```
      ┌──────────────────────┐
      │                      │
   $  │                      │
      └──────────────────────┘
```

Caption Within Fill-In Field

- Place dollar sign within fill-in field.
- Increase field size to compensate for dollar sign inclusion.

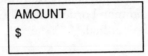

Assumed value indicators and dollar signs, while of value to the document coder, are irrelevant to data entry. The general design philosophy, then, is to sublimate their appearance on the document. This can be accomplished, at least, when using the floating box approach, by positioning them outside the fill-in field. They are visible to the document coder but are not "noise" to data entry. For documents using captions within the fill-in field, this sublimation cannot be accomplished because adjacent fields share common borders.

Coding Aids (Continued)

Decimal Points

- Inscribe the decimal point at its proper location within the fill-in field.

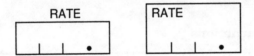

Required Completion Field Indicators (for coding)

- Incorporate a heavier rule around the fill-in field.

TERRITORY   ZONE

TERRITORY   ZONE

(Required)   (Not Required)

To indicate that a document fill-in field must always be completed, incorporate a heavier rule around the fill-in field. This convention is for the ease of the document coder, not data entry. Computer edits will normally provide the necessary feedback at data entry.

Care must be exercised in using bold borders on fields with captions within the box, since fields share common borders. For these kinds of documents this convention cannot always be applied.

OTHER CONSIDERATIONS

Title

- Locate at the document's top.
- Clearly describe document's intent or use.
- Spell out fully all words.
- Do not include redundant words (such as document or form).

A document must be identified by a title that describes its intent or use. An organization's conventions may dictate its exact placement. Normal positioning will be centered. Some organizations may require inclusion of a corporate logo on documents completed externally. Care must be exercised to allow for its inclusion as well.

Completion Instructions

- Describe instructions in the sequence in which they must be performed.
- Be brief and use clear and concise words.
- Locate instructions on the document cover, top, or before the section or item to which they apply.
- Instructions pertaining to an action to be taken with a completed document may appear at the document end or bottom.

Although it should be obvious how to complete a well designed document, it may occasionally be necessary to provide brief instructions or clarification information. These instructions should always precede that part of the document to which it applies. Brevity of completion instructions is a virtue.

Section Headings

- Identify logical groupings of related fill-in fields through section headings.
- Provide short, clear, fully spelled-out descriptions of the section's content.

- Locate section headings above the associated fill-in fields and justify to left margin.

Documents will normally be segmented into groupings or sections of related information. These groupings or sections may be preceded by a section heading. If so, the section heading will be left-justified above its grouping of related data fields. Section headings are recommended because they aid in developing perceptual groupings of document elements.

Fill-In Area Alignment

- Align fill-in areas in rows.

- Align (left-justified) the starting points on fill-in areas.

- Align, where possible (right-justified), the end points of fill-in areas in each row.

- On forms completed by typewriter, the starting points of fields should be aligned under one another, where possible, to facilitate the setting of typewriter tab stops.

Fill-in area alignment must follow a left-to-right, top-to-bottom orientation. Always align the starting points of fill-in areas in each row. Attempt to align the end points of the last field in each row. Do not, however, leave large gaps between fields in a row to achieve this right-justified alignment. Where these large gaps do occur, close the fill-in fields to the left and omit the right-justification for that particular row.

Fill-in area spacing should always be accomplished with the idea of facilitating tab stop setting for typewriter completion. It is usually easier to accomplish this with the caption within the fill-in box approach rather than with the floating box approach, since the former provides more leeway in establishing field widths. Bear in mind, however, that more documents generally are completed by hand than by typewriter, so compromises for ease of typing at the expense of ease of hand completion can be self-defeating.

Screen Design Steps 13

NECESSARY DESIGN STEPS

I. Review screen design documentation and services.

II. Identify system inputs and outputs.

III. Identify unique user requirements.

IV. Describe data elements.

V. Develop transactions.

VI. Develop final paper screens.

VII. Define computer screens.

VIII. Test screens.

IX. Implement screens.

X. Evaluate screens.

In this chapter the design steps necessary to develop and implement screens are reviewed and illustrated. Some guidelines and design aids are also presented.

Screen design is an orderly process, flowing through the requirements, design, testing, and implementation phases of a system development cycle. Screen design will normally move through those design steps summarized above. Most of these steps are common to all parts of a system development effort. Since this handbook is focusing only on screen design, the emphasis is on steps 4, 5, and 6. The remaining steps are reviewed only to the detail necessary to provide continuity of thought.

The subject matter to illustrate the design steps is a data entry screen developed for use with a dedicated source document. This kind of screen has been chosen because it is the most complex design activity and is subject to the most design tradeoffs. Design of other kinds of screens is normally less complex.

I. Review screen design documentation and services.
  A. Standards
    1. Screens
    2. Source documents/forms
    3. System development
  B. Handbooks
    1. Screen design
  C. Manuals
    1. Display terminal
    2. Data entry utility/system
    3. Screen definition
    4. Data element
  D. Consulting services
    1. Internal
    2. External

Before beginning any screen design activity, the designer must be aware of the services and documentation available for referral and assistance. Included are various standards, handbooks, manuals, and consulting services.

The design *standards* contain all the rules that must be adhered to in the screen design process. They may describe the specific methods, timing, and products for an organization's system development cycle.

Handbooks normally contain guidelines to aid the design process (such as are found in this document).

Important *manuals* are those that describe the characters of the terminal for which the screens will be designed, the characteristics of the system or utility with which the screens will be used, the characteristics of screen creation utilities on which screens may be created, and manuals that provide guidance in the specification of system data elements.

Consulting services are those available both within and outside the organization that can provide guidance concerning all aspects of the screen design process, including technical assistance and standard interpretations.

I. Review screen design documentation and services.

II. Identify system inputs and outputs.

Data entry screen formats are developed for the purpose of providing inputs to a system. System outputs affect the content of inquiry screens. The product of the phase that identifies a system's inputs and output—the data elements—will be the building blocks used in the screen design process.

I. Review screen design documentation and services.

II. Identify system inputs and outputs.

III. Identify unique user requirements.

User requirements of importance to the screen designer are those of the people performing the data entry, inquiry, or interactive function. The screen design guidelines described in previous chapters have been developed for optimum ease of use by a wide range of users. They assume the following:

- job level may be clerical or managerial;
- touch-typing skills may or may not exist;
- turnover rate may be high or low;
- business knowledge may be minimal or extensive;
- the potential for using more than one system exists;
- system usage may be frequent or infrequent.

Since the screen standards have been developed at a fairly "low" common denominator, users exceeding these requirements will still find the screens very usable.

This phase, then, will ascertain where the screen users fall within this broad spectrum. This knowledge may then be applied as design tradeoffs are performed throughout the design process. For example, in-depth business knowledge and low turnover rates may allow incorporation of more cryptic screen captions as an occasional design tradeoff. The designer is cautioned, however, not to let user characteristics wield too much influence, as these characteristics can change in time.

In this requirements step, the necessity for developing associated source documents for data entry must also be determined. This decision will direct data entry screen design to the proper design guidelines.

I. Review screen design documentation and services.

II. Identify system inputs and outputs.

III. Identify unique user requirements.

IV. Describe data elements.
   A. Title/name.
   B. Screen caption.
   C. Size.
   D. Required or optional status.
   E. Logical relationship with other data elements.

Data elements, the building blocks of screens, were defined in step 2. The screen design process itself begins with the specification of some important data element characteristics. Most of this information can probably be captured from worksheets that are normally prepared during the input/output design process.

The *title* will be the name of the data element. This name must be a clear description of the data element for the screen user (and document coder). Titles on system worksheets may have to be clarified because they often include extraneous information (to the user), such as system descriptors.

Screen captions must be developed from the data element title. Rules for developing screen captions are included in the chapters on guidelines for the kind of screens being created.

Size is the length of the field in character positions. It is a numeric value ranging from 1 to n.

Required or optional status will define the frequency of occurrence of a data element. A required field is one into which data is always keyed or always displayed every time a screen is used.

Logical relationship with other data elements is the rule for cross-field validation checking and customary associations between data elements.

This data element descriptive information must be recorded in some meaningful and easily used format. A computer printout of data elements may be available, but its size, information content, and format normally make a printout difficult to use. A manual solution is to prepare a simple listing of all relevant data elements, as illustrated in figure 13.1. Throughout the remainder of this chapter many of the design steps will be illustrated with figures and examples. The information shown is based upon an actual design, but it has, however, been extensively edited and shortened for illustrative simplicity, and should not be construed as a technically valid transaction.)

Figure 13.1 Example data element list.

Title	Screen Caption	Size	Req/ Opt.	Logical Relationships
Street Address (Mailing)	MAIL-ADD:	30	R	With Mail City, St, Zip
City (Mailing)	CITY:	13	R	With Mail Add, St, Zip
State (Mailing)	ST:	2	R	With Mail Add, City, Zip
Zip Code (Mailing)	ZIP:	5	R	With Mail Add, City, St
Company	CO:	2	R	With Branch Code
Branch Code	BR-CD:	3	R	With Company
Marital Status	MAR-STS:	1	O	With Spouse Emp.
Spouse Employed	SP-EMP:	1	O	With Marital Status
Effective Date	EFF-DT:	6	R	With Expiration Date
Expiration Date	EXP-DT:	6	R	With Effective Date
HO Policy Form Number	POL-FORM:	1	R	With Coverages
Producer Code	PROD-CD:	6	R	With Sub-Prod Code
Sub-Producer Code	SUB-PROD:	4	O	With Producer Code
Account Number	ACCT#:	9	R	
Primary Policy Number	PRI-POL#:	8	O	With Sec. Res. Policy
Insured Premises Other Than Mailing Address	PRMS-OTH:	8	O	With Premises Address
Premises Address	PRMS-ADD	30	O	With Prms City, St, Zip
Premises City	CITY:	13	O	With Prms Add, St, Zip
Premises State	ST:	2	O	With Prms Add, City, Zip
Premises Zip Code	ZIP:	5	O	With Prms Add, City, St
A. Building Limits	A-BLDGS:	7	O	Coverage Type I
B. Other Structures Limits	B-OTH-STR:	5	O	Coverage Type I
C. Unsched. Personal Property Limits	C-UNS-PR:	7	R	Coverage Type I
D. Add'l Living Expenses Limits	D-ADD-LIV:	5	R	Coverage Type I
E. Pers. Liab.-Each Occur. Limits	E-PER-LI:	7	R	Coverage Type II
F. Med. Payment-Each Pers. Limits	F-MED-PAY:	5	R	Coverage Type II
Deductible Amount	DED-AMT:	5	R	Coverage with Ded Form #
Deductible Form Number	DED-FORM#:	3	O	Coverage with Ded Amt.
Producer Issued Dec	PROD-ISS:	1	R	
Secondary Residence Policy	SEC-RES	1	O	With Primary Policy No
Property Legal Descript. Attach.	LEG-DESC:	1	O	
250 Theft Deductible	250-DED:	1	O	Coverage with Ded Amt.
Policy Type	POL-TYPE:	1	R	
New York Coinsurance	NY-CINS:	1	O	
County In Which Insured Premises Located	PRMS-CNY:	5	R	With Prms City, St, Zip
Policy Number	POL#:	13	R	
Insured Name–1	NM-1:	30	R	With Insured Name-2
Insured Name–2	NM-2:	30	O	With Insured Name-1

I. Review screen design documentation and services.

II. Identify system inputs and outputs.

III. Identify unique user requirements.

IV. Describe data elements.

V. Develop transactions.

    VI. Summarize design requirements affecting screen design.

    B. Specify data elements that will comprise a transaction.

    C. Organize transaction data elements into sections.

    D. Identify and lay out screens.

A *transaction*, sometimes called a function, is a screen or series of screens comprising an activity whose conclusion results in an output or action fulfilling a system requirement. Transaction design, like most design, is a deductive process, proceeding from a general set of requirements to a specific solution —one screen format or a series of screen formats. It is also an iterative process, with frequent starts, stops, and steps backward. The steps summarized above reflect the normal sequential flow of transaction design. The loops in design may cause many steps to be performed several times. This is normal and to be expected. (This fact, however, should not discourage the designer from trying to achieve minimal iterations. This is a goal toward which one should strive.)

I. Review screen design documentation and services.

II. Identify system inputs and outputs.

III. Identify unique user requirements.

IV. Describe data elements.

V. Develop transactions.

    A. Summarize design requirements affecting screen design.

        1. Important design requirements

            a. Human

            b. Hardware

            c. Software

            d. Source document (if applicable)

            e. Application

        2. Considerations and requirements are reflected in

            a. Standards

            b. System requirements documents

            c. Handbooks

    d. Manuals

    e. Manually prepared data element listing

The design considerations impacting screen design have been a topic of discussion in this handbook. Before beginning design, the handbook along with all relevant standards should be reviewed.

System requirements must be abstracted from the design documents prepared during the system development phases. All design must be accomplished within the standards, limits, and guidelines described. The manually prepared data element list will be an important reference source throughout the design.

If the application transactions being developed are to include as their data source an especially designed source document, then source document considerations are important. One important factor affecting screen design is the non-data-entry data elements, which must be included only on the source document.

To aid in application transaction development, these non-data-entry data elements should also be summarized on the data element list. This has been done for the example and is illustrated in figure 13.2.

The non-data-entry data elements can usually be obtained from the application requirements document. Screen captions are, of course, not necessary.

  I. Review screen design documentation and services.

 II. Identify system inputs and outputs.

III. Identify unique user requirements.

IV. Describe data elements.

V. Develop transactions.

    A. Summarize design requirements affecting screen design.

    B. Specify data elements that will comprise a transaction.

        1. Considerations in transaction development

            a. Application requirements

            b. Computer transaction requirements

            c. User requirements

Application transaction development is a major facet of all the system design activity that has occurred to this point. It will reflect the requirements of the application, the unique requirements of the structure of computer transactions, and the requirements of people generating and using the data. Throughout development activities, application transaction development has been a primary objective.

Figure 13.2 Example data element list with non data-entry data elements.

Title	Screen Caption	Size	Req/ Opt.	Logical Relationships
Street Address (Mailing)	MAIL-ADD:	30	R	With Mail City, St, Zip
City (Mailing)	CITY:	13	R	With Mail Add, St, Zip
State (Mailing)	ST:	2	R	With Mail Add, City, Zip
Zip Code (Mailing)	ZIP:	5	R	With Mail Add, City, St
Company	CO:	2	R	With Branch Code
Branch Code	BR-CD:	3	R	With Company
Marital Status	MAR-STS:	1	O	With Spouse Emp.
Spouse Employed	SP-EMP:	1	O	With Marital Status
Effective Date	EFF-DT:	6	R	With Expiration Date
Expiration Date	EXP-DT:	6	R	With Effective Date
HO Policy Form Number	POL-FORM:	1	R	With Coverages
Producer Code	PROD-CD:	6	R	With Sub-Prod Code
Sub-Producer Code	SUB-PROD:	4	O	With Producer Code
Account Number	ACCT#:	9	R	
Primary Policy Number	PRI-POL#:	8	O	With Sec. Res. Policy
Insured Premises Other Than Mailing Address	PRMS-OTH:	8	O	With Premises Address
Premises Address	PRMS-ADD	30	O	With Prms City, St, Zip
Premises City	CITY:	13	O	With Prms Add, St, Zip
Premises State	ST:	2	O	With Prms Add, City, Zip
Premises Zip Code	ZIP:	5	O	With Prms Add, City, St
A. Building Limits	A-BLDGS:	7	O	Coverage Type I
B. Other Structures Limits	B-OTH-STR:	5	O	Coverage Type I
C. Unsched. Personal Property Limits	C-UNS-PR:	7	R	Coverage Type I
D. Add'l Living Expenses Limits	D-ADD-LIV:	5	R	Coverage Type I
E. Pers. Liab.-Each Occur. Limits	E-PER-LI:	7	R	Coverage Type II
F. Med. Payment-Each Pers. Limits	F-MED-PAY:	5	R	Coverage Type II
Deductible Amount	DED-AMT:	5	R	Coverage with Ded Form #
Deductible Form Number	DED-FORM#:	3	O	Coverage with Ded Amt.
Producer Issued Dec	PROD-ISS:	1	R	
Secondary Residence Policy	SEC-RES	1	O	With Primary Policy No
Property Legal Descript. Attach.	LEG-DESC:	1	O	
250 Theft Deductible	250-DED:	1	O	Coverage with Ded Amt.
Policy Type	POL-TYPE:	1	R	
New York Coinsurance	NY-CINS:	1	O	
County In Which Insured Premises Located	PRMS-CNY:	5	R	With Prms City, St, Zip
Policy Number	POL#:	13	R	
Insured Name–1	NM-1:	30	R	With Insured Name-2
Insured Name–2	NM-2:	30	O	With Insured Name-1
Non-Data Entry				
Residence Telephone Number		10		
Insured Occupation		15		
Spouse Occupation		15		
Birth Date of Insured		6		
Existing Account		1		
Med. Payment— Each Accid. Limits		7		

The screen designer's role in this activity is to ensure that the application transactions adequately reflect user requirements and that application transactions "make sense" to all systems users; that is, that they reflect the environment as it is commonly perceived.

The product of this activity is one or more application transactions, each consisting of a series of defined data elements. Completion of this step initiates what has commonly been called screen design.

In our example, let us assume that all the specified data elements will comprise one transaction called "Homeowner's New Business." This transaction with its data element list is illustrated in figure 13.3. (Had it been required to develop two application transactions for all the data elements, these data elements would have had to be split into two separate application transactions data element listings.)

  I. Review screen design documentation and services.

 II. Identify system inputs and outputs.

III. Identify unique user requirements.

IV. Describe data elements.

V. Develop transactions.

   A. Summarize design requirements affecting screen design.

   B. Specify data elements that will comprise a transaction.

   C. Organize transaction data elements into sections.

      1. Calculate data element lengths

         a. Data element length is the sum of

            1) The number of characters in the screen caption

            2) The number of characters in the field

            3) The data element attribute characters (always 2)

         b. Add length to each data element in the data element listing

---

The development and organization of screens can be facilitated by adding to the prepared DATA ELEMENT LISTING a descriptive field called DATA ELEMENT LENGTH. Data element length will be the sum of:

- the number of characters in the screen caption,
- the number of characters in the field,
- the attribute characters.

Screen caption—The number of characters in the screen caption is figured by counting the total number of characters in the caption, including dashes,

Figure 13.3 Example "Homeowner's New Business" application transaction data element list.

Title	Screen Caption	Size	Req/ Opt.	Logical Relationships
Street Address (Mailing)	MAIL-ADD:	30	R	With Mail City, St, Zip
City (Mailing)	CITY:	13	R	With Mail Add, St, Zip
State (Mailing)	ST:	2	R	With Mail Add, City, Zip
Zip Code (Mailing)	ZIP:	5	R	With Mail Add, City, St
Company	CO:	2	R	With Branch Code
Branch Code	BR-CD:	3	R	With Company
Marital Status	MAR-STS:	1	O	With Spouse Emp.
Spouse Employed	SP-EMP:	1	O	With Marital Status
Effective Date	EFF-DT:	6	R	With Expiration Date
Expiration Date	EXP-DT:	6	R	With Effective Date
HO Policy Form Number	POL-FORM:	1	R	With Coverages
Producer Code	PROD-CD:	6	R	With Sub-Prod Code
Sub-Producer Code	SUB-PROD:	4	O	With Producer Code
Account Number	ACCT#:	9	R	
Primary Policy Number	PRI-POL#:	8	O	With Sec. Res. Policy
Insured Premises Other Than Mailing Address	PRMS-OTH:	8	O	With Premises Address
Premises Address	PRMS-ADD	30	O	With Prms City, St, Zip
Premises City	CITY:	13	O	With Prms Add, St, Zip
Premises State	ST:	2	O	With Prms Add, City, Zip
Premises Zip Code	ZIP:	5	O	With Prms Add, City, St
A. Building Limits	A-BLDGS:	7	O	Coverage Type I
B. Other Structures Limits	B-OTH-STR:	5	O	Coverage Type I
C. Unsched. Personal Property Limits	C-UNS-PR:	7	R	Coverage Type I
D. Add'l Living Expenses Limits	D-ADD-LIV:	5	R	Coverage Type I
E. Pers. Liab.-Each Occur. Limits	E-PER-LI:	7	R	Coverage Type II
F. Med. Payment-Each Pers. Limits	F-MED-PAY:	5	R	Coverage Type II
Deductible Amount	DED-AMT:	5	R	Coverage with Ded Form #
Deductible Form Number	DED-FORM#:	3	O	Coverage with Ded Amt.
Producer Issued Dec	PROD-ISS:	1	O	
Secondary Residence Policy	SEC-RES	1	O	With Primary Policy No
Property Legal Descript. Attach.	LEG-DESC:	1	O	
250 Theft Deductible	250-DED:	1	O	Coverage with Ded Amt.
Policy Type	POL-TYPE:	1	R	
New York Coinsurance	NY-CINS:	1	O	
County In Which Insured Premises Located	PRMS-CNY:	5	R	With Prms City, St, Zip
Policy Number	POL#:	13	R	
Insured Name–1	NM-1:	30	R	With Insured Name-2
Insured Name–2	NM-2:	30	O	With Insured Name-1
Non-Data Entry				
Residence Telephone Number		10		
Insured Occupation		15		
Spouse Occupation		15		
Birth Date of Insured		6		
Existing Account		1		
Med. Payment— Each Accid. Limits		7		

special characters, and the separator (:). For example,

- EFF-DT: is 7 characters;
- PROD-CD: is 8 characters;
- CO: is 3 characters.

Field—The number of characters in the field is the expected number of entry characters as described in the size field. For example,

- EFFECTIVE DATE is a 6-character entry field;
- PRODUCER CODE is a 6-character entry field;
- COMPANY is a 2-character entry field.

Attributes—Each part of the data element—the screen caption and the entry field—will be preceded by an attribute character.

- Allow 2 characters for attribute positions.

Lengths for the illustrated data element will be:

- EFFECTIVE DATE—15(7 + 6 + 2),
- PRODUCER CODE—16(8 + 6 + 2),
- COMPANY—7(3 + 2 + 2).

Data element lengths have been calculated for the example and are illustrated in figure 13.4.

V. Develop transactions.

    C. Organize transaction data elements into sections. (Cont'd)

        1. Calculate data element lengths.

        2. Apply grouping techniques and design considerations.

            a. Information grouping techniques

                1) Sequence of use

                2) Frequency of use

                3) Function

                4) Importance

            b. Screen design considerations

                1) Human

                2) Hardware

                3) Software

                4) Source document

                5) Application

Figure 13.4 Example data element list with data element lengths.

Title	Screen Caption	Size	Req/ Opt.	Logical Relationships	DE Length
Street Address (Mailing)	MAIL-ADD:	30	R	With Mail City, St, Zip	41
City (Mailing)	CITY:	13	R	With Mail Add, St, Zip	20
State (Mailing)	ST:	2	R	With Mail Add, City, Zip	7
Zip Code (Mailing)	ZIP:	5	R	With Mail Add, City, St	13
Company	CO:	2	R	With Branch Code	7
Branch Code	BR-CD:	3	R	With Company	11
Marital Status	MAR-STS:	1	O	With Spouse Emp.	11
Spouse Employed	SP-EMP:	1	O	With Marital Status	10
Effective Date	EFF-DT:	6	R	With Expiration Date	15
Expiration Date	EXP-DT:	6	R	With Effective Date	15
HO Policy Form Number	POL-FORM:	1	R	With Coverages	12
Producer Code	PROD-CD:	6	R	With Sub-Prod Code	16
Sub-Producer Code	SUB-PROD:	4	O	With Producer Code	15
Account Number	ACCT#:	9	R		17
Primary Policy Number	PRI-POL#:	8	O	With Sec. Res. Policy	19
Insured Premises Other Than Mailing Address	PRMS-OTH:	8	O	With Premises Address	19
Premises Address	PRMS-ADD	30	O	With Prms City, St, Zip	41
Premises City	CITY:	13	O	With Prms Add, St, Zip	20
Premises State	ST:	2	O	With Prms Add, City, Zip	7
Premises Zip Code	ZIP:	5	O	With Prms Add, City, St	11
A. Building Limits	A-BLDGS:	7	O	Coverage Type I	17
B. Other Structures Limits	B-OTH-STR:	5	O	Coverage Type I	17
C. Unsched. Personal Property Limits	C-UNS-PR:	7	R	Coverage Type I	18
D. Add'l Living Expenses Limits	D-ADD-LIV:	5	R	Coverage Type I	17
E. Pers. Liab.-Each Occur. Limits	E-PER-LI:	7	R	Coverage Type II	18
F. Med. Payment-Each Pers. Limits	F-MED-PAY:	5	R	Coverage Type II	17
Deductible Amount	DED-AMT:	5	R	Coverage with Ded Form #	15
Deductible Form Number	DED-FORM#:	3	O	Coverage with Ded Amt.	15
Producer Issued Dec	PROD-ISS:	1	R		12
Secondary Residence Policy	SEC-RES	1	O	With Primary Policy No	11
Property Legal Descript. Attach.	LEG-DESC:	1	O		10
250 Theft Deductible	250-DED:	1	O	Coverage with Ded Amt.	11
Policy Type	POL-TYPE:	1	R		11
New York Coinsurance	NY-CINS:	1	O		11
County In Which Insured Premises Located	PRMS-CNY:	5	R	With Prms City, St, Zip	36
Policy Number	POL#:	13	R		20
Insured Name–1	NM-1:	30	R	With Insured Name-2	37
Insured Name–2	NM-2:	30	O	With Insured Name-1	37
Non-Data Entry					
Residence Telephone Number		10			
Insured Occupation		15			
Spouse Occupation		15			
Birth Date of Insured		6			
Existing Account		1			
Med. Payment— Each Accid. Limits		7			

The objective of this design step is to segment the transaction's data elements into logical groupings and then to place the groupings into a logical order. No attempt is made to organize the data elements within a section or grouping.

Information grouping techniques were summarized in section 1 of chapter 5. Screen format design considerations are the subject of this entire handbook. The *most important factor* in grouping and ordering is the *natural working habits* of the people who generate, record, and use the source data.

If the application transaction is going to reflect the structure of an associated source document, attention must be directed to source document design as well as screen format layout.

Any one design will normally reflect a combination of these grouping techniques. Information may be organized functionally, and within each function individual items may be arranged by sequence or importance. Numerous permutations are possible.

It is important to recognize that many of the design considerations may be partially incompatible with one another. Computer editing needs may not be fully achieved in light of the grouping requirements, or processing and edit requirements may be inconsistent. In these cases, the final organization of items within the transaction will be a compromise between all the considerations. The designer must weigh the alternatives and use judgment based upon transaction accuracy, time, cost, and ease requirements. It is important to remember, however, that *human requirements take precedence over machine processing requirements*, and that the avenue chosen, regardless of direction, must be consistent within itself.

V. Develop transactions.
  C. Organize transaction data elements into sections. (Cont'd)
    1. Calculate data element lengths.
    2. Apply grouping techniques and design considerations.
      c. Design product:
        1) Data elements are segmented into logical groupings
        2) The groupings are ordered in the manner in which they will occur in the transaction

---

The order and groupings of data elements for this example are summarized in figure 13.5.

V. Develop transactions
  C. Organize transaction data elements into sections. (Cont'd)
    1. Calculate data element lengths

2. Apply grouping techniques and design considerations
3. **Specify necessary supplemental information**
   a. **Title**
   b. **Screen/page number**
   c. **Section headings**
   d. **Messages and instructional information**
   e. **Space lines**

The *title* will be the source document title or a meaningful abbreviation of that title. For multiscreen transactions the title should only appear on the first screen.

The *screen or page number* may also be used to give identity to a screen by incorporating within it a mnemonic descriptive of the name of the transaction. Screen/page numbers will be located in a consistent position in the upper right-hand corner of the screen.

Data entry screen formats should not be packed with data. Inclusion of *section headings* serves to provide visual breaks in the screen formats and gives the user an additional reference "point" in visually moving from the source document to the screen. Section headings should be those found on the source document.

Space lines or blank lines also serve to provide visual breaks in the screen and give the user another reference "point" in visually moving from the source document to the screen. They may be substituted for section headings at section boundaries, or they may be used where a wider than normal visual break exists between lines of the source document data entry field. (These breaks may occur when the source document contains rows of non-data-entry data elements or other supplementary information not used in the data entry process.)

Messages and instructional information are usually not necessary and are not recommended for inclusion on this kind of screen format.

At the conclusion of this activity, there will have been specified:

- the content of the screen title,
- the structure and content of page numbers,
- whether section headings will be included (and their content),
- whether instructions and messages will be included (and their content),
- whether space lines will be included.

Supplemental information requirements for this example are illustrated in figure 13.6. Included are screen title, page numbers, section headings, and space lines. There will be no instructions and messages. The screen number

Figure 13.5 Example order and general grouping of data elements in an application transaction.

1. *Policy-Related Data Elements*
   Expiration Date
   Effective Date
   Account Number
   Primary Policy Number
   Producer Issued Dec
   Policy Type
   Policy Number
   Existing Account (NON-DE)
   Secondary Residence Policy

2. *Producer- and Company-Related Data Elements*
   Producer Code
   Branch Code
   Sub-Producer Code
   Company

3. *Residence- and Insured-Related Data Elements*
   Street Address (mailing)
   City (mailing)
   State (mailing)
   Zip Code (mailing)
   Marital Status
   Spouse Employed
   Insured Premises other than mailing address
   Premises Address
   Premises City
   Premises State
   Premises Zip Code
   County in which Premises located
   Property Legal Description Attached
   Residence Telephone Number (NON-DE)
   Insured Occupation (NON-DE)
   Spouse Occupation (NON-DE)
   Insured Birth Date (NON-DE)
   Insured Name–1
   Insured Name–2

4. *Coverage-Related Data Elements*
   HO Policy Form Number
   Deductible Amount
   Deductible Form Number
   Building Limits
   Other Structure Limits
   Unscheduled Personal Property Limits
   Additional Living Expenses Limits
   Personal Liability—Each Occurrence Limits
   Medical Payments—Each Person Limits
   $250 Theft Deductible
   New York Coinsurance
   Medical Payments—Each Accident Limits (NON-DE)

Figure 13.6 Example supplemental information requirements.

Title:	Homeowners Application
Page/Screen Number:	HMAP nn
Section Headings:	Will Be Included
Instructions/Messages:	None
Space Lines:	Will Be Included

is a contraction of the transaction name (HMAP) with specific pages designated by a numeric value beginning with 01.

I. Review screen design documentation and services.

II. Identify system inputs and outputs.

III. Identify unique user requirement.

IV. Describe data elements.

V. Develop transactions.

    A. Summarize design requirements affecting screen design.

    B. Specify data elements that will comprise a transaction.

    C. Organize transaction data elements into sections.

    D. Identify and lay out screens.

        1. Apply to each grouping (section) of data elements

            a. Information grouping techniques

            b. Screen design considerations

The information grouping techniques summarized in the previous step (V. C. 2.) are now applied to each specific section of the transaction. This grouping is carried out within the described hardware limitations, according to the described field specification rules, and in conjunction with all the reviewed design considerations. The guidelines following are also helpful.

---

2. Conform to the following guidelines:

    a. Confine screen line usage to data elements consuming about three-fourths of its available width (60–65 characters in an 80-character-wide line)

        1) The data element lengths calculated in step V. C. 1. are used to determine line space consumed.

    b. For multiscreen transactions, break screens at natural points.

1) **Between sections on a source document**

2 **At the end of a source document page**

3) **Never break a screen such that its parts are contained on two sides of a source document.**

c. **If the guidelines result in the final transaction screen containing only a few lines (2–3), consider the following tradeoffs (in recommended order of implementation):**

1) **Omit a space line or lines.**

2) **Combine section headings.**

Limiting each screen line to fields containing 60 to 65 characters leaves space for 1) developing perceptual groupings, and 2) transforming the completed screen into an image of its source document. For a source document-oriented data entry system with an 8-character caption limitation, source document space limits are usually reached before screen limits are reached. The screen limit can be quickly exceeded, however, if a line contains a large number of small fields. In screen format (or source document) design, therefore, try to avoid including a large number of small fields on one line.

Again, design tradeoffs may have to be performed. The discussion in step V. C. 2. is again appropriate, as are the above tradeoff guidelines.

The ordering of data elements within screen formats may be performed on a standard printed layout sheet. Because of the general nature of the product, these kinds of screen format drafts can, however, be completed on a plain piece of paper. This is the recommended methodology.

Figure 13.7 illustrates the first screen draft of the first screen prepared for the example data elements. This draft was developed in conjunction with a related source document that is illustrated in figure 13.8.

SOME TRADEOFFS

This first draft fits well with the designed source document. However, some problems are immediately obvious: lines 12, 13, and 16 exceed the recommended 60- to 65-character maximum. In fact, two exceed the 80-character absolute and final maximum.

Lines 12 and 13. This situation frequently occurs when two sets of addresses are placed next to one another. The form provides a nice fit; the screen gets tight. The solution is to reduce the size of the screen captions. Since the fields on the document use up the entire line, creating a source document image will be fairly easy once the screen field data is compressed to within 80 characters.

So, to achieve an image relationship and effectively use the document, reduce MAIL-ADD to ML-AD, PRMS-ADD to P-ADD, CITY to CT and ZIP to

Figure 13.7 Example preliminary screen format draft.

Line Information and Data Elements	Total Character Count
1. *** HMAP01 ***	14
2. HOMEOWNERS APPLICATION (TITLE)	23
3. 1. POLICY INFORMATION (SECTION HEADING)	21
4. EFF-DT(15)EXP-DT(15)ACCT#(17)POL#(20)	67
5. PROD-ISS(12)SEC-RES(11)PRI-POL#(19)POL-TYP(11)	53
6. 2. PRODUCER AND COMPANY INFORMATION (SECTION HEADING)	35
7. CO(7)BR-CD(11)PROD-CD(16)SUB-PROD(15)	49
8. 3. RESIDENCE AND INSURED INFORMATION (SECTION HEADING)	36
9. NM-1(37)	37
10. NM-2(37)MAR-STS(11)SP-EMP(10)	58
11. (BLANK)	0
12. MAIL-ADD(41)PRMS-ADD(41)	75
13. CITY(20)ST(7)ZIP(13)CCITY(20)ST(7)ZIP(13)	74
14. PRMS-OTH(19)PRMS-CNY(36)LEG-DESC(10)	65
15. 4. COVERAGES(SECTION HEADING)	12
16. POL-FORM(12)A-BLDGS(17)B-OTH-STR(17) C-UNS-PR(18)D-ADD-LIV(17)	73
17. E-PER-LI(18)F-MED-PAY(17)NY-CINS(11)	46
18. DED-AMT(15)250-DED(11)DED-FORM#(15)	41

ZP. The result is illustrated in figure 13.9. Line 12 now contains 75 characters and line 13 contains 74. Identifiable contractions of the source document caption still exist. (Remember, the document will always be available to aid in interpretation.)

Line 16. The exceeded capacity problem in line 16 is different—fields on the source document do not fill up the document line. Screen caption reduction in this case will primarily be directed toward creating a screen document image relationship. To reduce the size, change POL-FORM to FORM and B-OTH-STR to B-OTH. The result is also illustrated in figure 13.9. Line 16 now contains 73 characters. This is still high but should be workable. Identifiable contractions of the source document captions still exist.

V. Develop transactions.

   D. Identify and lay out screens. (Cont'd)

      1. Group data elements.

      2. Conform to guidelines.

Figure 13.8 Source document example.

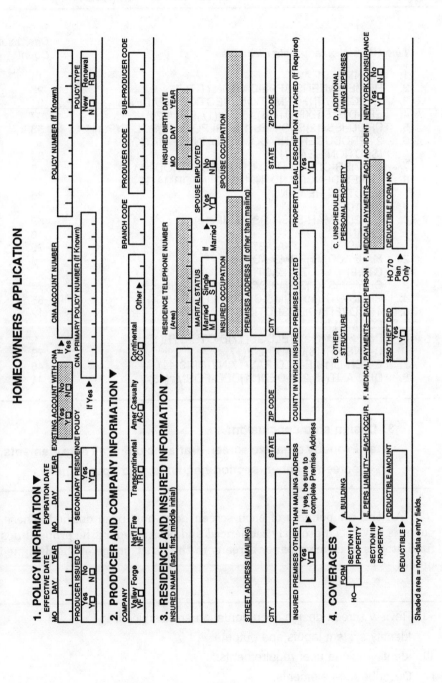

Figure 13.9 Example preliminary screen format draft (revision).

Line Information and Data Elements		Total Character Count
1.	*** HMAP01 ***	14
2.	HOMEOWNERS APPLICATION (TITLE)	23
3.	1. POLICY INFORMATION (SECTION HEADING)	21
4.	EFF-DT(15)EXP-DT(15)ACCT#(17)POL#(20)	67
5.	PROD-ISS(12)SEC-RES(11)PRI-POL#(19)POL-TYP(11)	53
6.	2. PRODUCER AND COMPANY INFORMATION (SECTION HEADING)	35
7.	CO(7)BR-CD(11)PROD-CD(16)SUB-PROD(15)	49
8.	3. RESIDENCE AND INSURED INFORMATION (SECTION HEADING)	36
9.	NM-1(37)	37
10.	NM-2(37)MAR-STS(11)SP-EMP(10)	58
11.	(BLANK)	0
12.	ML-AD(38) P-AD(37) ~~MAIL-ADD(41)PRMS-ADD(41)~~	75 ~~75~~
13.	CT(18) ZP(12)CT(18) ZP(12) ~~CITY(20)ST(7)ZIP(13)CCITY(20)ST(7)ZIP(13)~~	~~74~~
14.	PRMS-OTH(19)PRMS-CNY(36)LEG-DESC(10)	65
15.	4. COVERAGES(SECTION HEADING)	12
16.	FORM(8) B-OTH(13) ~~POL-FORM(12)A-BLDGS(17)B-OTH-STR(17)~~ C-UNS-PR(18)D-ADD-LIV(17)	~~73~~
17.	E-PER-LI(18)F-MED-PAY(17)NY-CINS(11)	46
18.	DED-AMT(15)250-DED(11)DED-FORM#(15)	41

3. **Design step conclusion:**

   a. **Properly organize screen drafts including all data elements, title, screen number, section headings, and space lines**

All the components of each screen have now been defined. These components have been properly sequenced and positioned on the proper lines. The final step is to develop paper screens in the exact image of the designed document.

I. Review screen design documentation and services.

II. Identify system inputs and outputs.

III. Identify unique user requirements.

IV. Describe data elements.

V. Develop transactions.

VI. Define final paper screen.

    A. Using the spacing guidelines summarized in section 5-2 of this handbook, transfer the fields and information from the draft layout worksheet to a standard printed screen layout form.

        1. Some important reminders

            a. Allow a cursor rest position at the end of each line (in this 80-character-wide example, an entry field cannot extend beyond column 78)

            b. In maintaining an image relationship between document and screen, align entry fields (not captions)

    B. Use the attribute definition conventions of the system for which the screens are being defined.

The information on the draft layout worksheet is now transferred to a standard printout screen layout form available from many vendors. The spacing and clarity guidelines described in the previous chapters must be implemented in this transfer process. The experienced designer who has an on-line screen generation facility may find it easier to perform this design on-line, using a terminal.

The attribute definition conventions of the system for which the screens are being designed must also be implemented at this time. This involves following rules for specifically identifying protected fields, unprotected fields, highlighted fields, and so forth. Since the specific methods may vary, they are not addressed here. Screen designers must see that they are properly specified for their own environment at this point.

The following pages describe a paper screen developed for the example problem, and review some final design tradeoffs. For clarity, no specification of attributes is included in the layout. Entry (or unprotected) fields are designated by periods (.). The remaining fields (captions, titles, etc.) may be assumed to be protected.

    I. Review screen design documentation and services.

    II. Identify system inputs and outputs.

    III. Identify unique user requirements.

    IV. Describe data elements.

    V. Develop transactions.

    VI. Develop final paper screens.

    VII. Define computer screens.

Figure 13.10 Development of paper screens (screen number and title).

```
                                                            *** HNAPO1 ***

1.  POLICY INFORMATION
    EFF-DT: _____  EXP-DT: _____           ACCT#: _____  POL#: _____  POL-TYP: _
    PROD-ISS: _____  SEC-RES: _____  PRI-POL#: _____                    POL-TYP: _
2.  PRODUCER AND COMPANY INFORMATION
    CO: ____  PRODUCER AND COMPANY INFORMATION  BR-CD: __  PROD-CD: __  SUB-PROD: __
3.  RESIDENCE AND INSURED INFORMATION
    NM-1: _____           MAR-STS: _  SP-EMP: _
    NM-2: _____
    ML-AD: _____          P-AD: _____
    CTY: _____  ST: _  ZP: _____  CTY: _____  ST: _  ZP: _____
    PRMS-OTH: _  PRMS-CNY: ____                 LEG-DISC: _
4.  COVERAGES
    FORM: _  A-BLDG: _____  B-OTH: _____  C-UNS-PR: _____  D-ADD-LIV: _____
             E-PER-L: _____  F-MED: _____                    NY-CINS: __
             DED-AMT: _____  250-DED: _  DED-FORM#: _____
```

1. The screen number is placed in the upper right hand corner.
2. The title is placed in centered position below the screen number and above the body of the screen.

288

Figure 13.11 Development of paper screens (section headings and data elements).

```
                                                              *** HMAP01 ***

                        HOMEOWNERS APPLICATION

1.  POLICY INFORMATION
    EFF-DT: -----    EXP-DT: -----    ACCT#: -----         POL#: -----
    PROD-ISS: -----  SEC-RES: -----   PRI-POL#: -----       POL-TYP: -
2.  PRODUCER AND COMPANY INFORMATION
    CO: -----              BR-CD: --      PROD-CD: -----    SUB-PROD: -----
3.  RESIDENCE AND INSURED INFORMATION
    NM-1: -----                MAR-STS: -    SP-EMP: -
    NM-2: -----
    ML-AD: -----
    CTY: -----     ST: --  ZP: -----     P-AD: -----     ST: --  ZP: -----
    PRMS-OTH: -    PRMS-CNY: -            CTY: -----      LEG-DISC: -
4.  COVERAGES
    FORM: -    A-BLDG: -----    B-OTH: -----    C-UNS-PR: -----    D-ADD-LIV: -----
               E-PER-L: -----   F-MED: -----                      NY-CINS: -
               DED-AMT: -----   250-DED: -      DED-FORM#: ----
```

3. Section headings begin in column 2. Column 1 will be reserved for an attribute (or a blank).
4. The longest field caption (PROD-ISS) is indented three spaces from the section heading.
5. The other data element beginning a line (EFF-DT) is aligned by entry fields.
6. The end point for entry fields is Column 78.

289

Figure 13.12 Development of paper screens (section headings and data elements).

```
                                              *** HMAP01 ***

                      HOMEOWNERS APPLICATION

1. POLICY INFORMATION
   EFF-DT: ------    EXP-DT: ------     ACCT#: ------     POL#: ------
   PROD-ISS: ------  SEC-RES: ------  PRI-POL#: ------  POL-TYP: ------
2. PRODUCER AND COMPANY INFORMATION
   CO: ------    BR-CD: ------    PROD-CD: ------    SUB-PROD: ------
3. RESIDENCE AND INSURED INFORMATION
   NM-1: ------               MAR-STS: -   SP-EMP: -
   NM-2: ------
   ML-AD: ------                        P-AD: ------
   CTY: ------   ST: --   ZP: ------   CTY: ------   ST: --   ZP: ------
   PRMS-OTH: -   PRMS-CNY: -                         LEG-DISC: -
4. COVERAGES
   FORM: -   A-BLDG: ------   B-OTH: ------   C-UNS-PR: ------   D-ADD-LIV: ------
             E-PER-L: ------  F-MED: ------                      NY-CINS: -
             DED-AMT: ------  250-DED: ------  DED-FORM#: ------
```

7. Fields are located in the same relative position that they occupy on the source document.
8. Larger gaps are left where larger spaces exist on the source document.
9. Entry fields under one another in a line are relatively positioned as best as possible. Due to varying caption and entry fields sizes, exact representation cannot always be achieved. Tradeoffs must be performed and the best overall representation achieved.

Figure 13.13 Development of paper screens (section headings and data elements).

```
                              *** HMAP01 ***

         HOMEOWNERS APPLICATION

1.  POLICY INFORMATION
    EFF-DT: ----- EXP-DT: ----- ACCT#: -----    POL#: -----
    PROD-ISS: ----- SEC-RES: ----- PRI-POL#: -----    POL-TYP: -----
2.  PRODUCER AND COMPANY INFORMATION
               BR-CD: -----    PROD-CD: -----    SUB-PROD: -----
3.  RESIDENCE AND INSURED INFORMATION
    NM-1: -----            MAR-STS: -----    SP-EMP: -----
    NM-2: -----
    ML-AD: -----                 P-AD: -----
           CTY: -----            CTY: -----
           ST: ----- ZP: -----   ST: ----- ZP: -----
    PRMS-OTH: -----    PRMS-CNY: -----    LEG-DISC: -----
4.  COVERAGES
    FORM: -----    A-BLDG: -----    B-OTH: -----    C-UNS-PR: -----    D-ADD-LIV: -----
                   E-PER-L: -----   F-MED: -----                       NY-CINS: -----
                   DED-AMT: -----   250-DED: -----   DED-FORM#: -----
```

10. Since there are no data entry data elements in this line on the document, a space line is left on the screen.
11. The city-state-zip line size requires the beginning position of the entry field for the first data element (CT) be moved back to column 12. It cannot be aligned under the above entry field (EFF-DT, PROD-ISS and CO.)
12. For consistency, the remaining data element entry fields beginning lines within that section are moved back to align with CT (NM-1, NM-2, and ML-AD). It is desirable to align all entry fields beginning a line with each other. It is not a requirement. However, it is necessary to align those within a section. Do try, however, to keep misalignments between sections to a minimum.
13. PRMS-OTH is not aligned because it is indented on the document.

Figure 13.14 Development of paper screens (section headings and data elements).

```
                                                              *** HMAPO1 ***

                        HOMEOWNERS APPLICATION

1.  POLICY INFORMATION
    EFF-DT: ------   EXP-DT: ------   ACCT#: ------   POL#: -
    PROD-ISS: -      SEC-RES: -   PRI-POL#: ------           POL-TYP: -
2.  PRODUCER AND COMPANY INFORMATION
    CO: ------    BR-CD: --    PROD-CD: --   SUB-PROD: ------
3.  RESIDENCE AND INSURED INFORMATION
    NM-1: ------                     MAR-STS: -   SP-EMP: -
    NM-2: ------

    ML-AD: ------                    P-AD: ------
    CTY: ------                      CTY: ------
    ST: -- ZP: ------                ST: -- ZP: ------
    PRMS-OTH: -        PRMS-CNY: -    LEG-DISC: -
4.  COVERAGES
    FORM: -    A-BLDG: ------   B-OTH: ------   C-UNS-PR: ------   D-ADD-LIV: ------
               E-PER-L: ------  F-MED: ------                      NY-CINS: -
    DED-AMT: ------   250-DED: -   DED-FORM#: ---
```

14. Because of the earlier reduction in caption sizes, line 16 now fits. The first data element (FORM) entry field is aligned under the previous section.
15. It is desirable to align the entry fields in line 17 under those in line 16 since they appear "aligned" on the document. To do this requires reducing the captions E-PER-LIAB and F-MED-PAY to E-PER-L and F-MED. This is done. (In changing captions, always make sure that if the same data elements are used on other screens, these captions are also changed).

292

Figure 13.15 Development of paper screens (section headings and data elements).

```
                                                   *** HMAP01 ***

                    HOMEOWNERS APPLICATION

1.  POLICY INFORMATION
    EFF-DT: -----    EXP-DT: -----    ACCT#: -----    POL#: -----
    PROD-ISS: -    SEC-RES: -    PRI-POL#: -----                POL-TYP: -
2.  PRODUCER AND COMPANY INFORMATION
    CO: -----    BR-CD: --    PROD-CD: --    SUB-PROD: -----
3.  RESIDENCE AND INSURED INFORMATION
    NM-1: -----    MAR-STS: -    SP-EMP: -
    NM-2: -----

    ML-AD: -----                     P-AD: -----
    CTY: -----    ST: --  ZP: -----  CTY: -----    ST: --  ZP: -----
    PRMS-OTH: -    PRMS-CNV: -----                  LEG-DISC: -
4.  COVERAGES
    FORM: -    A-BLDG: -----    B-OTH: -----    C-UNS-PR: -----    D-ADD-LIV: -----
               E-PER-L: -----   F-MED: -----                       NY-CINS: -
    DED-AMT: -----   250-DED: -    DED-FORM#: -----
```

16. Line 18 easily aligns under the above two lines in the section. The screen is finished.

293

Figure 13.16 Source document for designed screen.

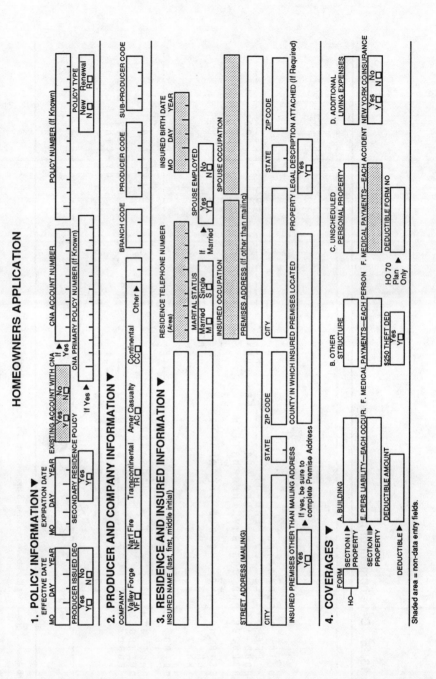

Completed paper screens are next defined within the system. Screen generation facilities are frequently used for this purpose. Figure 13.17 is a printout of the screen created through a screen generation facility.

   I. Review screen design documentation and services.
  II. Identify system inputs and outputs.
 III. Identify unique user requirements.
  IV. Describe data elements.
   V. Develop transactions.
  VI. Develop final paper screens.
 VII. Define computer screens.
VIII. Test screens.
 IX. Implement screens.
  X. Evaluate screens.

Screen testing occurs as part of the normal course of unit, subsystem, and system testing. Modifications are made as necessary. Care must be exercised to assure that any changes implemented conform to the design philosophy and guidelines being followed.

Screens like any part of a system, must be evaluated to ensure that they are achieving their design objectives—including clarity and ease of use. Any system evaluation plans should address them as part of the evaluation process.

Figure 13.17 Screen printout.

```
                                                    *** HMAP01 ***

                        HOMEOWNERS APPLICATION

1. POLICY INFORMATION
   EFF-DT: ------     EXP-DT: ------     ACCT#: ------     POL#: ------
   PROD-ISS: ------   SEC-RES: -   PRI-POL#: ------        POL-TYP: --
2. PRODUCER AND COMPANY INFORMATION
   CO: ------         BR-CD: --   PROD-CD: ------   SUB-PROD: ------
3. RESIDENCE AND INSURED INFORMATION
   NM-1: ------                   MAR-STS: -   SP-EMP: -
   NM-2: ------
   ML-AD: ------      P-AD: ------
   CTY: ------        ST: --   ZP: ------    CTY: ------   ST: --   ZP: ------
   PRMS-OTH: -        PRMS-CNY: ------        LEG-DISC: ------
4. COVERAGES
   FORM: -   A-BLDG: ------   B-OTH: ------   C-UNS-PR: ------   D-ADD-LIU: ------
             E-PER-L: ------   F-MED: ------                     NY-CINS: -
             DED-AMT: ------   250-DED: ------   DED-FORM#: ------
```

References

Ayres, Leonard P., *The War with Germany,* Washington, DC, 1919, p. 102.

Backs, Richard W., Walrath, Larry C., and Hancock, Glenn A. Comparison of Horizontal and Vertical Menu Formats. *Proceedings of the Human Factors Society—31st Annual Meeting,* 1987, Santa Monica, CA.

Bailey, R.W., Ph.D., Is Ergonomics Worth the Investment? *Proceedings: World Conference on Ergonomics in Computer Systems,* pp. 37–108, Los Angeles, CA.; Chicago, IL.; New York, NY; Amsterdam, The Netherlands; Dusseldorf, West Germany; Helsinki, Finland. Sept. 24–Oct. 4, 1984.

Baker, J.D., and Goldstein, I., Batch vs. Sequential Displays: Effects on Human Problem Solving. *Human Factors,* 1966, 8: pp. 225–235.

Barber, Raymond E., *Response Time, Operator Productivity and Job Satisfaction.* Ph.D. dissertation, NYU Graduate School of Business Administration, 1979.

Barber, Raymond E., and Lucas, H.C., System Response Time, Operator Productivity and job satisfaction. *Communications of the ACM 26,* Nov. 1983, 11: pp. 972–986.

Barmack, J.E., and Sinaiko, H.W., *Human Factors Problems in Computer-Generated Graphic Displays.* Inst. for Defense Analysis. AD-636170, 1966.

Barnard, P., *Presuppositions in Active and Passive Questions.* Paper read to the Experimental Psychology Society, 1974.

Barnard, P.; Wright, P., and Wilcox, P., The effects of spatial constraints on the legibility of handwritten alphanumeric codes. *Ergonomics,* 1978, 21: pp. 73–78.

Barnard, P.; Hammond, N.; Morton, J.; Long, J.; and Clark, I., Consistency and Compatibility in Human-Computer Dialogue. *International Journal of Man-Machine Studies,* 1981, 15: pp. 87–134.

Barnard, P.; Hammond, N.; MacLean, A.; and Morton, J., Learning and Remembering Interactive Commands. In *Proceedings: Human Factors in Computer Systems,* pp. 2–7. Gaithersburg, MD., March 15–17, 1982.

Bergman, Hans, Brinkman, Albert, and Loelega, Harry S., System Response Time and Problem Solving Behavior. *Proceedings of the Human Factors Society–25th Annual Meeting–1981,* pp. 749–753, Santa Monica, CA.

Billingsley, P.A., Navigation Through Hierarchical Menu Structures: Does It Help to

Have a Map? In *Proceedings of the Human Factors Society–26th Annual Meeting,* 1982, pp. 103–107. Santa Monica, CA., 1982.

Black, J.B., and Moran, T.P. Learning and Remembering Command Names. In *Proceedings: Human Factors in Computer Systems,* pp. 8–11. Gaithersburg, MD., March 15–17, 1982.

Bly, Sara A. and Rosenberg, Jarrett K., A Comparison of Tiled and Overlapping Windows. *Proceedings CHI '86 Human Factors in Computing Systems,* pp. 101–105.

Boies, S.J., User Behavior on an Interactive Computer System. *IBM Systems Journal 13,* 1, 1974, pp. 1–18.

Bonsiepe, G., A Method of Quantifying Order in Typographic Design. *Journal of typographic research,* 1968, *2,* pp. 203–220.

Bouma, H., Interaction Effects in Parafoveal Letter Recognition. *Nature, 226,* 1970, pp. 177–178.

Bower, G.H.; Clark, M.C.; Lesgold, A.M.; and Winenz, D., Hierarchical Retrieval Schemes in Recall of Categorical Word Lists. *Journal of Verbal Learning and Verbal Behavior,* 1969, 8: pp. 323–343.

Brod, Craig, *Technostress: The Human Cost of the Computer Revolution.* Addison-Wesley Publishing Company, Reading, MA, 1984.

Brooks, R., Search Time and Color Coding. *Psychonomic Science,* 1965, 2:281–282.

Burns, Michael J. and Warren, Dianne L., Formatting Space-Related Displays to Optimize Expert and Nonexpert User Performance. *Proceedings CHI '86 Human Factors in Computing Systems,* April 1986, pp. 274–280.

Bury, K.F., Boyle, J.M., Evey, R.J., and Neal, A.S. Windowing Versus Scrolling on a Visual Display Terminal. *Human Factors, 24* pp. 385–394 (1982).

Butler, T.W. Computer Response Time and User Performance. *ACM SIGCHI '83 Proceedings: Human Factors in Computer Systems,* Dec. 1983, pp. 56–62.

Cairney, P. & Sless, D. Communication Effectiveness of Symbolic Safety Signs with Different User Groups. *Applied Ergonomics,* 13, 1982:91–97.

Callan, J.R., Curran, L.E. and Lane, J.L., Visual Search Times for Navy Tactical Information Displays (Report # NPRDC-TR-77-32). San Diego, CA: Navy Personnel Research and Development Center, 1977. (NTIS No. AD A040543)

Carbonell, J.R.; Elkind, J.I.; and Nickerson, R.S. On the Psychological Importance of Time in a Time-Sharing System. *Human Factors* 10, 1969: pp. 135–142.

Card, S.K. User Perceptual Mechanisms in the Search of Computer Command Menus. In *Proceedings: Human Factors in Computer Systems,* pp. 190–196. Gaithersburg, MD., March 15–17, 1982.

Card, S.K., Pavel, M., and Farrell, J.E. Window-Based Computer Dialogues. *Human Computer Interaction—INTERACT '84*/B. Shackel (ed.) Elsevier Science Publishers B.V. (North Holland IFIP, 1985, pp. 239–243.

Card, Stuart, Moran, Thomas P., and Newell, Allen, The Keystroke-Level Model for User Performance with Interactive Systems. *Communications of the ACM 23,* 1980, pp. 396–410.

Carroll, J.B. and White, M.N., Word Frequency and Age of Acquisition as Determiners of Picture Naming Latency. *Quarterly Journal of Experimental Psychology, 25,* 1973, pp. 85–95.

Carroll, J.M., *Learning, Using and Designing Command Paradigms.* IBM Research Report RC 8141. 1980.

Carroll, John M., Minimalist Design for Active Users. *Human-Computer Interaction–*

*INTERACT '84/*B. Shackel (ed.) Elsevier Science Publishers B.V. (North Holland) IFIP, 1985, pp. 39–44.

Carroll, John M. and Carrithers, Caroline, Blocking Learner Error States in a Training-Wheels Systems. *Human Factors, 26(4),* 1984, pp. 377–389.

Carter, R.L., Visual search with color. *Journal of Experimental Psychology: Human Perception and Performance,* 8, 1982, pp. 127–136.

Chafin, R., and Martin, T. *DSN Human Factors Project Final Report.* Los Angeles, Calif.: University of Southern California, 1980. Contract No. 955013mRD—142.

Chapanis, A.; Parrish, R.N.; Ochsman, R.B.; and Weeks, G.D. Studies in Interactive Communication: II. The Effects of Four Communication Modes on the Linguistic Performance of Teams During Cooperative Problem Solving. *Human Factors 19,* No. 2 (1977): pp. 101–126.

Christ, R.E., Review and Analysis of Color Coding Research for Visual Displays. *Human Factors* 17, No. 6 (1975): pp. 542–570.

Christ, R.E. and Teichner, W.H., Color Research for Visual Displays. *JANAIR Report No. 730703,* Department of Psychology, New Mexico State University, 1973.

Cohill, Andrew M., and Williges, Robert C., Retrieval of HELP Information for Novice Users of Interactive Computer Systems. *Human Factors 27(3),* 1985, pp. 335–343.

Cotton, Ira W., Measurement of Interactive Computing: Methodology and Application. National Bureau of Standards Special Publication 500–548, 1978, 101 pages.

Cuff, R.N., On Casual Users. *International Journal of Man-Machine Studies* 12, (1980), pp. 163–187.

Cushman, William H., Reading for Microfiche, a VDT, and the Printed Page: Subjective Fatigue and Performance. *Human Factors, 28(1),* (1986), pp. 63–73.

Danchak, M.M., CRT Displays for Power Plants *Instrumentation Technology* 23, No. 10, (1976), pp. 29–36.

Davies, Susan E., Bury, Kevin F., and Darnell, Michael J., An Experimental Comparison of a Windowed vs. a Non-Windowed Operating System Environment. *Proceedings of the Human Factors Society—29th Annual Meeting—*1985, pp. 250–254, Santa Monica, CA.

Dickey, G.L., and Schneider, M.H., Multichannel Communication of an Industrial Task. *International Journal of Production Research, 9,* 1971, pp. 487–499.

Dodson, D.W., and Shields, N.J., Jr., Development of User Guidelines for ECAS Display Design. (Vol. 1) (Report No. NASA-CR-150877). Huntsville, AL: Essex Corp., 1978.

Doherty, W.J., The Commercial Significance of Man-Computer Interaction. In *Man/Computer Communication.* Vol. 2, pp. 81–94. Maidenhead, Berkshire, England: Infotech International, 1979.

Dondis, Donis A., *A Primer of Visual Literacy,* The MIT Press, Cambridge, MA (1973).

Draper, Stephen W. The Nature of Expertise in Unix. *Human-Computer Interaction—INTERACT '84/*B. Shackel (ed.) Elsevier Science Publishers B.V. (North Holland) IFIP, 1985, pp. 465–471.

Dray, S.M., Ogden, W.G., and Vestewig, R.E. Measuring Performance with a Menu Selection Human-Computer Interface. In *Proceedings of the Human Factors Society–25th Annual Meeting, 1981,* pp. 746–748. Santa Monica, CA., 1981.

Dunsmore, H.E., Using Formal Grammars to Predict the Most Useful Characteristics of Interactive Systems. In *Office Automation Conference Digest,* pp. 53–56. San Francisco, April 5–7, 1982.

Dunsmore, H.E., Designing an Interactive Facility for Non-Programmers, *Proceedings ACM National Conference,* (1980), pp. 475–483.

Durding, B.M., Becker, C.A., and Gould, J.D., Data Organization. *Human Factors 19,* No. 1 (1977): pp. 1–14.

Eason, K., *Man-Computer Communication in Public and Private Computing.* HUSAT Memo 173. Loughborough, Leicester, England, 1979.

Ehrenreich, S.L. Computer Abbreviations: Evidence and Synthesis. *Human Factors 27(2),* (1985), pp. 143–155.

Elam, P.G., Considering Human Needs Can Boost Network Efficiency. *Data Communications,* October 1978, pp. 50–60.

Ells, J.G. and Dewar, R.E., Rapid Comprehension of Verbal and Symbolic Traffic Sign Messages. *Human Factors, 21,* 1979, pp. 161–168.

Engel, F.L., Information Selection From Visual Displays. In *Ergonomic Aspects of Visual Display Terminals,* E. Grandjean and E. Vigliani (Eds.), London: Taylor and Francis Ltd, 1980.

Engel, S.E., and Granda, R.E., *Guidelines for Man/Display Interfaces.* IBM Technical Report, 19 December 1975. TR 00.2720.

Foley, J., and Wallace, V., The Art of Natural Graphic Man-Machine Conversation. *Proceedings of the IEEE 62,* No. 4 (April 1974).

Francik, Ellen P. and Kane, Richard M. Optimizing Visual Search and Cursor Movement in Pull-Down Menus. *Proceedings of the Human Factors Society–31st Annual Meeting,* 1987, Santa Monica, CA.

Frankenhaeuser, M., Psychoneuroendocrine Approaches to the Study of Emotion as Related to Stress and Coping. In *Nebraska Symposium on Motivation* (1978), edited by H.E. Howe and R.A. Dienstabier, pp. 123–161. Lincoln: University of Nebraska Press, 1979.

Fromme, F., Incorporating the Human Factor in Color CAD Systems. *IEEE Proceedings of the 20th Design Automation Conference,* 1983, pp. 189–195.

Furnas, G.W., Gomez, L.M., Landauer, T.K., and Dumais, S.T., Statistical Semantics: How Can a Computer Use What People Name Things to Guess What Things People Mean When They Name Things? In *Proceedings: Human Factors in Computer Systems.* Gaithersburg, MD., March 15–17, 1982.

Galitz, W.O., IBM 3270 On-Line Evaluation. *INA Technical Report,* E5320-A02/M72-0001, January 20, 1972.

Galitz, W.O., *Summary Report of the Personal Lines Form Questionnaire and Agency Visits.* INA Technical Report, 20 September 1973. E5710-A05/N73-0001.

Galitz, W.O., *An Evaluation of the Impact of Mnemonic CRT Labels on the Design and Use of EIS Forms and Screens* INA Technical Report, March 1975.

Galitz, W.O., DEBUT II—The CNA Data Entry Utility. *Proceedings of the Human Factors Society-23rd Annual Meeting (1979),* pp. 50–54. Santa Monica, Calif., 1979.

Galitz, Wilbert O., CRT Viewing and Visual Aftereffects. *UNIVAC Internal Report.* Roseville, MN, 1 August 1968.

Gardell, B., Tjanstemannens Arbetsmiljoer (Work Environment of White-collar Workers). Preliminary report. The research group for social psychology work. Department of Psychology, University of Stockholm, Report No. 24, 1979.

Gaylin, Kenneth B., How are Windows Used? Some Notes on Creating an Empirically-Based Windowing Benchmark Task. *Proceedings CHI '86 Human Factors in Computing Systems,* pp. 96–100.

Geldard, F.A., *The Human Senses*. New York: John Wiley, 1953.

Gilfoil, D.M., Warming Up to Computers: A Study of Cognitive and Affective Interactions Over Time. In *Proceedings: Human Factors in Computer Systems*, Gaithersburg, MD., March 15–17, 1982, pp. 245–250.

Goodwin, N.C., Effect of Interface Design on Usability of Message Handling Systems. In *Proceedings of the Human Factors Society–26th Annual Meeting—1982*, Santa Monica, CA, 1982, pp. 69–73.

Goodwin, N.C., Designing a Multipurpose Menu Driven User Interface to Computer Based Tools. In *Proceedings of the Human Factors Society–27th Annual Meeting*, Santa Monica, CA, 1983, pp. 816–820.

Gould, J.D.; Lewis, C.; and Becker, A., *Writing and Following Procedural, Descriptive and Restricted Syntax Language Instructions*. Yorktown Heights, NY: IBM, 1976.

Gould, John D. and Grischkowsky, Nancy, Doing the Same Work with Hard Copy and with Cathode-Ray Tube (CRT) Computer Terminals. *Human Factors, 26(3)*, 1984, pp. 323–337.

Granda, R.E., Teitelbaum, R.C., and Dunlap, G.L., The Effect of VDT Command Line Location on Data Entry Behavior. In *Proceedings of the Human Factors Society–26th Annual Meeting, 1982*, Santa Monica, CA. (1982), pp. 621–624.

Greene, J.M. *Psycholinguistics: Chomsky and Psychology*. Harmondsworth, Middlesex, U.K.: Penguin, 1972.

Grudin, Jonathan and Barnard, Phil, When Does an Abbreviation Become a Word? and Related Questions. *CHI '85 Proceedings*, pp. 121–.

Halsey, R.M. and Chapanis, A., On the Number Absolutely Identifiable Spectral Hues. *Journal of Optical Society of America*, 41, 1951, pp. 1057–1058.

Hammond, N., Barnard, P., Clark, I., Morton, J., and Long, J., *Structure and Content in Interactive Dialogue*. Paper presented at American Psychological Association Annual Meeting, Montreal, September 1980, and IBM Human Factors Report HFO 34. October 1980.

Hammond, N., Long, J., Clark, I., Barnard, P., and Morton, J., Documenting Human-Computer Mismatch in *Interactive Systems*. In *Proceedings of the Ninth Annual Symposium on Human Factors in Telecommunications*. 1980B.

Hansen, J., Man-Machine Communication. *IEEE Transactions on Man, Systems and Cybernetics*. Vol. SMC-6, No. 11, November 1976.

Haubner, P., and Benz, C., Information Display on Monochrome and Colour Screens. *Abstracts: International Scientific Conference on Ergonomic and Health Aspects in Modern Offices*, Turin, Italy, November 7–9, 1983, p. 72.

Haubner, Peter and Neumann, Frank, Structuring Alphanumerically Coded Information on Visual Display Units. *Proceedings: International Scientific Conference: Work With Display Units*, Stockholm, Sweden, May 12–15, 1986, pp. 606–609.

Herriot, P., *An Introduction to the Psychology of Language*. London: Methuen, 1970.

Hiltz, S.R., *Online Communities: A Case Study of the Office of the Future*. Ablex Publishers, Norwood, NJ, 1984.

Hiltz, Starr Roxanne and Kerr, Elaine B., Learning Modes and Subsequent Use of Computer-Mediated Communication Systems. *Proceedings CHI '86 Human Factors in Computing Systems*, pp. 149–155.

IBM, Software Design Principles. *Proceedings: Software Ease of Use Workshop*, Boca Raton, FL, Oct. 22, 1984.

Johansson, G., Aronsson, G., and Lindstrom, B., Social, Psychological and Neuroendocrine Stress Reactions in Highly Mechanized Work. *Ergonomics*. 21 (1978): pp. 583–599.

Jones, P.F., Four Principles of Man-Computer Dialogue. *Computer Aided Design* 10 (1978): pp. 197–202.

Kaplow, R., and Molnar, M., A Computer Terminal Hardware/Software System With Enhanced User Input Capabilities. In *Computer Graphics*. New York: ACM, 1976.

Karasek, R.A. Job Demands, Decision Latitude, and Mental Strain: Implications for Job Redesign. *Administrative Science Quarterly* 24, 1979 pp. 285–311.

Karasek, R.A., Baker, D., Marxer, F., Ahlbom, A., and Theorell, T., Job Design Latitude, Job Demands, and Cardiovascular Disease: A Prospective Study of Swedish Men. *American Journal of Public Health* 71, 1981: pp. 694–705.

Karat, John, Transfer Between Word Processing Systems. *Proceedings: International Scientific Conference: Work With Display Units,* pp. 745–748. Stockholm, Sweden, May 12–15, 1986.

Kaster, Jürgen and Widdel, Heino, The Effect of Visual Presentation of Different Dialogue Structures on Ease of Human-Computer Interaction. *Proceedings: International Scientific Conference: Work With Display Units,* Stockholm, Sweden, May 12–15, 1986, pp. 772–776.

Keister, R.S., and Gallaway, G.R. Making Software User Friendly: An Assessment of Data Entry Performance. In *Proceedings of the Human Factors Society—27th Annual Meeting—1983,* Santa Monica, CA., 1983, pp. 1031–1034.

Kelly, M.J., and Chapanis, A. Limited Vocabulary Natural Language Dialogue. *International Journal of Man-Machine Studies.* 9, 1977: pp. 479–501.

Kiger, J.I., The Depth/Breadth Tradeoff in the Design of Menu Driven User Interfaces. *International Journal of Man-Machine Studies,* 1984, 20, pp. 201–213.

Kintish, W., Comprehension and Memory of Text. In *Handbook of Learning and Cognitive Processes,* edited by W.K. Estes, vol. 6. Hillsdale, NJ: Lawrence Erlbaum Associates, 1978.

Kopala, C.J., The Use of Color Coded Symbols in a Highly Dense Situation Display. *Proceedings of the Human Factors Society—23rd Annual Meeting—1981,* Santa Monica, CA, pp. 736–740.

Kruk, Richard S. and Muter, Paul, Reading of Continuous Text on Video Screens. *Human Factors, 26(3),* 1984, pp. 339–345.

Kühne, Andreas, Krueger, Helmut, Graf, Werner, and Merz, Loretta, Positive Versus Negative Image Polarity. *Proceedings: International Scientific Conference: Work With Display Units,* Stockholm, Sweden, May 12–15, 1986, pp. 208–211.

Lalomia, Mary J. and Happ, Alan J., The Effective Use of Color for Text on the IBM 5153 Color Display. *Proceedings of the Human Factors Society—31st Annual Meeting—1987,* Santa Monica, CA, pp. 1091–1095.

Landauer, T.K. and Nachbar, D.W., Selection from Alphabetic and Numeric Menu Trees Using A Touch Screen: Breadth, Depth, and Width. *Proceedings CHI '85 Human Factors in Computing Systems,* pp. 73–78.

Ledgard, H., Whiteside, J.A., Singer, A., and Seymour, W., The Natural Language of Interactive Systems. *Communications of the ACM 23,* No. 10, Oct. 1980, pp. 556–563.

Lee, Eric and MacGregor, James, Minimizing User Search Time in Menu Retrieval Systems. *Human Factors, 27(2)* (1985), pp. 157–162.

Liebelt, L.S., McDonald, J.E., Stone, J.D., and Karat, J., The Effect of Organization on Learning Menu Access. In *Proceedings of the Human Factors Society—26th Annual Meeting,* 1982, Santa Monica, CA, 1982, pp. 546–550.

Loftus, E. F., Freedman, J.L., and Loftus, G.R., Retrieval of Words from Subordinate and Supraordinate Categories in Semantic Hierarchies. *Psychonomic Science,* 1970, pp. 235–236.

Luria, S.M., Neri, David F., and Jacobsen, Alan R., The Effects of Set Size on Color Matching Using CRT Displays. *Proceedings of the Human Factors Society—30th Annual Meeting—1986,* Santa Monica, CA, pp. 49–61.

Magers, Celeste S., An Experimental Evaluation on On-Line HELP for Non-Programmers. *Proceedings CHI '83 Human Factors in Computing Systems,* pp. 277–281.

Martin, J. *Design of Man-Computer Dialogues.* Englewood Cliffs, NJ: Prentice-Hall, 1973.

McDonald, J.E., Stone, J.D., and Liebelt, L.S., Searching for Items in Menus: The Effects of Organization and Type of Target. In *Proceedings of the Human Factors Society—27th Annual Meeting,* 1983, Santa Monica, CA, pp. 834–837.

McTyre, John H. and Frommer, W. David., Effects of Character/Background Color Combinations on CRT Character Legibility. *Proceedings of the Human Factors Society—29th Annual Meeting,* 1985, Santa Monica, CA, pp. 779–781.

Microswitch (A Honeywell Division), *Applying Manual Controls and Displays: A Practical Guide to Panel Design,* Freeport, IL, 1984.

Miller, D.P. The Depth/Breadth Tradeoff in Hierarchical Computer Menus. In *Proceedings of the Human Factors Society—25th Annual Meeting, 1981,* Santa Monica, CA, 1981.

Miller, G.A., The Magical Number Seven, Plus or Minus Two: Some Limits on our Capability for Processing Information. *Psychological Science 63,* 1956, pp. 81–97.

Miller, L.A., and Thomas, J.C., Behavioral Issues in the Use of Interactive Systems. *International Journal of Man-Machine Studies 9,* No. 5, Sept. 1977, pp. 509–536.

Miller, L.H., A Study in Man-Machine Interaction. *Proceedings of the National Computer Conference,* 46, AFIPS Press, Montvale, NJ, 1977, pp. 409–421.

Miller, R.B., *Human Ease-of-Use Criteria and Their Trade-offs.* TR00.2185. Poughkeepsie, NY: IBM Corp., 12 April 1971.

Moskel, Sonya, Erno, Judy, and Shneiderman, Ben, Proofreading and Comprehension of Text on Screens and Paper. *University of Maryland Computer Science Technical Report,* June 1984.

Murch, G., The Effective Use of Color: Physiological Principles. Tektronix, Inc. 4 p., 1983.

Murch, G., The Effective Use of Color: Perceptual Principles. Tektronix, Inc. 6 p., 1984A.

Murch, G., The Effective Use of Color: Cognitive Principles. Tektronix, Inc., 7 p., 1984B.

Muter, Paul, Latremouille, S.A., Treurniet, W.C., and Beam, P., Extended Reading of Continuous Text on Television Screens. *Human Factors 24,* 1982, pp. 501–508.

Nemeth, C., *User-Oriented Computer Input Devices.* Master's thesis. Chicago, IL: The Institute of Design, Illinois Institute of Technology, 1982.

Nickerson, R.S., Man-Computer Interaction: A Challenge for Human Factors Research. In *IEEE Transactions of Man-Machine Systems,* MSS-10, No. 4, Dec. 1969.

Nielsen, Jakob, Mack, Robert L., Bergendorff, Keith H., and Grischkowsky, Nancy L., Integrated Software Usage in the Professional Work Environment: Evidence from Questionnaires and Interviews. *Proceedings CHI '86 Human Factors in Computing Systems,* pp. 162–167.

Ogden, W.C., and Boyle, J.M., Evaluating Human-Computer Dialogue Styles: Command vs. Form/Fill-in for Report Modification. In *Proceedings of the Human Factors Society—26th Annual Meeting,* 1982, Santa Monica, CA, pp. 542–545.

Paap, Kenneth R., and Roske-Hofstrand, Renate J., The Optimal Number of Menu Options per Panel. *Human Factors, 28(4),* 1986, pp. 377–385.

Parton, Diana, Huffman, Keith, Pridgen, Patty, Norman, Kent, and Shneiderman, Ben, Learning a Menu Selection Tree: Training Methods Compared. *Behaviour and Information Technology 4,* 2, 1985, pp. 81–91.

Parkinson, Stanley R., Sisson, Norwood, and Snowberry, Kathleen, Organization of Broad Computer Menu Displays. *International Journal Man-Machine Studies, 23,* 1985, pp. 689–697.

Perlman, Gary, Making the Right Choices with Menus. *Human Computer Interaction—INTERACT '84*/B. Shackel (ed.) Elsevier Science Publishers B.V. (North Holland) IFIP, 1985, pp. 317–321.

Polya, G., *How to Solve It.* Doubleday, New York, 1957.

Quinn, Lisa and Russell, Daniel M. Intelligent Interfaces: User Models and Planners. *Proceedings, CHI '86 Human Factors in Computing Systems,* pp. 314–318.

Quintanar, Leo R., Crowell, Charles R., and Pryor, John B., Human-Computer Interaction: A Preliminary Social Psychological Analysis. *Behavior Research Methods & Instrumentation 14,2,* 1982, pp. 210–220.

Reed, A.V., Error-Correcting Strategies and Human Interaction with Computer Systems. In *Proceedings: Human Factors in Computer Systems,* Gaithersburg, MD., March 15–17, 1982, pp. 236–238.

Rehe, R.F., *Typography: How to Make It More Legible.* Carmel, IN.: Design Research International, 1974.

Remington, Roger and Williams, Douglas, On the Selection and Evaluation of Visual Display Symbology: Factors Influencing Search and Identification Times. *Human Factors, 28(4),* 1986, pp. 407–420.

Robert, Jean-Marc, Some Highlights of Learning by Exploration. *Proceedings: International Scientific Conference: Work With Display Units,* Stockholm, Sweden, May 12–15, 1986, pp. 348–353.

Roemer, J., and Chapanis, A., Learning Performance and Attitudes as a Function of the Reading Grade Level of a Computer-presented Tutorial. In *Proceedings: Human Factors in Computer Systems,* Gaithersburg, MD., March 15–17, 1982, pp. 239–244.

Romano, C. and Sonnino, A., Efficiency of Data Entry by VDUs—A Comparison Between Different Softwares. In *Ergonomics and Health in Modern Offices* (edited by Etienne Grandjean) Taylor & Francis, London and Philadelphia, 1984.

Rosenberg, J. Evaluating the Suggestiveness of Command Names. In *Proceedings: Human Factors in Computer Systems,* Gaithersburg, MD., March 15–17, 1982, pp. 12–16.

Savage, R.E., *A Survey of User Opinions of Various Input Field Designs.* Unpublished study, IBM. Rochester, MN., 1980.

Savage, R.E., Habinek, J.K., and Blackstad, N.J., An Experimental Evaluation of Input Field and Cursor Combinations. In *Proceedings of the Human Factors Society— 26th Annual Meeting,* 1982, Santa Monica, CA, pp. 629–633.

Scapin, D.L. Computer Commands Labelled by Users versus Imposed Commands and Their Effect of Structuring Rules on Recall. In *Proceedings: Human Factors in Computer Systems,* Gaithersburg, MD., March 15–17, 1982, pp. 17–19.

Schleifer, Lawrence M., Effects of VDT/Computer System Response Delays and Incentive Pay on Mood Disturbances and Somatic Discomfort. *Proceedings: Interna-

tional Scientific Conference: Work With Display Units, Stockholm, Sweden, May 12–15, 1986, pp. 447–451.

Schoonard, J.W., and Boies, S.J., Short-Type: A Behavioral Analysis of Typing and Text Entry. *Human Factors* 17, No. 2, 1975, pp. 203–214.

Schwarz, Elmar, Beldie, Ian P., and Pastoor, Siegmund, A Comparison of Paging and Scrolling for Changing Screen Contents by Inexperienced Users. *Human Factors, 25(3),* 1983, pp. 279–282.

Seppala, Pentti and Salvendy, Gavriel, Impact of Depth of Menu Hierarchy on Performance Effectiveness in a Supervisory Task: Computerized Flexible Manufacturing System. *Human Factors, 27(6),* 1985, pp. 713–722.

Shinar, David and Stern, Helman I., Alternative Option Selection Methods in Menu-Driven Computer Programs. *Human Factors, 29(4),* 1987, pp. 453–459.

Shinar, David, Stern, Helman I., Bubis, Gad and Ingram, David, The Relative Effectiveness of Alternative Selection Strategies in Menu Driven Computer Programs. *Proceedings of the Human Factors Society—29th Annual Meeting,* 1985, Santa Monica, CA, pp. 645–647.

Shneiderman, B., *Software Psychology.* Cambridge, MA.: Winthrop Publishers, 1980.

Shneiderman, Ben, Control Flow and Data Structure Documentation: Two Experiments. *Communications of the ACM,* Vol. 25, No. 1, Jan. 1982A, pp. 55–63.

Shneiderman, Ben, System Message Design: Guidelines and Experimental Results, in Badre, A. and Shneiderman, B. (Editors). *Directions in Human/Computer Interaction,* Ablex Publishers, Norwood, NJ, 1982B, pp. 55–78.

Shneiderman, Ben, *Designing the User Interface: Strategies for Effective Human-Computer Interaction.* Addison-Wesley Publishing Co., Reading, MA, 1987, pp. 448.

Shneiderman, Ben, Mayer, R., McKay, D., and Heller, P., Experimental Investigations of the Utility of Detailed Flowcharts in Programming. *Communications of the ACM,* Vol. 20, 1977, pp. 373–381.

Sidorsky, R.C., Color Coding in Tactical Displays: Help or Hindrance. *Army Research Institute Research Report,* 1982.

Sless, David, Name and Address Please . . . A Guide for Form Designers. Prepared for Information Co-ordination Branch, Department of Sport Recreation and Tourism, Canberra, Australia, Feb. 1987, 28 p.

Smith, D., Faster Is Better—A Business Case for Subsecond Response Time. *Computerworld,* 1983.

Smith, Sidney L., and Mosier, Jane N., Guidelines for Designing User Interface Software. Prepared for Deputy Commander for Development Plans and Support Systems, Electronic Systems Division, AFSC, USAF, Hanscom AFB, MA. Mitre ESD-TR-86-278 MTR 10090, Aug. 1986.

Smith, Wanda, Computer Color: Psychophysics, Task Application, and Aesthetics. *Proceedings: International Scientific Conference: Work With Display Units,* Stockholm, Sweden, May 12–15, 1986, pp. 561–564.

Snowberry, K., Parkinson, S.R., and Sisson, N., Computer Display Menus. *Ergonomics,* 26, 1983, pp. 699–712.

Spiliotopoulos, V. and Shackel, B., Towards a Computer Interview Acceptable to the Naive User. *International Journal of Man-Machine Studies 14,* 1981, pp. 77–90.

Springer, Carla J. and Sorce, James F., Accessing Large Data Bases: The Relationship Between Data Entry Time and Output Evaluation Time. *Human Computer Interaction—INTERACT '84,* pp. 263–267.

Stern, Kenneth R., An Evaluation of Written, Graphics, and Voice Messages in Pro-ceduralized Instructions. *Proceedings of the Human Factors Society—28th Annual Meeting,* 1984, pp. 314–318, Santa Monica, CA.

Stewart, T.F.M., Displays and the Software Interface. *Applied Ergonomics,* Sept. 1976.

Taylor, I.A., Perception and Design. *Research Principles and Practices in Visual Communication,* J. Ball and F.C. Pyres, Eds., Association for Educational Communication and Technology, 1960, pp. 51–70.

Tedford, W.H., Berquist, S.L., and Flynn, W.E., The Size-Color Illusion. *Journal of General Psychology 97,* No. 1, July 1977, pp. 145–149.

Teitelbaum, Richard C., and Granda, Richard, The Effects of Positional Constancy on Searching Menus for Information. *Proceedings CHI '83 Human Factors in Computer Systems.* pp. 150–153.

Tinker, M.A., Prolonged Reading Tasks in Visual Research. *Journal of Applied Psychology 39,* 1955, pp. 444–446.

Treu, S., ed., User-Oriented Design of Interactive Graphics Systems. In *Proceedings of the ACM.* SIGGRAPH Workshop, October 14–15, 1976, Pittsburgh, PA. New York: ACM, 1977.

Treisman, A., Perceptual Grouping and Attention in Visual Search for Features and for Objects. *Journal of Experimental Psychology: Human Perception and Performance, 8,* 1982, pp. 194–214.

Trollip, Stanley and Sales, Gregory, Readability of Computer-Generated Fill-Justified Text. *Human Factors 28(2),* 1986, pp. 159–163.

Tufte, Edward R., *The Visual Display of Quantitative Information.* Graphics Press, Cheshire, CT, 1983, 197 pp.

Tullis, T.S., An Evaluation of Alphanumeric, Graphic and Color Information Displays. *Human Factors 23,* 1981, pp. 541–550.

Tullis, Thomas S., Designing a Menu-based Interface to an Operating System. *Proceedings CHI '85 Human Factors in Computing Systems,* pp. 79–84.

Tullis, Thomas Stuart, Predicting the Usability of Alphanumeric Displays. Ph.D. dissertation, Rice University, 1983, 172 p.

Turner, Jon A. Computer Mediated Work: The Interplay Between Technology and Structured Jobs. *Communications of the AACM 27,* 12, Dec. 1984, pp. 1210–1217.

Vartabedian, A.G., The Effects of Letter Size, Case and Generation Method on CRT Display Search Time. *Human Factors 13,* No. 4, 1971, pp. 363–368.

Vitz, P.C., Preference for Different Amounts of Visual Complexity. *Behavioral Science 2,* 1966, pp. 105–114.

Walker, R.E., Nicolay, R.C. and Stearns, C.R. Comparative Accuracy of Recognizing American and International Road Signs. *Journal of Applied Psychology 49,* 1965, pp. 322–325.

Wallace, Daniel, Time Stress Effects on Two Menu Selection Systems. *Proceedings of the Human Factors Society—31st Annual Meeting,* 1987.

Wason, P.C., and Johnson-Laird, P.N., *Psychology of Reasoning: Structure and Content.* London: Batsford, 1972.

Watley, Charles and Mulford, Jay, A Comparison of Commands' Documentation: Online vs. Hardcopy. Unpublished student project, University of Maryland, Dec. 8, 1983, In Shneiderman, 1987.

Watson, R.W., User Interface Design Issues for a Large Interactive System. In *AFIPS Conference Proceedings 45,* 1976, pp. 357–364.

Weinberg, G.M., *The Psychology of Computer Programming*. New York: Van Nostrand Reinhold, 1971.

Weiss, Stuart Martin, Boggs, George, Lehto, Mark, Shodja, Sogand, and Martin, David J., Computer System Response Time and Psychophysiological Stress II. *Proceedings of the Human Factors Society—26th Annual Meeting—1982*, pp. 698–702.

Wertheimer, M., *Productive Thinking*, Harper and Row, New York, 1959.

Whiteside, John, Jones, Sandra, Levy, Paula S., and Wixon, Dennis, User Performance with Command, Menu, and Iconic Interfaces. *Proceedings CHI '85 Human Factors in Computing Systems*, April 1985, pp. 185–191.

Wichansky, Anna M., Legibility and User Acceptance of Monochrome Display Phospher Colors. *Proceedings: International Scientific Conference: Work With Display Units*, Stockholm, Sweden, May 12–15, 1986, pp. 216–219.

Wingfield, A., Effects of Frequency on Identification and Naming of Objects. *American Journal of Psychology, 81*, 1968, pp. 226–234.

Wright, P., and Barnard, P., Just Fill in This Form: A Review for Designers. *Applied Ergonomics 6*, 1975, pp. 213–220.

Wright, P. and Lickorish, A., Proof-Reading Texts on Screen and Paper. *Behaviour and Information Technology 2, 3*, 1983, pp. 227–235.

Wright, Patricia, User Documentation. *Proceedings: World Conference on Ergonomics in Computer Systems*, 1984, pp. 110–126, Los Angeles,, CA; Chicago, IL; New York, NY; Amsterdam, The Netherlands; Dusseldorf, West Germany; Helsinki, Finland, Sept. 24–Oct. 4, 1984.

Zahn, C.T., Graph-Theoretical Methods for Detecting and Describing Gestalt Clusters. *IEEE Transactions on Computers, X-20*, 1971, pp. 68–86.

Zwaga, H.J. and Boersema, T., Evaluation of a Set of Graphics Symbols. *Applied Ergonomics, 14*, 1983, pp. 43–54.

Zwahlen, Helmut T. and Kothari, Nimesh, The Effects of Dark and Light Character CRT Displays Upon VDT Operator Performance, Eye Scanning Behavior, Pupil Diameter and Subjective Comfort/Discomfort. *Proceedings: International Scientific Conference: Work With Display Units*, Stockholm, Sweden, May 12–15, 1986, pp. 220–222.